COURAGE, A MEMOIR BY PATRICIA ALCIVAR

COURAGE, A MEMOIR BY PATRICIA ALCIVAR

PATRICIA ALCIVAR

CONTENTS

PROLOGUE   1

1 Chapter One - Round 1   3

2 Chapter Two - Round 2   17

3 Chapter Three - Round 3   33

4 Chapter Four - Round 4   39

5 Chapter Five - Round 5   75

6 Chapter Six - Round 6   127

7 Chapter Seven - Round 7   171

8 Chapter Eight - Round 8   213

9 Chapter Nine - Round 9   235

10 Chapter Ten - Round 10   259

11 Chapter Eleven - Round 11   293

12 Chapter Twelve - Round 12   319

13 Chapter Thirteen - Round 13   325

14 Chapter Fourteen - Round 14   347

15 Chapter Fifteen - Round 15   363

Epilogue   373

PROLOGUE

C OURAGE

My mother, Nancy immigrated to the United States from Barranquilla, Colombia alone when she was barely 18 years old. She was one of 5 children. However, just one of them, Hector her older brother was her real brother and the other 3 were half siblings from a different father. They lived in a poor neighborhood in Barranquilla, Colombia called Barrio Monte. Her stepfather, Gregorio worked in a brewery and my grandmother, Maria Mercedes sold fruits and vegetables on the streets of Barrio Monte.

Life was grim in Colombia. There was never enough food on the table and my mother's anxieties grew each day wondering what would become of her life. Until one day while walking back from school, she walked into an agency that offered to connect her with a family in the United States as part of the housekeeping staff. All my mother had to do was come up with the money for her flight and visa and the agency would take care of the rest.

She was not close to Gregorio, but she gathered up the courage to tell my grandmother, "Mamá I want a better life for all of us. I want to go to the United States and work as a housekeeper for a few years. I will save up enough money to bring everyone to the United States, but right now, I need you to ask Gregorio to loan me the money for my flight and visa. I promise I will pay him back and bring everyone to the United States once I save up the money," said my mother.

My grandmother always trusted my mother. Of the 5 children, she would give my mother her keys to her sacred drawer where she kept her small earnings. She knew deep inside that my mother would not only keep her promise, but that she was their only hope and ticket out of poverty.

A short time after that in the late 1960's, my mother arrived in Michigan to work for a wealthy family where she would work as a nanny and a housekeeper. She was grateful for her room and the opportunity to make money, but she felt extremely lonely and cried herself to sleep almost daily for the first couple of years. She internalized all her feelings and did her best to stay strong.

Her main priority was on saving money to pay Gregorio back and bring her family to the United States. In five years, she saved up enough money to move to New York City and kept her promise and brought her entire family as well.

Her life had improved considerably especially with now having family close by. My mother lived in the borough of Queens in New York City and helped find my grandmother, aunts and uncles a place to live in the same area. She had started to take English classes and met a man named William whom would sweep her off her feet with his charm. Everyone seemed to like him in the beginning as he was a big and generous spender.

One night during a barbecue party, my mother was tired and wanted to leave, but William had gotten drunk as usual and wanted to keep drinking, so my mother changed her tone and told him, "I want to go home NOW with or without you." His face changed and he grabbed the knife that was near the barbecue and slit my mother's left hand.

Her hand was bleeding profusely and had fainted when the ambulance came to rush her to the hospital. She received 24 stitches and a life time scar internally and externally. William would later say that he lost his balance and that it was all a big accident. He cried to my mother and made countless excuses and empty promises. He proposed marriage to her right there in the hospital and she said yes. That would be the most impactful decision of her life and the beginning of a violent and destructive marriage.

Chapter One - Round 1

COURAGE
A Fighter is Born

My mother had just given birth to me at Elmhurst Hospital in Queens, New York in her early 30's. The nurse said, "It's a Girl, what will you name her?" My mother didn't have a name for me but, she managed to see an old Newsweek Magazine cover with a woman holding a machine gun and it read 'The Saga of Patty Hearst." My mother smiled and named me:

Patricia Evelyn Alcivar

For some odd reason, I love the story of how I was named. It goes along with the deep inner desire of always wanting to be unique in my own way. I did not know it at the time, but I was unique and that usually does not sit well with people. When my mom brought me home from the hospital to introduce me to my older sister, she went ahead and slapped me.

I don't have too many fond memories of my childhood. I remember being scared often when my father, William picked me up from my older sister's past down crib and he touched me in a way that even as an innocent child, I knew it wasn't right. I grew up listening to the sounds of Latin music blasting on every Thursday, Friday and Saturday evenings and the smell of rum on my father's breath.

He was 5.11" and over 200 lbs. and he would bring me into his bedroom and start rubbing his heavy body on top of me whether he was intoxicated or not during the week when my mother was at work. Later in my life, I would learn the proper terms of what he had done to me. Throughout the next 10 years, my father would molest me which is when there is a sexual assault or abuse especially of a child. There would never be any penetration out of fear that he would get caught.

He was a maintenance worker for IBM on Madison Avenue and worked the morning shift of 6 am to 2 pm and my mother also worked in maintenance for Fisher Brothers and worked the evening shift from 4 pm to 12 am. He was an abusive alcoholic just like most of the men in my family- my grandfather, uncle and cousins. I felt bad for my mother who would come home from work tired usually after 1 am and pleaded with him to lower the music, but he would get angry and ignore her. When my mother insisted one night for him to turn off the music, he got so angry and turned on the gas from the stove and threatened to burn the apartment down and kill us all.

I hated to hear them yell and argue. I remember praying and squeezing my Snuggles Teddy Bear extra tight. "God, please take me, my sisters and mom away from him." For whatever reason which I will never know, my father chose me out of the four sisters to consistently torture.

He abused me physically, sexually, verbally and emotionally on a daily basis. There were countless beatings, but there are a handful that I will never forget because they literally scarred me for life. One that comes to mind was when I was about 8 years old, my father purchased a beautiful glass dining table with chairs that had suede coverings on the seats. "If I find anyone horsing around on these chairs, I will make them pay!" he said one evening. I wss a skinny kid weighing less than 50lbs at the time. When he turned away to go to his bedroom, I stood up on the chair and did a quick dance. My oldest sister yelled "Dad, Patricia is dancing on the new chairs!" My heart sunk when I heard his footsteps and saw the rage in my father's face. He stripped me down to my panties and hit me with a leather belt until he exhausted himself. I was trembling and every muscle in my body hurt, but I didn't cry and that made him furious. He took away my Snuggles Teddy Bear and threw it away to hurt me more and it did.

I couldn't sleep on my back that night and waited up for my mother to come home from work. She was upset and blamed me for being disobedient, but she at least put warm compresses on my back. She thought the same thing would happen to her if she tried to do or say anything. The next day on Saturday, my grandmother, who was a feisty eccentric woman whom I loved, came over and started crying when she saw how bruised my little back and body were. She was angry and even though she didn't speak any English, she went to school with me that Monday and reported my father to the school counselor. I remember feeling proud of my grandmother for standing up for me. I momentarily felt hope that perhaps this nightmare would end soon.

Police officers and a school counselor came to our home later that day, but my mother told them that it was my fault because I had been disrespectful. My hope was gone and so was my respect for my mother. The one person that should have really stood up for me didn't. My grandmother disliked my father, but the feeling was mutual between those two. I kept praying and dreaming. Those were my favorite things to do. I would dream often that I was a famous athlete. When my father allowed us to watch television with him, he watched Bruce Lee movies or boxing. Even though it was mostly "men movies or sports", I didn't care. I imagined myself being just like them-strong.

My mother used to tell me that I could avoid the beatings and most of the trouble I got myself into if I just obeyed and followed the rules. I never thought that I was purposely disobedient. I felt as I was following my instincts spontaneously. One day while walking back from Bellevue Hospital where my sisters and I received our required vaccines for school, my face lit up when I saw a playground with a climbing wall. My mother yelled at me and said, "Don't even think about it! There is no time to play. I have to drop you all back home and run to work." But I rarely got to play anywhere and the playground looked so beautiful, so I ran ahead to take a quick look at the playground.

I ran as fast as I possibly could and I was momentarily filled with joy when I saw how awesome this playground was. "I guess I could get a quick climb in before everyone gets here," I thought to myself. So, I started climbing the rocks and I was thrilled when I reached the top!

Then I heard my oldest sister yelling, "Hey Patricia you are in trouble! Mom is right here!" I was startled and lost my balance and the next thing I knew I was laying on the hard concrete and felt something impeding my vision. I wiped the blood off my eyes and jumped to my feet watching as my sister laughed. "I was just joking dummy, but now you are in real trouble when mom sees that blood," said my older sister. My oldest sister was a bully and I would constantly be teased and hit by her. My head hurt so much, and I felt dizzy. My mother saw the blood dripping down my head and proceeded to grab and pull me by my sideburns and took me to a nearby fish store to get ice. "You better clean that up and not let your father see that! I told you there was no time to play but you never listen!" said my mother. That was just one of the many times I paid dearly for being a kid.

The years passed with the same abuse, but as I would one day realize-everything (bad or good) comes to an end. One Friday night, my father invented a new game where he made me a human bullseye target and sat me in the middle of the couch and started to throw toys as hard as possible to see if he could knock me out. After a few hard blows that left me woozy, I ran away and locked myself in the bathroom for a couple of hours wishing he would pass out from being drunk as he usually did. I slowly opened the door and it was quiet.

Two of my sisters were in our bedroom but one of my sisters was missing. He was locked in his bedroom with her. I tried to open the door and then started banging and kicking on it as hard as I could. I may die, but I will not let him do to my sister what he had done to me for so many years.

I also remembered that in school, the teacher taught us to call 911 if we were in any danger. So, I picked up the phone and dialed 911, "Please HELP! My father is drunk and is trying to hurt my sister and is going to kill us."

It all happened so fast! The police came and he had to come out of the room. The female officer took a blanket to cover me and hugged me and said "you are a brave girl...he won't hurt you again." I was only 10 years old, and I felt comforted receiving a hug even from a stranger.

He was removed from our home and I never saw him alone again. We had to go to court a few times for my mother to obtain full custody of all 4 of us sisters. I remember talking with the judge and telling him what my father did to me. However, my mother never pressed any charges. My Father's defense was that the alcohol made him do it, but I knew that was a lie and just an excuse to stay out of jail.

Existing became a struggle for me. The two most significant people in a child's life are their parents who are supposed to protect, love and teach them. I had nothing. I yearned for my mother's approval, love and affection. I felt guilty and responsible for my parent's divorce. I knew my father didn't love me, but to this day, my mother has never said, "I love you" to me or provided the affection that all children deserve. Healthy touch is essential for human survival; babies who are deprived of touch can fail to thrive, lose weight and even die, but defying the odds would become a constant standard of life for me.

My mother became focused on putting food on the table, a roof over our heads and clothes on our backs. She also became bitter and verbally abusive. That is all she knew. I remember always feeling like I didn't belong; like an outsider. My only outlet was the extra activities I was allowed to do after school at times. The counselor at school told my mother that I had a mild case of ADD when I was 6 years old and any extra activities would help drain the excess energy. But the extra activities would become much more. It was my healthy outlet and essential to my well-being.

Through a program at my mother's job, they offered free ballet for children. I was in ballet for a couple of years. There was a subtle change in my behavior, but not significant. When that program ended, I begged my mother to register me for gymnastics. I loved it and dreamed of being like Nadia Comaneci, but it became too expensive. So, one day walking home from school, I heard the loud sounds of "Kiai!" As I peeked through the window, I saw students kicking and punching just like the Bruce Lee movies I used to watch.

I came home from school and begged my mother to register me in Master Kim's Taekwondo School in Sunnyside, Queens near where my grandmother lived. My mother said it was much cheaper than gymnastics, but I needed to get a job and help pay for it. I had just turned 13 and I was eligible to get my working papers through school. My first job was delivering the New York Daily Newspaper to the residents of Woodside, Queens.

It would require me to wake up at 5 a.m., pick up the newspapers for my route by 6 a.m. and deliver to about 20 homes by 7:30 a.m. and be in school by 8 a.m. Although it was tough, I was earning my little money and paying for Martial Arts. I learned the value of a dollar at a very young age and I am thankful for that even though everyone in my family thought I was weird and even asked my mother if I was a lesbian for liking "boy sports".

Nothing I was doing as far as athletics and working was supported by anyone in my family. According to them, women in Colombia learned how to cook, clean, iron and maintain the house from a young age in order to be a good wife when the time came. Not even my male cousins practiced any sports, so when they found out I was practicing martial arts, everyone made fun of me and consistently laughed at me during Sunday family get togethers at my grandmother's house after church.

I felt alone often even though I was living at home sharing a bedroom with my 3 sisters. My older sister fought with me often and forced me to do her chores on top of mine as well as her homework. But soon enough, she would start to like boys and become rebellious. She started to sneak out of the house and one day ran away with an older guy who would get her pregnant. She became the first of my sisters to have a kid being a kid herself.

Teen pregnancy in my neighborhood or in New York City for that matter, was not uncommon. If anything, it was the norm to see young girls raising children of their own. I knew early on that children would not be in my future. I could never fathom being so broken inside and trying to be a mother. It would not be fair to anyone, so instead I put my focus into school, homework, karate and doing my chores.

I didn't see my mother much during the week because we were in school during the day and she kept her evening job to make ends meet, but when I did see her during the weekend, she was distant and usually would just give us more chores. I didn't know how to talk to her. All I wanted was to feel her love, but that would never happen. Ever.

It had been 3 years since my father was removed from our home and as much as everyone wanted to pretend everything was normal, it was far from normal. We were a dysfunctional family. I consistently got yelled at for a variety of petty reasons like leaving a dirty cup or not throwing out the trash and would get woken up at 2 am to wash it or throw out the trash. I would never get praised for bringing home good grades or bringing home a trophy for performing my "kata" perfectly at local karate tournaments or contributing a part of my small newspaper route salary. My mother often criticized and belittled me, just like her family did to her. I felt as if I didn't matter to her and no matter how hard I tried, it was just never good enough.

One day while my grandmother was babysitting us and watching a novela (Spanish soap opera), I went into the medicine cabinet and opened up a new bottle of Bufferin Aspirin and some other medication and consumed everything. I sat in the glass dining table remembering the beating I got because I had danced on the chair. Tears were running down my cheeks and my grandmother's face got so blurry and then I just went to sleep.

I woke up in the hospital with a terrible pain in my throat and stomach. I had just gotten my stomach pumped. My mother was standing there over me and she was furious that she was called at work to rush over to the hospital. "Why didn't you just die? Next time do it right!" she said. The nurse heard what my mother said to me and asked my mother to leave. The nurse hugged me tight and whispered in my ear, "Don't ever sacrifice your life for anyone. You are too precious and owe it to yourself to live your life to the fullest." I would never forget what she said.

The kind nurse came over the next morning and handed me a book as a gift. It was a biography on Eleanor Roosevelt who was a human rights activist, feminist, and filled to the brim with moxie. The book also contained many of her inspiring quotes that would become my daily tokens of motivation. "I hope her story will inspire you," said the Nurse. I started reading the book immediately. The words and quotes were motivating to me and I re-read and memorized her quotes and used them as mantras throughout my life. I wished I could have stayed in the hospital longer. I felt safe there.

At least in the hospital I was able to sleep with the lights off and not have nightmares. Sleeping is usually a time of peace for most but it was very difficult for me when my father was home and after he left. I had dark scary nightmares that felt evil and paralyzing. I couldn't speak or move as if someone was holding me down. I would suffer from what is known as "sleep paralysis" on and off throughout my life. I slept with a night light on, but still afraid. For that night in the hospital though, I slept in peace.

Once I returned home 2 days later, I did the things that helped me stay sane. "I owe it to myself to live life to the fullest," I remembered the nurse's words to me as I made my way to my Martial Arts class. I had just switched from Taekwondo to Kyokushin Karate, a Japanese full contact art that was more challenging and intense.

On Sundays, watching Rocky movies and making pizza from scratch by kneading white flour and using Ragu marinara sauce and grating mozzarella cheese was one of my favorite things to do with my sisters even if I did most of the work. After pizza, I had to wash all the dishes but then I got to choose what to watch on television. I was flipping through the channels and all of a sudden stopped when I heard loud roars and cheering. A petite woman was running and broke a large red tape held by two people with her chest lifted and arms raised. She fell to the ground overwhelmed with tears of happiness. She was proud and I felt like I was there with her.

I was in awe and I just blurted with excitement, "I am going to do that one day!" My sisters and mother started laughing and my mother said, "You are not good for that so just forget it." I knew that no one supported my athletics, but their words and laughter stung. I went to sleep with Olga Markova's image of winning the 1992 Boston Marathon that night and set my alarm for 4 am. The fact that everyone laughed at me just added to the fuel I had within. I could feel how proud she was of herself and so were the people cheering for her. I didn't know how I was going to do it, but I was going to at least I thought as I fell asleep.

My alarm went off at 4 a.m. and I put on old torn gray sweats, just like 'Rocky" and my worn-out tennis shoes and started running down Queens Boulevard on a cold early spring morning. It was so dark and quiet as ran past a Calvary Cemetery. I thought I saw red eyes glow behind one of the tombstones which made me now start sprinting! I made it 20 blocks down on Queens Boulevard to the corner of where Bally's

Fitness gym used to be before getting a serious side stitch underneath my ribs that impeded my breathing.

I looked down at my watch and saw that I had ran those 20 blocks equivalent to a mile in 8 minutes. I knew zilch about pacing and was disappointed that I had only lasted 8 minutes before stopping. I turned around and hobbled back home. My face was on fire and I was sweating when I got home and I liked the feeling. I couldn't wait to try again. I tried to tell my sisters all about it, but no one would listen. I wanted to run with anyone of them and even tried to bribe them by doing their chores, but no one agreed. I ran a block further every other day and by the summer 2 months later, I was running 60 blocks, 3-miles! During one of my morning runs, I saw a flyer on a storefront window for a 5k run! I ripped the flyer off the glass and mailed in the registration form. It would be my first running race ever- the Hellgate 5k in Astoria, Queens.

On race morning, I was nervous and barely warmed up nor stretched. An older man with a bullhorn and an airhorn was making announcements and all of a sudden said, "Runners... On your mark, get set, GO!" Everyone was sprinting and I did not want to fall behind, so I sprinted too! After 7 minutes, I saw the first mile marker and realized, I went out insanely fast as I usually hit the first mile in 10 minutes during my training morning runs. At 7-minutes per mile, I knew that was unknown territory for me. Then that side stitch returned and on top of that, my knee also started hurting for no apparent reason. I struggled big time throughout the entire 2nd mile. I wasn't sure how I would make it to the 3rd mile, but then I imagined myself as Rocky and kept saying to myself "You can do it! One more Mile!"

I crossed the finish line for the first time in my life at the age of 14. I wanted to hug someone so badly, but no one was there. I closed my eyes and whispered to myself "Thank you God." When I opened my eyes, an older man was looking and smiling at me. "Am I in trouble?" I asked. He smiled again and handed me a bottle of water and a banana. "Stick around young lady, I have a feeling that you won something," he said.

It was a hot summer day in June and I was happy to stick around and delay my return home.

The same older man holding the bullhorn started announcing the age group and overall winners of the Hellgate 5k. The 1st category was 15–19-year-old women. He announced 3rd place and then he said "in 2nd place from Woodside, Queens- PATRICIA ALCIVAR!" I won even though I was only 14 years old, and I felt a wave of emotions. At the time, I was really shy and my face turned red, but I went up and received my 2nd place trophy.

The same kind man was smiling, almost proud and shook my hand. He told me I reminded him of his daughter. "I want to run the New York City Marathon," I said. He told me I was too young but the more he heard me talk, he realized what it meant to me. He handed me a bunch of flyers for different races and the name of the person in charge of the New York City Marathon and the address where I can go see him.

I was smiling from ear to ear and had a bounce in my step coming home. I showed the trophy to my mother proudly and she said "That's all you get? How come only 2nd place? You should focus more on learning how to cook and not burning the rice instead". No hug, no special treatment, no nothing. No one in my entire family had ever participated in any sports and girls in Colombia would never do things like this. My mother did not know how to react as everything I was doing was uncommon in her eyes. I took a nap with my trophy next to me. I earned at least that and then went for a walk around the neighborhood and got an Italian Ice at the pizzeria as a treat to myself.

While I was walking, I saw a sign on the same storefront window where I had seen the sign for the race named Sneaker Stop that read "Salesgirl/Cashier Wanted." I walked in and applied for the job and to my surprise, got it. The newspaper delivery job was not going to be enough to purchase much needed running sneakers. I felt guilty asking my mother for expensive running sneakers so I had to take measures into my own hands.

The knee pain I had developed was from running with worn out tennis shoes. One of the perks from working at Sneaker Stop was that employees got a 50% discount. Within a month of working there, I purchased my first running sneakers, a slice of pizza, a trip to the movies and I also made sure I gave some money to my mother. I initially started working at the store on the weekends from opening to closing which would be 16 long hours.

It wasn't an easy job either. I had to be on my feet most of the time and when it was busy with customers requesting to try on multiple sneakers at a time, I had to run up and down steep stairs. On one occasion, I was tired and sat down when the store was slow and the store owner, Jorge came over and said to me in a firm tone, "If the store is not busy with customers, you need to clean the windows, sweep the inside and outside of the store or dust the sneaker holders and racks. There is always something to do!"

Besides scaring the daylights out of me when he said that I was appreciative because that speech taught me about making the best use of my time at work and in everything I do. I was thankful to have this job which enabled me to purchase my new running sneakers and running on my new white Etonics made a huge difference.

With my new sneakers, I could run further without any pain. By mid-summer I was running all the way down to the Court Houses on Queens Boulevard and back which was over 6 miles! Whenever I was running, I felt better about myself, but the minute I was home, I felt terrible and useless again. I had a collection of about 10 trophies, I was an excellent student at school, did my chores and contributed financially, but it just wasn't good enough.

I kept working, running and practicing martial arts with much dedication for the next entire year. While I was working at the sneaker store one day, I overheard some women talk about a lady looking for someone to rent a room in her apartment.

Through running, I felt my courage grow and I asked the woman for more information and mentioned that I was looking for a place. She gave me the name, address and telephone number of Dona Oliva in Jackson Heights, Queens.

I came home tired from a full weekend of work and training and my mother welcomed me home by yelling at me saying that I had a list of chores that had to get done. She would often say, "This is MY House! If you don't like it, Get out!" I wanted to cry, but I did my chores and went to sleep fully clothed. I woke up the next morning, packed a duffle bag with clothes, my books and a few trophies and left. Instead of going to school, I showed up in Dona Olivia's home crying and asked her to please rent the room to me. She hugged me and agreed to rent the tiny room to me.

I was now 15 years old and living by myself. That day, I didn't go to school and just stayed in my new room and prayed and cried myself to sleep with the lights on. I was alone, but I was in peace. No more yelling. No more chores. No more making me feel bad. I already missed my sisters, but I was sure no one missed me.

CHAPTER 2

Chapter Two - Round 2

The New York City Marathon
"The future belongs to those who believe in the beauty of their dreams," Eleanor Roosevelt

I was attending school at Fiorello LaGuardia Middle College High School and my goal was to be the best student I could be. With the teenage pregnancy being high, I didn't want to be another statistic. That was not going to be part of my journey. My days consisted of waking up at 5am, running, going to school, working 4-5 times a week at the Sneaker Store and still managing to practice Martial Arts at least twice a week in the evenings.

"I owe it to myself to live life to the fullest." I always remembered the nurse's words to me and I woke up with a mission to go see the President of the New York Road Runners Club after school. I took the number 6 train to 89th Street in Manhattan and walked to the New York Road Runners Club which at the time was located on 9 East 89th Street between Madison and Fifth Avenues. An older man with kind blue eyes named Joe Kleinerman asked me if I had an appointment. I said, "I am here to see Mr. Allan Steinfeld, the President of New York Road Runners Club. I live by myself but my dream is to run the New York City Marathon."

Little did I know that Joe Kleinerman was one of the founding members of the New York Road Runners Club-one of the biggest running companies in the world as well as the Producers of the New York City

17

Marathon. I could see and feel his heart soften. He asked the receptionist to let Mr. Allan Steinfeld know that he had a visitor who needed to speak to him. Moments later, a young woman who was his assistant came to escort me to his office.

Mr. Steinfeld extended his arm to shake my hand. "Nice to meet you young lady. How can I help you?" he said. My eyes watered but I didn't cry, and I told him my story from calling the police to how I started running after seeing Olga Markova win the Boston Marathon on television to now living by myself. I was surprised at myself for sharing so much about my past, but it was also so liberating.

I unconsciously wanted to let go and rise above it. I would learn that the more you share something that is supposed to hold you down, the less power it has over you. He put his hand on my shoulder and smiled at me in a very tender fatherly way and then called his assistant into his office. He granted me a free entry into the 1993 New York City Marathon and waived the fee for running classes with Coach Bob Glover and a year's worth of running race entries to any New York Road Runner races. Mr. Allan Steinfeld told me that it was early spring and the New York City Marathon was in November, so I had about 6 months to train. He expected a full report on how I was doing before and after the marathon.

I was not going to let this incredible opportunity go to waste. For the first time in my life someone-a complete stranger, gave me a chance and believed in me. I registered immediately for the Marathon and for Bob Glover's Running Classes which would be every Monday and Wednesday evenings in Central Park.

I was a senior in high school in 1993. I had skipped a grade for being at the top of my class and excelled in all my classes but kept to myself and barely had friends. I did not want anyone to know that I was living by myself and risk getting reported to ACS (Administration of Child Services) and worse, get sent to a foster home as the legal age to be independent was 18. My focus was on graduating honorably, training, finding a better job and on not becoming another statistic.

My rent was $60 a week and I was making between $85-$100 a week at Sneaker Stop. Any money left over after paying for my room was used for transportation and food. I knew I had to find a better job eventually. I showed up for my first running class that Monday evening at 7pm after going to school in the morning and working a few hours at the sneaker store. I was tired, but the excitement distracted me from all of that.

Bob Glover was a tall fair skinned man in his late 40's with piercing blue eyes. I had my usual gray sweats but at least I had my white Etonic running sneakers. "Alright Folks, listen up! Line up by your running pace.

7 minutes per mile or under come with me, 8-9 minutes per mile will go with Coach Alex and over 10 minutes per mile go with Coach Shelly." I could have gone in the 2nd group, but when I saw Coach Shelly, the only female coach, I went with that group. She had a kind face.

We ran a 2-mile warm-up and then caught up with the main groups. We were to do 12x Hill repeats of Cat Hill in Central Park within our groups. I started out too fast that there was no one behind me. I was so happy, but that lasted about two repetitions and then I fell behind coming in next to last on the rest of the repetitions. I was now struggling to just survive the workout.

Shelly tapped my shoulder after class and asked my age. I was afraid but I told her the truth. "Do your parents know you are here?" she asked. I told her that I had spoken to Mr. Allan Steinfeld and he gave me the running classes to help me train for my first New York City Marathon and that was all I told her. I knew just by the look in her face that she understood. I went home to my room tired but with a sense of accomplishment. Despite some rainy and cold days, I never missed a class.

After 5 months of non-stop dedicated training, I was ready for the 18-mile Marathon Tune-up Run which consisted of 3 full loops of Central Park. Before each training run or race, I always prayed. It was the one thing I had to do and it never failed me. I prayed before the sound of the horn and off we went!

I was feeling good for the entire first loop even though I had gone out too fast yet again. I remembered Coach Shelly telling me that I needed to learn how to pace myself properly. But to me, it felt necessary to go out and give 100% even if then I would pay for it. I struggled through the 2nd loop and then the 3rd loop was miserable but I had to finish no matter what! A fellow runner gave me the thumbs up as he passed me and said "Keep Going!" I finished the 3rd lap and completed the 18-miles!

I was only a month away now from the New York City Marathon. Sometimes, I remembered what my mother had said about me running a marathon one day, "You are not good for that, so forget it." I realized that when things are going well, the old painful things will want to come back and haunt you if you let it. It is a process, and you need to recognize it and do everything you can to move on.

It was time to taper and start recovering so I could be in peak conditions on Marathon Day. I didn't realize what an enormous event this was. On the last week before the New York City Marathon, Bob Glover took us on a tempo run around the finish line of the Marathon by Tavern on the Green in Central Park. There was a plethora of bleachers set up already as well as scaffolding, barricades and a jumbotron! Coach Shelly said, "Visualize yourselves crossing the finish line on Sunday with your arms in the air." I did and felt a rush of emotions running through my body.

On that Saturday before the Marathon, I went to pick up my bib number and went to the pasta party by myself. I wanted to take in all this experience as Coach Shelly told us that the 1st Marathon is usually the most special. I was not able to sleep that night from nervousness and from a horrible stomach ache.

I woke up and discovered I had my period. I had started my period when I was just 10 years old after my father left. I thought I was dying from a fall I took after climbing the fences I was told not to. My mother found my bed full of blood a few days later and told me I was not dying and that it was part of starting to become a woman. It was difficult to comprehend that and I didn't enjoy what I was feeling physically nor mentally. Ever since then, I really did feel like I was dying each time I got my red best friend.

I woke up at 4am, prayed and had my coffee and got the #7 train to the 42nd Street and walked a few blocks to the New York City Public Library where all the runners would be transported to Staten Island- The Start of the New York City Marathon. As I waited on line to get on the bus, I saw runners hugging their loved ones before getting on board. I had no one. It was a familiar feeling of being alone.

I was cold waiting at the Verrazano Bridge on Staten Island and my lower back and stomach started to ache already and I had not even started. The loud bang of the cannon sounded to start the Marathon and my 26.2-mile journey begun! The entire bridge shook from all the feet pounding of the 25,000 runners. As we ran 3 miles on the bridge and exited into Brooklyn, there were crowds screaming and holding signs in support of all of us. I was amazed that complete strangers were trying to high-five me, giving me the thumbs up and just smiling with care.

At mile 13.1-half way through the New York City Marathon, we were crossing over the Pulaski Bridge which felt like running barefoot on rocks. My body felt broken, but as I was coming off the bridge, I realized that we had just arrived in Queens- My Borough! We were running in Long Island City, near where I had been going to school. There were so many people cheering and handing out water. Deep down, I wished to see my mother, my sisters or just anyone familiar. I desperately looked in the crowds, but no one I knew was there.

The run in Queens was very short and we were heading towards the Queens Borough Bridge which was a very steep mile and a half that would take us into Manhattan and into mile 16! "Live your life to the fullest," thoughts flooded my mind as I struggled to keep putting one foot in front of the other. The roars and cheers from the crowds only grew louder all throughout 1st Avenue. The stitch on my side returned along with the knee pain, lower back and stomach pains. As I started to cross yet another bridge at mile 20 on 125th Street into the Bronx, I started to feel overwhelmed.

Being a teenager still, I had never pushed my body to this extreme. I think the pain showed so much in my face, that a medical volunteer asked if I needed help. I held back tears and just kept moving. All of a sudden, we were in Central Park- Mile 23 and the final 5k left to run. 3.1 miles left to accomplish my dream that had started almost 2 years ago and to prove that I was good for something.

As I ran through the hills in Central Park, I remembered Coach Shelly's words to visualize myself crossing the finish line. It helped distract the unbelievable pain and fatigue in my legs. We exited Central Park momentarily to run Mile 25 on 6th Avenue into Columbus Circle before re-entering Central Park for the final half mile stretch. I could feel my legs trying to give out on me. "Fight for it!" I said to myself. "You're Gonna Do It!" said a woman standing in the crowd and looking directly at me. I had an instant lump in my throat hearing that and then seeing my image on the Jumbotron running towards the finish line with all those thousands of people clapping.

I FINISHED! I collapsed as I crossed the Finish Line realizing I am a Marathon Finisher despite all the odds! At that precise moment, I vowed to myself to never forget this moment and to run a marathon each year to keep honoring this achievement and to remind me of what is possible even if you are the only one who believes. A military officer put the finisher medal on me and carried me all the way to the family reunion area to retrieve my belongings. I limped to take the subway and back home to my little room. I wished I could show my medal to my mother and sisters, but I also knew they wouldn't have cared. I remembered them all laughing when I said I would run a marathon one day. If they could just see me now.

I wrote a letter to Mr. Allan Steinfeld thanking him and letting him know what I was feeling and that I wanted to return next year. I prayed and fell into the deepest sleep that night. I was alone, but I was in peace.

Earlier that year before completing my 1st ever Marathon, I had graduated from Middle College High School with Honors as the Salutatorian of my class a year ahead of schedule. Because of my high grades, I was allowed to take college courses for free at LaGuardia Community College, so right after graduation, I enrolled as a part-time college student.

Now, I had accomplished 2 of my goals- Graduating with honors and finishing my 1st Marathon. It was a nice start, but something deep inside made me feel that there was much more to do. I didn't know what was next and prayed for guidance. As a small gift to myself for my marathon finish, I treated myself the next morning to a large coffee and cinnamon raisin bagel with cream cheese at Dunkin Doughnuts that I purchased with a coupon from my NYC Marathon goody bag.

I read the Sunday New York Daily Newspaper from the day before and looked through the classifieds and while I was doing this, I found two amazing things- a basement apartment for rent in Rego Park, Queens and a job opening as a receptionist at a place called Sanctuary for Families.

As much as I was comfortable living in a tiny room by myself and working at the sneaker store, I knew I had to leave both as soon as possible or else I would get stuck. With a sense of urgency, I went to school to use their computer and wrote a cover letter and mailed it immediately to Sanctuary for Families expressing my interest in the Receptionist position and also called the contact for the apartment, Mrs. Lenore and asked to see the basement apartment that she was renting in her home.

Mrs. Lenore asked me to come see the apartment that afternoon. I took the train right after school to Rego Park and as I walked around the neighborhood, it reminded me of when I first saw it during my training runs. I always looked forward to running by this section and hoped in my heart to one day to live nearby. I knocked on the door and Mrs. Lenore came out and I could tell by the expression in her face that she was not expecting to see a teenager standing in front of her. "Hello, are you with someone else?" she asked.

I felt my head spin, but I managed to tell her that I have been living on my own because I left an abusive home, but that I have been working after school and was looking to get a better job. I had no references, so all I had was my word. She invited me inside her home and told me that paying rent is very important. She made a deal with me and said she would hold the apartment for me until I found out if I had the new job. The rent was going to be $500/per month- a big jump from $60 a week. Right after I left her home, I remembered seeing a church further down on Queens Boulevard during my runs and I walked the mile there. I sat in church for a while and then prayed and felt tears rolling down my cheeks.

Martial Arts would now occupy my focus since I was invited by Instructor, Shihan Henry-Oh to be part of the Fight Team which would be training for the World Full Contact Tournament in Manhattan Center. I had to make the most out of every opportunity that was presented to me, so I was going to the Sunnyside Kyokushin Dojo every other day and on the weekends.

A few weeks passed and I came to my room after training to find a letter taped on my door. I opened it and it was a letter from Sanctuary for Families inviting me for an interview that Monday morning. I was excited but nervous about getting questioned about my age. I was still under what New York City considered the legal age to be living by myself and I had made it this far without being reported. Teenagers found living on their own were usually placed in foster care homes which had a horrible reputation for being dangerous and sometimes worse than living on the streets.

The next day on Sunday, I went to church and prayed. On Monday, I woke up earlier than usual and asked Dona Oliva if I can borrow her make-up. I told her I needed to look older for my job interview in Manhattan. She didn't hesitate and helped apply the mascara, eye shadow and blush on my face. I looked in the mirror and I felt satisfied. She also loaned me her long elegant brown trench coat. I didn't have much of a professional wardrobe, so I wore my best church outfit which was my black pants, and laced trimmed turquoise blouse.

I arrived at 50 Chambers Street in Downtown, Manhattan and asked one of the ladies who was a counselor to see Carla, the Office Manager. Within a few minutes, Carla showed up and looked at me from head to toe and extended her hand, "Nice to meet you. Let's go into my office," said Carla. "So, tell me a little about yourself and your background," said Carla. I took a deep breath, smiled and said, "I graduated as a Salutatorian, skipped a grade, worked an internship at Hewlett Packard and at Astoria General Hospital, but most important of all, I am a hard worker and fast learner and really need this job to pay for my new apartment." Carla opened her eyes wide and was still smiling and took me into see Kristin the Assistant Director and Laurie, the Executive Director.

Both Kristen and Laurie simultaneously asked, "How old are you?" I could feel my face get warm and I blurted out "I am 18 years old." I could feel them eyeing me but I wasn't sure what was going through their heads. I didn't know if they knew I was lying about my age. "How soon can you start," asked Kristen. "I can start as soon as you'd like," I replied without hesitation.

While I was on the subway to Rego Park to let Mrs. Lenore know that I was hired for the job, I kept replaying everything that had just happened. I was going to give 100% effort to this opportunity- my first real job in the professional working world and I would have to continue my college courses on some evenings and weekends. I was also dreading telling the good news to my employers at the Sneaker Store.

Mrs. Lenore opened the door and she knew I had the job by the expression in my face. My sister had always told me that with my face, I really didn't need to speak at times. "Congratulations! You can move in as soon as you want," she said and also handed me the keys. Now, I also had to tell the good news to Dona Oliva. I had a sinking feeling in my stomach. This time I took the bus to the Sneaker Store to start my afternoon shift. "Why are you all dressed up?" asked the Manager and Co-owner Yamille. How can such a happy day be so stressful? I thought before answering. "I got offered a new job as a receptionist for an organization in Manhattan today! I start next Monday-a week from now."

The look on Yamille's face was not of joy. She marched over to the register and took out $100 and said, "You can leave now. I've always told you that no one is indispensable. Good luck." I was hurt and disappointed but figured she must have felt hurt at me wanting to leave, but all I wanted was a better future. This type of behavior would be a constant in my life where people would not be happy anytime anything good happened to me.

I didn't know if Dona Oliva was going to have the same reaction. I didn't want to hurt her in any way. I decided to go to the Karate Dojo instead of going to my room. Shihan Henry-Oh was surprised to see me at an unusual time, but he made sure I trained extra hard. I wouldn't stress at all for the next two hours. The World Tournament was also quickly approaching, so it was a good last-minute decision and now felt I had the courage to speak with Dona Oliva.

Dona Oliva was waiting to see how the interview went. I nervously smiled and said, "I got the job! But I have something else to tell you... I also found a small basement apartment in a house in Rego Park and I would like to move in soon." She looked down for a moment and then gave me a hug and said, "I never expected you to live here forever. I will miss having someone in that room. I know you will do great things and I wish you the best." I breathed a big sigh of relief. People like her in my life would be rare. I didn't want to leave but knew I had to. I didn't have much to pack. Before I left that evening, I wrote a little note to Dona Oliva thanking her for her generosity and for being so sweet to me along with $100 that was given to me at the Sneaker Store.

I showed up to my new basement apartment in Rego Park. It had a small kitchen, a small dining area, a bathroom and a separate bedroom. It was cozy and big at the same time. I never had this much space all to myself. I had no furniture and slept on the rug inside the bedroom and used my duffle bag as a pillow and my coat as a blanket. I slept with the lights on in the living room on the first night in my new place.

Mrs. Lenore knocked on my door the next morning and said, "I have some furniture that I am getting rid of. You are welcomed to it if you want." Right outside my door was a futon, a small dining table for two people and a small television. I was in disbelief. "If you don't need these items, I would like to have them," I said softly trying not to cry. Mrs. Lenore smiled and walked away. She was an angel in disguise that the heavens from above always manages to put in my path at the right moment.

The next morning, I ran for the first time since the New York City Marathon. I was replaying all my Marathon memories and everything that had occurred in the last week since. Without realizing it, I had just ran 6 miles and felt like I could run forever. All of a sudden, a noise of some sort of cries woke me up from the trance state I was in.

I stopped and searched to see where the sound was coming from. I walked closer to a bush that was around the corner from the house and it was 2 male kittens! Without a second thought, I took them home with me.

I named them Billy and Jay. I had a few days free before I started my new job, so I spent all my free time with these guys. They were an amazing breath of fresh air. I played with Billy and Jay, shared my tuna fish and watched television with them.

When I lived with my parents, they never allowed me to have anything I could call my own including pets. We had a dog named Blacky once when I was about 6 years old. I loved him so much and he slept on my bed and one day he was just gone. No reason, no explanations-just gone...

Monday came and I started my new job at a place that would become a life changing experience. Sanctuary for Families is a not-for-profit organization dedicated to the safety, healing and self-determination of victims of domestic violence and related forms of gender violence through comprehensive services ranging from legal services, shelter and counseling. Offering clients and their children outreach, education and advocacy.

The phones were ringing off the hook with women wanting to find out information about services and if there was any space available in any of the shelters. I realized that I was the first-person victims of domestic violence would hear when trying to flee a dangerous situation. It was a stressful first day. I remembered the times we were scared of my father and felt there was no place to go.

When the end of the day came, one of the counselors, Teresa, who was also a nun, came over to introduce herself. She had bright kind blue eyes and a gentle smile. "It will get easier. Hang in there. We need you," she said. I had come to find out through one of the clients that the receptionists didn't last more than a couple months. They had 6 different receptionists in the past year alone. All I knew is that I needed this job and I was not going anywhere anytime soon.

As the weeks went by, I started to read the literature that Sanctuary for Families offered to their clients. I was educating myself and discovering that domestic violence is an awful cycle that can be passed on from generation to generation. Victims of abuse generally become abusers themselves, but with knowledge and awareness, you have the power to stop and break the cycle. I remembered my mother saying that my grandfather was abusive to my grandmother and I saw a lot of abuse in my family which I was taught to believe was the norm. I wondered if my mother and father were abused themselves in anyway growing up and I knew the answer.

I had always believed in the power of your choices and being humble enough to ask for help. I felt an enormous amount of gratitude for the opportunity to work here as it was a blessing in so many ways.

Throughout the next few months, I took it upon myself to organize everything in the supply room and cabinets as well as maintain all the common areas in the office. I learned how to use all the office machines like the copier, fax, postage machine and order the supplies when anything was running low. "Did you organize all that?" asked Carla. I smiled and said, "Yes, it was kind of slow and have been meaning to do that for a while." She was surprised and then placed a computer on my desk. "It is not new, but I figured you can use it to update the contact list and a few other office documents."

The receptionists usually did not have computers as their main responsibility was answering the phone, taking messages and greeting the clients. However, I went above and beyond my receptionist responsibilities and helped the other departments translate documents and offered to help out with everything and anything. Although a used computer might not seem like a big deal, it was very meaningful for me. To me, it meant acknowledgement of my hard work and efforts and that meant the world to me.

CHAPTER 3

Chapter Three - Round 3

World Champion

"Do one thing every day that scares you," Eleanor Roosevelt

My work hours at Sanctuary for Families were from 9am-5pm, so I was able to get to Karate practice by 6:30 p.m. almost every day and I felt ready for the World Championships which was the following weekend in Manhattan Center, right across the street from Madison Square Garden. I didn't realize it back then, but I had a God-given ability to just keep going even through fatigue, stress or sadness. I packed my days from sunrise to past sunset because I've always felt I had something to prove to myself and to my higher power.

I tried to make the best out of training tonight but then Shihan Henry-Oh pulled me aside after practice and spoke to me in a serious tone and said, "There are 8 women in your division and 2 of them are on the Elite Brazilian Team. You have been training well and I believe you can take it all."

I went straight home after practice and felt like something was wrong almost immediately. For the past 3 months now, Billy and Jay always greeted me when I came home except for tonight. I started looking underneath my bed, inside the closets, in the bathroom, but nothing. I saw a hole in the window screen of the living room. Could it be? Did they run away? I knocked on Mrs. Lenore's door, "Billy and Jay are missing! Can I borrow a flashlight?" I was in tears and went out looking for them for what seemed like the entire night. I did not find them. I felt so alone that night.

For as long as I could remember, I was always drawn to all animals. When I was an adolescent, I was crazy about dogs, cats, birds and teddy bears. For a short moment, having Billy and Jay helped fill the emptiness that I felt often and I was incredibly sad to have them yanked out of my life. I went for a long run the next morning. Running and Karate were my healthy outlets. The more I hurt, the more I ran and the harder I kicked and punched.

Every day after work during that week, I made it to the Dojo to stretch, meditate, practice my kicks and punches. Like Coach Shelly had taught me, I also visualized myself winning and the only thing missing now was prayer, so the Friday night before the big day, I went to church.

That Saturday morning, I did not feel nervous and I met Shihan Henry-Oh and the team at Manhattan Center to get weighed in and officially check in. I saw my opponents who were giving me the nastiest looks which I found unnecessary. It was not my style to trash talk or to be anyone's enemy. Eight of us would officially register for the Women's Light Weight division which meant that in order to become the Champion, I would have to fight and win 4 consecutive bouts.

Once I weighed in at 118lbs, I started hearing my mother's words echoing in my ear, "You are not good for that, so forget it." I wasn't sure why at this precise moment I was having these thoughts and hearing these words. I ran to the bathroom and got on my knees, "God, please help me have clarity, strength and courage to fight to the best of my ability. If it is your will for me to be victorious, so be it. Amen." I changed into my Gi (white Karate uniform), took a few deep breaths and waited in the warm-up area to be called for my bout.

Shihan Henry-Oh was nowhere to be found and was too busy speaking with other instructors and international guests from all over the world. I was on my own again and then I heard "PATRICIA ALCIVAR on deck for the next bout in the red corner," coming through the speakers in my dressing room. As I walked down the hallway and onto the mat, I kept saying to myself "You deserve to live life to the fullest...all or nothing!" I looked across the mat and saw my opponent who was shorter than me and from Chicago. The Sansei who was refereeing quickly gave us instructions and then said, "SHOBU HAJIME!" When I heard that, a fire ignited within and I started off with a roundhouse kick that landed flush on her face and I followed up with a series of low kicks and punches. The referee jumped in and stopped the bout. One down, 3 to go.

I took a quick breather and within a few minutes was back on the Mat looking across to my 2nd opponent, a girl in her early 20's, about my height from New Jersey. The same referee gave us instructions and once again he yelled out, "SHOBU HAJIME!"

She was nice and fresh and started at a relentless pace kicking and punching, but it didn't hurt. When I kicked her, it moved her entire body. So, I made every kick and punch count. The round lasted the full 5 minutes and at the end of it, I had clearly won. 2 down, 2 to go.

My teammates from the Sunnyside Kyokushin Karate Dojo were now visible for me to see for the first time. My teammate, John came over and said, "The next two opponents are from the Brazilian Elite Team. You Got this. Your next opponent has a soft stomach, so focus on taking her wind away." That was the first time throughout the tournament anyone gave me any coaching, so I soaked up all the information.

My 3rd bout begun and this girl was bigger and stronger. She was hitting me with furious low kicks, but then I started punching her ribs and mid-section. I saw her wince each time I hit her right side, so I concentrated on chopping her down and after the full five minutes, I won my 3rd bout. I would later find out that she had fractured ribs. 3 down, 1 to go!

I had 5 whole minutes to drink water, stretch and get ready for the Championship Bout. My legs were hurting. My last opponent injured the inside of my legs with her vicious low kicks. John came over and told me to stop rubbing and holding my legs because my opponent was watching. "Your final opponent is taller, so do the same thing. Don't stop until you break her ribs! You can do it!" whispered John firmly in my ear.

Everything was hurting, but just like the Marathon, I can put all the pain on hold until I am finished. "You deserve to live your life to the fullest. All or nothing," I repeated before the final "SHOBU HAJIME!" My final opponent came out as if she was possessed. She went straight for my legs-inside and outside HARD! I almost went down, but the fear of losing and the fear of giving in fueled me not to and I started a furious attack of hooks to the body. I could see her face in pain and bending every time she saw my fist coming. The punches to her ribs took away her legs and then I finished her off with a right hand to the solar plexus. The bout ended and the referee raised my hand as the Women's Kyokushin Full Contact World Champion!

John came over and hugged me. I closed my eyes. "Thank you, God." I was in disbelief. I went to the bathroom and cried. Although I had just won a World Championship, I didn't understand why I wasn't truly happy. I also didn't think many people expected me to win. My girly features and kind face deceived many people into thinking I was weak. Many spectators came up to me afterwards asking how I could go at the pace I did without showing any weakness or pain.

What they didn't know was that I learned from a very young age how to withstand insurmountable pain from the beatings my father gave me. If I could survive that and living on my own, this tournament in some ways didn't compare. My life had already prepared me to be a fighter.

I was somewhat confused and momentarily sad because with the exception of John, none of my other teammates, students from the Dojo or instructors where anywhere near me. Nonetheless, I was going to do my best to enjoy this incredible achievement. I iced my legs as I watched the rest of the bouts and cheered on my teammate John as he also won the World Championship for the Men.

The awards ceremony started and I was handed a beautiful Trophy as well as a $500 check. I smiled inside and wondered if my mother would be proud. I took in this moment, but thought, "There is much more to do."

CHAPTER 4

Chapter Four - Round 4

Boxing, the Loneliest Sport
   "People grow through experience if they meet life honestly and courageously. This is how character is built,"
Eleanor Roosevelt

John invited me to go out and celebrate afterwards to a local bar, but I was still under age and didn't want to risk getting in trouble on a night I had just won a World Championship. The pain is now making an appearance! I can hardly walk and just want to go home and rest. John had a bruised eye and just gave me one last hug and I treated myself to a taxi home.

The next day, I wanted to run, but I was very sore and instead decided to walk a few miles to Sunday church. I prayed for guidance and clarity. My journey was not over, but I just did not know what was next. I walked more after church. I didn't have Billy and Jay waiting for me anymore, so I was not rushing to get home. I walked another 3 miles to Dona Oliva's home to say hello and tell her about my tournament, but no one was home. I walked back home for a total of 8 miles today. I had exhausted myself and finally passed out.

I got to work early that Monday and when Teresa arrived, she said "Congratulations! You have broken a record." I opened my eyes wide and I said, "How did you know about the World Championships?" She looked so confused. "You have now been the longest receptionist we have had and you are doing a wonderful job." smiled Teresa. I had been working at Sanctuary for Families for over a year now! Working hard was just part of my DNA. If there was anything I inherited from my mother, it was not being afraid to work hard.

Carla came over and handed me a catalogue that said "The New School." I wasn't quite sure what to do with it but then she said, "Employees are allowed to take up to three classes from the New School for free." I had stopped my college courses after completing a Certificate in Secretarial Studies.

I eventually wanted to return to school, but with a full-time job and training, I barely had time and besides, I didn't have enough money to pay for college with now paying $500/per month in rent. Perhaps I could start taking a few classes towards a degree.

"Thank you, Carla! I will check it out at my lunch hour and let you know." One of the things I did on my own was to stay sharp on my bilingual skills and would volunteer to translate documents for the legal and counseling departments, so I had my morning all cut out for me. While I ate lunch at my desk, I went through the New School Catalogue. I saw a writing class that appealed to me and wrote down the code and then I saw a public speaking class and wrote the code for that as well and finally, I saw something that really caught my eye, "The Art of Boxing."

I gave my list to Carla and she faxed the registration forms right away. My classes would start in a couple of weeks, but I couldn't help remembering all those Saturday nights watching boxing on T.V. with my father and wishing I could be just like them. I missed my Martial Arts practice, but had not returned to the Dojo after the World Championship because I felt like there was nothing else for me to do there, but this was my chance to try what I've always thought was part of who I was- A Fighter.

After lunch, Carla wanted to have a meeting with me to evaluate my 1-year performance. Although I knew I had done the absolute best work I could, I couldn't help but think that it wasn't good enough. Being told I was good for nothing all throughout my life by the most important people in my life made me feel insecure often.

"Patricia, in the year that you have been with us, you have made wonderful progress and helped the departments and taken many things off my plate like ordering office supplies and maintaining office equipment. The Supervisory Team would like to promote you to Assistant Office Manager and of course, that comes with a 10% raise," said Carla. I was speechless. "How does that sound Patricia?"

"Thank you so much Carla! That sounds amazing!" I answered while still holding back tears. Carla smiled and shook my hand. I had not confided in anyone at work about my personal situation.

That feeling of uncertainty and feeling like an outsider stayed with me and I struggled to fit in. As with my newspaper job and the Sneaker Store job, I would just let my work speak for itself.

Two weeks passed and my first Boxing class was on a Saturday at an open space inside one of The New School locations near 14th Street in Manhattan. I woke up early and ran 3 miles to shake off the butterflies, took a shower and then took the train. The New York City subways were so unreliable and there were always some route changes due to construction on weekends. You could literally end up in Africa and sure enough, the train I was on went in a different direction. I got off and ran a couple of miles to the New School and arrived to the class already in progress. "Hey you Kid! You're late. Just try to follow along," said the giant instructor with a heavy Brooklyn accent that reminded me of Rocky Balboa.

"Step, step and jab, right hand to the body and hook to the head and right to the body and go back and start over again," said the instructor. We did that same drill for about a half hour and I was already feeling frustrated. "When do we get in the ring and start fighting?" was my thought. The tempo of the class was slow and I couldn't wait until it was over. I couldn't believe I wasted my Saturday on this.

90 minutes after, the class was finally over. He was high fiving people as they walked out the door. He tried to high five me and said "See ya next weekend kid!" I looked irately at him and said, "I am not coming back. I thought this was a real boxing class where we got to fight." He

looked bewildered. I continued to say "I am a World Champion in Martial Arts and thought I could better my punches and figure out what my next goal in the sport could be with this class, but I was wrong."

He had an annoying smirk on his face and said, "Okay kid, let me see what you got. Throw any punches you want." This was the tallest man I had ever seen at about 6 feet 5 inches and easily over 225 pounds or so and I was barely 5'4, but I started throwing my best and hardest punches. He was blocking everything hard. I remained calm and found an opening in his solar plexus and hit him as hard as I could right in the center! "WHOA!" he doubled over, but still had his eyes on me.

It actually was not a waste of my Saturday anymore after landing that shot. Now I was the one smirking. "Hey Kid, so Women's Boxing just became legal last year in 1995. I can train you to fight for the New York Golden Gloves this year if you want." It was the beginning of January and the women would fight sometime in March. We need to sign you up immediately if this is what you want.

I looked straight into his eyes and said, "That is what I want." He took all my information and said he would take care of it. "I want you to come to Wall Street Boxing on Monday and we can start training and talk more then."

I cracked my own self up at times of how spontaneous I could be, but it felt like something else took over momentarily. As I was making my way home, I saw Mrs. Lenore standing outside. She had a concerned expression on her face. "Hi Mrs. Lenore. Is everything okay?" I hesitated to say. "Listen Patricia, this is very difficult to say to you and please understand that I have no choice. My husband lost his job and we need to increase the rent. We kept the rent low because we knew your situation, but now, we have to increase it to $600."

I had been living there for now almost 2 years without a rent increase, but even with my new job, that was too high of a price. "I am sorry about your husband Mrs. Lenore. How long do I have?" I could tell that she felt terrible and I didn't want to add to her stress. "We can give you at least a month to look for another place and if you don't find one, you can always stay in one of the bedrooms in the main house." I felt like the wind had been knocked out of me from a big round house kick.

I didn't even know where to begin looking for a new place. Tomorrow was Sunday, a new day where I would run a 5k and then go to church and figure everything out. I was relieved and excited to be running a race again. I was able to get into a meditative state while trying to push through discomfort. When I arrived to the Start of the race in Flushing, Queens, I saw that kind man that had given me Allan Steinfeld's name and race flyers. He had already seen me and was walking towards me with his arm extended to shake my hand.

I wanted to hug this familiar face, but he was very respectful. "Nice to see you again Patricia! How have you been?" He gently asked. He knew my name but never told me his. "I never got to thank you for giving me Mr. Allan Steinfeld's information. He helped me get into the New York City Marathon and I ran it! I would love to run it again this year!"

He didn't look surprised and said, "I knew you would. Alan Steinfeld is a kind man and will be your friend always. Call him and I am sure he will help you again." He smiled one more time and before I can say anything else, he hurried away to help finish setting up the finish line. I stretched and did a quick warm-up jog. The gun went off and I ran as hard as I could. I couldn't think, I just ran. It felt good. I had improved my 5k time and this time I won 1st in my age division. While I was leaving, I got an application to join a running club that met at the Astoria Park Track every Wednesday evening for speed workouts. I liked the feeling from running fast as there was no time to think about anything else. I planned to show up the following Wednesday.

The weekend went by quickly and I packed a gym bag to go straight to the Wall Street Boxing Gym right after work. I didn't feel that working in my new role as Assistant Office Manager was much different than what I was already doing, but I wanted to keep doing the best job I could. I would make my rounds in the morning to each department asking if they needed help with anything. Their "Zero Tolerance" event was the organization's prime fundraiser, so I sent out additional invitations and typed Thank You letters to people that purchased tickets or sent donations.

At 5pm I raced out the door and took the elevator up to the Wall Street Boxing Gym which was in a very trendy Manhattan office building. There was a small ring. 4 heavy bags, 2 speed bag stations and a corner with full length wall mirrors for shadow boxing. "Hey Yo Kid! Go jump rope for 3 rounds and shadow-box in the mirror. You are sparring today." Holy Smokes! I was not expecting to spar. In Karate, when we had sparring practice, it was serious business. I have not sparred or fought since the Kyokushin Karate World Tournament which was a while ago.

As I was finishing up my warm-up, I saw another woman shadow boxing. Coach came over and started wrapping my hands with stinky wraps that smelled like hot garbage and then he helped me put a pair of equally smelly 14-oz gloves on. He then placed a Shevlin brand head guard on me. The only thing I owned was my mouth guard. "You are going to have to get your own gear, but you can borrow these for the meantime," said Coach.

Then, the muscular petite woman that I had seen warming up, came over and said, "Are you ready?" I would find out later that her name was Jill, last year's 1st Female New York City Golden Gloves Champion in the 106-pound division. Coach said, "This is the kid's 1st time sparring and I'm training her for this year's gloves. I think she's got something." Jill's expression and demeanor changed. The bell rang and she landed the hardest left hand on my head and followed up with a nasty body punch. It took my breath away and it took everything I had to finish that round on my feet. When I went to the corner, Coach was furious and cursing under his breath. "Hang on for one more round. I don't know what's up her ass," he said.

Bell rang for the second round and Jill came out with the same unwarranted aggression. I was confused and didn't know how to respond.

This was my very first time in the boxing ring. I barely survived the second round and Coach said, "I think that's enough for today." Jill smiled and said, "That's it? Okay, but call me anytime you want some work and good luck in the Gloves!" Jill had just turned professional as a female boxer. What she did was not right, but I still admired her achievement in the New York City Golden Gloves and now dreamed of becoming a Golden Gloves Champion.

Afterwards, Coach held the pads for me and we worked on foot work. "You didn't move and got caught because you didn't move your feet. You have to jab and move and find your openings. You gotta think! Boxing is like a game of chess. I want you to watch videos of classic boxing fights of Sugar Ray Leonard and Mohamed Ali. Learn from the best!" I nodded my head in agreement.

Afterwards, he gave me a list of gear that I needed and the "Ringside" catalogue. Coach started going over the ridiculously costly training fees. "I work for a not-for-profit organization and don't make a lot of money. I don't think I can continue to train. I don't work on Wall Street. I work on Chambers Street," I said. Coach saw the freaked-out expression on my face and quickly changed his mind. "Okay Kid, we can figure something out. For now, go home and get some rest. We will meet 4-5 times a week to get you ready for the Gloves."

As I got on the train, I realized I still had to find a place to live. That Wednesday, I decided to go to the track and join the speed workout with the Hellgate Road Runners Club. I saw some familiar faces from the race and would later introduce myself properly. I was one of the youngest runners there and I felt everyone was staring wanting to know my information.

"Hi, my name is Patricia and I ran the New York City Marathon last year. I would like to run it again this year but first I am training for the Golden Gloves tournament in March," I said. That definitely caught people's attention but one older man in his late 40's was overly enthusiastic about what I had just shared and kept asking me questions about where I trained and who was my coach. His name was Adrian and he seemed to be a big boxing fan.

I tried to be polite and said, "Thanks very much for wanting to know about my training, but I live in Rego Park for now and have to make the train. I don't want to be out in the dark too long." I tried jogging to the train station, but saw that he started following me. "Hey Patricia wait up! I can give you a quick ride home," he said. I was hesitant but getting a ride versus taking the long ride home sounded better so I accepted.

"So how long have you lived in Rego Park," he asked. "Well, I love my neighborhood and have only lived in Rego Park for about a year, but I have a month to look for a new place to live. The lady's husband who is renting the basement apartment to me, lost his job and has to increase the rent and I cannot afford it," I said.

Adrian's eyes sparkled and he said, "I have a fully furnished basement apartment in my house that you are welcomed to live in for half of what you are paying now so all you have to do is train and work without too much stress." I didn't understand why I had such an uneasy feeling. Was it because he was an older creepy man who seemed a little too interested in my boxing? We arrived at my home and I said, "Thank you so much for the ride, Adrian. Let me think about your kind offer on the basement rental and I will give you an answer next week at track practice." I needed to pray for clarity and guidance. One of the many lessons I learned throughout my life was that if it sounded too good to be true, it usually was.

The weekend arrived and I went to train at Wall Street Boxing. "Hey yo Kid! Come over to the office. This is Mr. C the owner of Wall Street Boxing and I talked to him about your situation and he is not going to charge you to train here. I won't charge you either for training as long as you work and fight hard. You gotta make something out of yourself," said Coach in his Brooklyn accent. I didn't know what to say. I was fighting back tears, but managed to say, "I won't let you down...I promise and thank you Mr. C. I really appreciate it."

I learned how to wrap my own hands and understood the routine of always jumping rope for at least 3 rounds to warm-up and then shadow box to refresh my memory on techniques I had learned before pad and ring work. Today, I would spar with a bigger girl who was in the 139-pound division. Her name was Denise, the defending Golden Gloves Champion at 139 pounds. "Oh great! Another champion that is going to try and knock my head off," I thought to myself, but then I saw her come in with her boxer dog who ran up to me and smooched me up! I had a genuine love for dogs and anyone who had them.

"Don't get distracted by anything, you hear me kid? This chick is bigger than you, so you are going to stick and move just like we've been practicing," said Coach. The bell to start round 1 of 3 rung and we came to the center of the ring and tapped gloves. Denise threw 2 quick stiff jabs at my head but I slipped both of them just as Coach had taught me and it worked! I kept doing that the entire round.

I went back to my corner for the 1-minute rest. "Good Kid, but now you gotta throw! When she jabs, slip and go to the body and back up to the head. Do It!"

Second round started and Denise starts with a jab which I slipped and I threw a left hook to her body and right to her chin which landed on point. Her eyes opened up wide and she responded with a hard right hand which I felt but didn't flinch and responded right back for a good exchange right before the end of the round. "Better round, but you gotta move those feet after you throw. You are getting caught because you stand there admiring your work. MOVE!" said Coach right before the final round started.

This time I started with 2 hard stiff jabs which snapped Denise's head back and then I moved from side-to-side. She started chasing me and the more she chased, the more I moved. I threw two jabs and moved. She couldn't catch me and I saw that she started to get tired and frustrated and then the bell rang. "One more round!" said her corner which at the time was her husband. "Nah, thanks, we're good. It's only this kid's second time sparring, so next time," said Coach while he was taking off my head guard and mouth piece. "When you do good, they always want one more round to get even, good job kid."

I went to the weight room to do 3 rounds of push-ups, sit-ups and neck exercises. Coach would always tell me, "We gotta get rid of this baby fat and get you strong." I didn't think I was fat at 125 pounds. I just didn't have much muscle. As I was finishing up Denise walked in and hugged me. She totally caught me off guard. She wasn't angry at me. "Girl! You are awesome! You're going to win the Golden Gloves! Thanks so much for the work. Can we spar again next weekend?" I was surprised. I was glad at the opportunity to potentially make a friend. "Thank YOU, Denise! You are strong and awesome too! You have to check with Coach about sparring, I have nothing else to do except train but I would love to," I replied.

As I was stretching, I felt my head thumping. I understood why I need to keep moving after I landed my punches or else my head would thump from the blows. I took my time changing and Coach knocked on the door and yelled through the door, "Nice job kid! I gotta run to teach the New School class. Go home and rest and Monday we will spar again but at Gleason's Gym. We will meet here and go there together."

Sparring in Boxing to me was so different and harder than sparring in Karate, but I will do whatever it takes. I really appreciated Coach taking the time to train me. I was feeling like I owed it to myself to make the best out of this opportunity, but now I couldn't let Coach down either. That Saturday after training, I went to the movies and brought myself a box of sour patch kids as a treat to myself. One of the things I really loved was candy. When I was growing up, I rarely got to eat candy, play or do things that kids do, so I had a tendency to be drawn to the things I never got do.

When I woke up the next day to get ready for my Sunday routine of running and then church, I saw Mrs. Lenore. "Hello Patricia. How are you doing with the apartment search? We have a couple passing by this afternoon to look at the basement apartment. Is it ok?" I had not given any thought to Adrian's offer, but I may just have to take it temporarily.

"Yes, of course Mrs. Lenore. I will be at church later and I will be back later in the afternoon. I will confirm by this Wednesday of my move out date. I think I found another basement apartment," I replied before I took off running.

I was sore from the boxing workout, but I ran hard. I didn't want to think. I would do the thinking and praying at church. "God, please guide me. I don't know if I am making the right decision, but I have nowhere else to live. Please protect me wherever I go and in everything I do," I said while praying on my knees at church. This new apartment would be about a half a mile away from where I grew up in Woodside, Queens. The chances of bumping into my sisters and mother would be high.

The weekend flew by and so did my day at work. I hurried to meet Coach after work and we took the train to Gleason's Gym on Fulton Street. Coach tried to make conversation on the train and on the half-mile walk to the gym. I kept my answers to Yes and No and as short as possible. I was not sure what he would think if he knew what I had gone through and my current situation, but I had a feeling that he had an idea.

We arrived at Gleason's Gym and it immediately reminded me of a scene out of "Rocky II," when Rocky went to train at Apollo Creed's boxing gym. 90% of the gym members were black and 99% were men, so naturally when I walked in with Coach who was super white and tall, we made a bit of a scene. The owner, Bruce was checking in people at the front desk and charged me $10 to workout.

"Go into the locker room to change and start warming up quick. You are going to spar a few rounds and we are going to run back to take the train and finish up at Wall Street. I have clients to train," said Coach. I didn't make eye contact with anyone and did exactly what Coach instructed me to do. Coach was putting on my head guard and a guy named John came over fully geared up jumping around throwing air punches and said, "Are you guys ready to go or what?" I felt the blood rush to my cheeks and asked, "Am I sparring with that guy?"

Coach put his hand on my shoulder and said, "Listen to me Kid...I would never put you in any danger. You're like my kid. You are going to move around with John for 3 rounds. Stick and move and practice everything you learned. I'll be right on the other side of the ropes watching." The bell rang and I danced around the ring for the entire round without throwing one single punch. I was afraid. "What the hell are you doing? If you don't throw any punches the next round, we are leaving and that will be the end for today" yelled Coach.

Round 2 begun and I came out with 2 hard jabs, right to the body, left hook and another right hand which all landed. John responded with a right left hook combination which landed flush on my chin and I answered right back. The bell rung and as I was walking back to my corner, I noticed that there was a crowd gathered around the ring. "Better round, but did you forget about the slips, the ducks, the weaves? Defense or else you're gonna keep getting clocked," said Coach firmly.

Round 3 begun and I slipped and weaved John's combinations and countered. I got caught a couple of times and even though John was holding back, he was still a man and I felt his punches, so moving was priority. I would hear the comments from the people watching, "who is that girl?" 3rd round ended and John said to Coach from across the ring, "You got yourself a future champion."

I had now been living in Adrian's basement apartment in Woodside for the past 3 months. It was not the ideal situation because he made me feel uncomfortable and I knew that was a bad sign. I found myself tip-toeing when I got home from work and training to avoid running into Adrian.

I had stopped going to the Wednesday track workouts to avoid going home with him. Instead, I just ran on the weekends or right after boxing. But on one night, he waited right outside my door. "Hey Patricia! How's everything going? When is your Golden Gloves fight?" I had just come from a long day of work and training, but he was the owner of the apartment I was renting, so I had to be polite. "Hey Adrian, I am good. I have been really busy working and training. All the women are to check-in and weigh-in at the quarterfinals on Friday, March 15th- a week from today at Holy Cross High School. I may not fight if there are not enough women in my division or if I get a bye," I said.

Adrian replied, "I will be there! I will find out all the information and get all the crew from the Track Club to come down. In the meantime, anything you need let me know." I was so tired and he could see it in my face. I just thanked him and went inside. The New York Golden Gloves boxing tournament was considered one of the most prestigious boxing tournaments and winning it was considered an honor of for life. However, Women's Boxing was still so new and it was part of the reason why people were intrigued when they found out I boxed.

The next day on Saturday, I went to Wall Street Boxing and mostly did pad work, hit the bags and did a lot of shadowboxing. I was registered for the 119-pound division, so at the end of the workout, Coach wanted me to weigh in. My weight after the workout was 121 lbs. "Okay, that's not bad. You get a 2-pound allowance in the Quarter Finals, but I want you to be on weight. You have to eat clean until the end of this tournament. You got me?"

I took a deep breath and said, "Yes, I understand. I just have a bad sweet tooth." Coach had a funny look on his face and said, "Just eat honey instead of sugar this weekend and I'll see you back here again on Monday." I was anxious the remaining of the weekend. Between trying to avoid Adrian and being careful of where I walked in order to lessen the chance of bumping into anyone in my family and now trying to stay on weight, I was starting to feel overwhelmed. Instead of buying frosted flakes, I went to the supermarket and got a jar of honey just like Coach said.

I ran 6 miles after training, so all I wanted to do was rest and watch television and that's exactly what I did with my jar of honey. I loved watching scary movies and one of my favorites was on "A Nightmare on Elm Street." I was immersed in watching the movie when I realized I had consumed the entire 32 ounces of honey! I didn't feel good at all and hoped I would just sleep it off.

I woke up feeling bloated and discovered my red best friend had arrived. I fell back asleep and woke up again almost 3 hours later because Adrian was knocking on my door. "Oh Gosh, just leave me alone," I mumbled under my breath. "I made extra eggs, hash browns and pancakes if you want," yelled Adrian from the other side of the door. I could use the extra food and not spend any money on shopping today I thought to myself. "Umm, okay thanks Adrian. I'll be up in a few minutes. I am rushing to go to church though."

I came upstairs and he gave me a hug and a kiss on the cheek which made me cringe. However, it was how he has always greeted me and another reason why I avoided him like the plague. "How's the champ feeling this morning?" he said. I couldn't hide it and said, "I don't feel good at all but have to go to church. I would love to take the breakfast to eat later if that's okay," I said reluctantly.

He had a concerned look, but said, "Yes! Of course! Take anything you'd like. Would you like me to drive you to church?" he said. I grabbed the breakfast quick and said, "Oh thank you so much for the offer! Church is my personal thing and I need to go there myself, but I appreciate it. Gotta run!" I went to church and stayed after the service and prayed and meditated.

The workday went by fast and I wished I was able to go home as I was not feeling 100%, but I was committed to putting in the needed work for this tournament. "Hey Kid! Let's get on the scale before you work out," said Coach the second he saw me come in to Wall Street Boxing Gym.

It was my 2nd day on my period and I still felt bloated, but had to do whatever Coach said, so I stripped down to my shorts and sports bra and got on the scale. "WHAT THE FUCK!" yelled Coach. The scale read 125. My eyes got watery and I was embarrassed and said, "I am sorry coach. I ate the honey you told me to this weekend instead of sugar and I am on the 2nd day of my period. I promise I didn't eat any candy." Coach was upset and confused. "Well, it must be water retention from the period then.

But how much honey did you eat?" I felt an incredible heaviness in my chest and said, "I ate a jar of honey." Coach's eyes couldn't get any bigger. "WHAT? Who the hell eats a jar of honey except Winnie the Pooh," he said but he wasn't laughing.

"Here's what we are going to do. You are going to work out here and then we are going to Central Park tonight and run for at least an hour and you are not to touch sugar or honey and you will eat in small portions. Understand?" I couldn't even look at him, but I said "I understand and it will never happen again." I jumped rope for 10 rounds, shadow boxed for 5 rounds and hit the pads for another 5 rounds wearing a sweatshirt. I put on a dry shirt and we took the train to Central Park near where Coach lived. He gave me his jacket and one of his big Akita dogs, Brando before we took off for the 6-mile run. I came back 90 minutes later exhausted and went home and straight to bed without eating anything.

I woke up like a zombie and realized that Sanctuary for Families' big fundraising event Zero Tolerance was tonight, so I wasn't going to go to the boxing gym today. I worked and barely ate or drank anything out of fear. At the catered open bar event, I ate a piece of cheese. All I kept remembering was how upset Coach had been. I didn't have a scale at home, so I had no idea how much I was weighing but I imagined it had to be less as I have barely eaten for the past 2 days.

On Wednesday, I went to the gym earlier than usual since I would have to take the rest of the week off. "Yo kid! Go straight to the scale," said Coach. "I have to pee first, but I'll meet you at the scale," I replied.

I really don't know why I had to pee since I've barely consumed any fluids, but it was probably nerves. "God please help me," I whispered. I was in my sports bra and shorts again and got on the scale. It read 120. Coach breathed a sigh of relief. "Nice kid. This can never happen again on fight week. You have to be responsible. Eating a jar of honey is not normal and we need to take care of that," said Coach.

I managed to also breathe a sigh of relief for now. "I know Coach. It won't happen again. I have lived by myself since I was 15 years old and barely have money for food. Sometimes I eat candy or Frosted Flakes because it is the cheapest thing I can find and it makes me feel better. Please don't say anything to anyone," I replied.

It was the first time I said more than a sentence to him while fighting back the urge to cry. "Okay Kid. Don't worry. I won't say anything. I understand and I have a friend who is a counselor that you can see soon. Just don't cry. I hate to see girls cry," he said.

I did my usual warm-up and moved around the ring for a few rounds with Coach. "You are ready Kid. I want you to eat very lite tonight and tomorrow. Sleep good and I'll see you Friday at Holy Cross." As I was sitting on the train, I had flashbacks of my boxing journey thus far. It was time for me to be strong just like the boxing movies I used to see even though no one thought I could be strong, but here is my chance. The worrying about my weight, my period and not eating made me feel drained. I couldn't wait to just sleep.

I was approaching my front door and then I hear from above, "Hey Champ are you ready for tomorrow? I got in touch with the crew and we will all be there!" said Adrian. I did not want to nor was I going to go upstairs and instead started opening up my door and said, "Awesome! I have to rest but thanks for the support. Good night!" I took a hot shower and then boiled and egg and had tea with no sugar or honey and went to sleep listening to my rumbling hungry stomach.

I woke up nearly at 10 am which was a rare occurrence, but I felt so rested. Then there was a knock on my door, "Hey Champ! Your name is in the newspaper. I'm leaving it in front of your door." I quickly jumped out of bed and got the newspaper. The New York Daily Newspaper was a sponsor of the tournament and published the boxers scheduled to box each week. I opened it up quickly to the sports section and sure enough, my name was there: Women's 119 division, Patricia Alcivar from Wall Street, BC.

This is really happening tonight. I boiled an egg again and some hot tea and had that for breakfast and lunch again. I took a lunch time nap, prayed and took the bus to Holy Cross High School which was in Flushing, Queens and about a good hour from where I was living. Right outside the school, I saw Coach and another guy just as big as him. "Hey Yo Kid, this is my brother who is going to help us tonight and work your corner." He looked like Coach but just younger.

We went inside and checked in. "Okay, Alcivar, Welcome to the Quarter Finals. You need to go to the room marked "Ladies room" where they will weigh you in and if you make weight then they will match you up. There are 5 girls in your division, so 2 girls will fight tonight and the other 3 will get byes to the semi-finals next week. Good Luck," said the guy.

I walked into the room where all the women were already. "Any men that are in this room need to step out while we weigh in the ladies," said one of the women officials named Denny. The women had started to strip down to their panties and sports bra. They all had mean faces except Denise! I was so glad to see her and she walked over and hugged me. It was my turn to get on the scale and it read 120.0. "You're good. Now get dressed and wait until your class is called to get matched," said Denny." Even though I made weight, I secretly hoped to get a bye into the semi-finals next week.

Coach came back in the room. "I weighed in at 120 Coach," I said. He rubbed my head as if I was a pet but that was okay with me. I knew he was happy, so that was all that mattered to me. Then all of a sudden Denny said in her loudest voice, "119 Women Come with Me!" She continued to say, "There are 5 of you. You will pick a number from this jar. Number 1 and 2 will box each other tonight. Numbers 3, 4 & 5 will get a bye into the semi-finals next week."

We all took out a folded paper. I slowly opened it up and there it was #1 and an older woman in her late 30's with a deep scar down her cheek with a last name of Barbosa had #2. "#1 and #2 step out please," said Denny. When Barbosa looked at me, she laughed and said "YES! It's gonna be a quick knockout tonight!"

I remained calm even though inside I felt like a scared puppy. Coach came into the room looking for me with his brother and I said, "I am fighting tonight against Barbosa, the woman with the scar on her cheek." They both looked over at her and she was shadowboxing with hand weights and talking to herself. "Is that really a woman?" he said jokingly but when he saw I wasn't laughing, he got serious and said, "Don't worry Kid, you got this! Go get changed and we will start to warm-up. You are the 5th bout tonight."

I went to the bathroom to change but I started to cry as well. "God, please give me the courage and strength I need to fight. I have no one except you. Please don't leave me," I whispered. When I came out, Coach's brother was standing right outside like a bodyguard. "Are you nervous?" he asked. I didn't want to start crying again and I couldn't lie. My eyes watered though and I nodded. He put his hand on my shoulder and said, "You wouldn't be human if you weren't nervous. It's okay. Just don't let that fear paralyze you. When that bell rings, take all your fear, all your love and everything you are feeling and unleash it on that girl! You hear me?" I looked straight into his eyes and nodded again.

"ALCIVAR AND BARBOSA START WALKING OUT. YOU ARE THE NEXT BOUT!" yelled one of the Officials. Coach put my head guard on and the yellow robe representing the color of my corner. Barbosa was in the blue and she walked out first to loud cheers from the sold-out crowd. I started walking out a few seconds later and the cheers disappeared. I heard faint sounds of clapping with concerned looks on people's faces. Some were saying, "Oh no! She's so cute... She's gonna get hurt."

I entered the ring and Coach took off my robe. The referee came to check that I had my mouthpiece in and my chest protector on and then the announcer said through a loud microphone, "Get ready for a special bout! We have the only female bout tonight in the 119-pound division. In the yellow corner we have PATRICIA ALCIVAR from the Wall Street BC and in the blue corner we have BARBOSA fighting unattached." We came to the center of the ring and tapped gloves and went back to our corner for the start of the bell. Coach tapped my head guard and said, "Take care of business Alcivar."

I nodded my head and thought about what Coach's brother said. "Let it unleash!" was my final thought and then the bell rang. Barbosa ran at me and I stopped her in her tracks with 4 straight hard punches to her face that made her head snap back. The referee immediately stepped in and gave her an 8-count. She shook her head and put up her gloves immediately to indicate that she was good to continue.

The referee said "BOX!" and this time I ran at her and started another set of furious punches that made her wobble back towards the ropes and again the referee stepped in for another standing 8-count. I maintained my focus and waited for the end of the eight-count.

The referee again said "BOX!" and Barbosa came out swinging, but my punches were harder and landed flush on her face and before she went down, the referee stepped in for the final time and stopped the bout in the 1st round. I scored a TKO (Technical Knockout) in my first ever boxing match. I started jumping up and down and was tearing up.

"Good job Alcivar," said Coach and now, the crowd that had hesitated to cheer me on, were on their feet clapping and screaming.

After the bout, people from the crowd wanted to shake my hand and take a picture with me. I was shy and hesitated but Coach kept poking me to go ahead. "You have to be social and get the crowd and fans to support you. This is part of your boxing journey. I wouldn't steer you wrong Alcivar." Coach alternated between calling me Kid & Alcivar but it didn't really matter to me. I just wanted him to be proud of me and for that night, it seemed like he was.

"Hey Champ! Congratulations!" yelled Adrian who was accompanied by a few of his friends and people from the running club. I felt uneasy, but remembered what Coach had just said to me. "Thanks so much!" I said as I high fived them and hurried away and stuck to Coach like glue. "We still have a lot of work to do so no celebrating. Tomorrow, rest and run on Sunday and I'll see you back in the gym on Monday. Next Friday is the semi-finals and only 1-pound allowance, so you MUST eat lite and stay on weight," said Coach in a serious tone as he sent me off in a cab.

I was exhausted as I laid in bed. Although my bout had lasted just one round, all the stress, excitement and not eating much took a toll on me tonight. I prayed and said "Thank you God for helping me win tonight" and then drifted off into a deep sleep.

In the middle of the night, I started to feel an uneasy feeling in my chest and stomach and felt as if someone was in my room. I opened my eyes and my room was dark. I never turned off the lights! What is going on? I tried to scream but no words came out. "Our Father who are in heaven...."

I was mentally saying. "Please God, don't let him get me," I was saying internally while I felt tears coming down my cheek and then all of a sudden, I let out a deep breath and sprung up from the bed.

My face was all wet from sweat and tears. It was 3am and I turned on the T.V. before I fell asleep for the next two hours. I woke up and went for a lite 3-mile run and decided to go to the boxing gym. I didn't think Coach would mind. As I was riding on the train to the boxing gym, I remembered my bout from the night before. It had all happened so fast, but what I would never forget was the proud feeling I felt knowing I didn't give in to the fears. I smiled to myself as I walked into the gym.

"Hey look whose here?", announced Coach to the members. Everyone came over to shake my hand. The results were in today's newspaper, but Coach was happy and was telling everyone too. "Hey Alcivar, nice to see you but I thought I told you to take it easy today," said Coach. I had already confided in Coach about my living situation, so might as well tell him about my sleeping issues too and said, "I couldn't sleep last night even after my win. Something is bothering me at night, so I left the lights on." To my surprise, Coach didn't freak out and instead said, "Okay Kid, don't worry. We are going to take care of this. I am going to call my friend Father Joe to see when he can see you. Go jump rope and then we are going to move around for a few rounds."

I felt better being in the gym instead of being anxious at home. I was also glad to have told Coach something I have kept inside for so long time. Coach seemed to understand and that's all that mattered for the time being. I hit the pads and hit the bag for 3 rounds and stretched and that was it for today. "I want you to have soup and a little protein when you get home and then rest. If you don't rest, we can't win again next week. Got it Alcivar," said Coach. I nodded and waved goodbye.

On the train ride home where I usually went over the events of my day, I remembered confiding in Coach. Trusting anyone about my past or the things happening in my life was challenging, but Coach was all I had and he seemed trustworthy. As I got off the train station and walked home, I also thought about my living situation which I knew had to change eventually. The purpose of leaving an abusive home was to be in peace and living in Adrian's basement, the peace had started to dissipate.

I opened the door to my bedroom and found roses on my bed with a note that read "Congratulations on your win last night Champ-Adrian." I was not happy with this surprise and didn't understand why the hell is this man in my bedroom leaving roses on my bed. Although I didn't have much street smarts, I knew enough to know that this wasn't right. A couple of minutes later, he knocked and said, "Hey Champ, I have extra chicken from Boston Market if you want some."

I felt my face burn with anger, but I made my way upstairs and replied, "Hey Adrian, Thanks so much for the flowers but I would feel better if you didn't do that. My room is my private space. I am really tired now and just need to relax downstairs." His face got red as well and said "No problem, Champ. How about some dinner?" I thanked him yet again and said, "I am just going to go downstairs, stretch and rest. I am trying to keep my weight in check and ate soup already." I didn't eat soup and instead ate a banana and called it a night.

I did everything I was supposed to and then some throughout the week as I approached Thursday night-a day before the semi-finals. I didn't own a scale, but I had eaten super light the entire week and was praying that I would be on weight. I met Coach at 5pm in the entrance lobby of Christ the King High School in Queens. He greeted me with a high-five and asked, "What's shaking Kid? Why the long face?" Growing up, my family had always said that I wore my feelings on my sleeve. I had a very expressional face and it was impossible to hide what I was feeling. I was nervous about my weight, the crowd, my opponent and losing. "I am okay Coach, just a little anxious," I replied while we walked to get checked in.

I saw Mr. Jimmy O circle my name. I was the last one of the 4 girls in my division to check in. He smiled and said, "Good luck tonight young lady. You got a good jab so use it." We walked in and the coaches and the rest of the girls were sitting waiting and talking amongst themselves when Denny called out, "119 women ONLY! Come on down and get weighed in! Coaches are not allowed in." My heart started racing and I quickly made my way down the hall and started undressing. There was a girl-Christine Bruno, last year's defending champion who weighed in completely naked! She just made weight at exactly 120 pounds or else they would have given her an hour to go lose the extra weight.

You get one chance to re-weigh yourself before getting eliminated. "Alcivar, you're next," said Mercedes who was another USA Boxing official like Denny. I got on the scale and Mercedes said in a loud voice, "119.5!" I momentarily felt relieved. "Okay Ladies, Listen up! We are going to match you up right away. We will have 2 bouts tonight. Number 1 and 2 and 3 and 4 will box each other," said Denny. Now, my hands were sweating, but I reached in and grabbed a paper and so did the remaining 3 women. "1 and 2 step forward," said Mercedes. I stepped forward for number 1 and Christine stepped out for number 2. "Shake hands ladies and let's have a good bout tonight."

I went back and said to Coach, "119.5 and I am fighting Bruno tonight." Coach jumped up out of his seat and without hesitation said, "GOOD! You can beat last year's champion and become the new one." I didn't understand why he believed in me so much and wondered if he knew how much I doubted myself. I changed into my boxing trunks and t-shirt and boots and started warming up. We were the 3rd bout and in amateur boxing, there are only three 2-minute rounds, so bouts went by fast.

"ALCIVAR/BRUNO ON DECK," I heard over the speakers. I didn't have time to pray, but I closed my eyes and mentally prayed, "God, you are my savior and protector. Please help me have courage and strength tonight. Amen." It was a sellout crowd and who were mostly cheering for Bruno. After all she was last year's champion. After our names were announced we came to the center of the ring and as the referee was giving us instructions, I heard someone from the crowd say "KNOCK HER OUT CHRISTINE!" and then the bell rang.

Bruno came out swinging strong and connected right away with a one-two (jab and right-hand combo) that stung and as I was about to respond with a big over hand right, I felt a horrible pain! My right shoulder popped out! In the years I spent as a gymnast, I was encouraged to dislocate my shoulders for a high bar routine but that caught up to me tonight. I winced in pain but thankfully the head guard and mouthpiece helped camouflage my facial expression. I worked on my foot work for the remainder of the round while the crowd was screaming "Stop Running!"

End of the 1st round and I went to my corner and Coach quickly pulled out the stool and said "You lost that round. You gotta throw more combinations and that freaking right hand!" I knew we only had a minute but managed to say, "Coach! My shoulder is dislocated!" Coach quickly reacted and said, "okay, okay, when she comes out you are going to stop her with a hard quick snapping jab to her nose. Jab her until your left arm falls off!"

The start of the 2nd round begun and as Bruno came at me, I threw the hardest jab of my life right in the center of her nose! Bruno's head snapped back and blood started gushing out. I kept jabbing to her nose and now she was the one wincing in pain. The referee stepped in and the doctor looked at her nose and stopped the fight before the end of the 2nd round. Her nose was broken. I wanted to cry, but I didn't. The crowd who was mostly her supporters clapped and some cheered, but I didn't care.

"I told you it was going to be good to beat the old champion," said Coach. My shoulder was sore, but I was okay. I had not purposely dislocated my shoulder since my gymnastics days which was a while ago, so it hurt. After I changed, the officials gave me instructions, "Congratulations Alcivar! You and Eileen Lacy will fight next Friday in the Finals at Madison Square Garden Theatre and there are NO weight allowances. You MUST be 119 or under." I shook the Official's hand and then left with Coach.

"We're going to have you see a physical therapist for that shoulder after this fight. Right now, you are going to go home and ice that shoulder and rest. Tomorrow, you rest and run lite on Sunday and come into the gym on Monday so we can have a plan for this chick," said Coach as he put me into a cab home. My 2nd TKO.

"Thank you, God for giving me the strength and helping me find courage even through adversity tonight," I whispered with my eyes closed in the cab. I was exhausted and wanted to just lay in bed with no interruptions and was hoping not to bump or hear from Adrian at all. I opened the door as quietly as possible and saw that the lights upstairs were off, so I sneaked in and went straight to bed.

As I laid in bed, I kept hearing the announcer say, "The winner by TKO at 1:50 of the 2nd round, PATRICIA ALCIVAR." I was good enough for something tonight and then I passed out with my small bed light on. I slept deeply from being mentally and physically exhausted.

I had learned early on that my best sleep came after intense exercise. It was as if I let everything I was feeling out during my workouts and the more intense, the better I could rest and the calmer I was.

My eyes automatically opened at 4:59 am without an alarm. My shoulder was sore but not too bad. I know Coach said to rest today, but I really would like to go out for a lite jog. I forced myself to close my eyes for another hour before I dressed up and went out for a 3-mile run. As I ran, I prayed and remembered my last two bouts where no one except Coach gave me a chance of winning. I am in the finals of the New York City Golden Gloves in Madison Square Garden and it will be on Television (MSG Cable). I let all that sink in and wanted to keep running, but didn't.

"Hey Champ! Another TKO last night! Congratulations! Did you hear me? I was yelling with my friend Angel. We are going to get tickets today for your final match!" Adrian shouted as he was going out on his run and I was thankfully coming back. "Thanks very much. I was totally focused on fighting and heard the entire crowd screaming. Very Cool you are getting tickets for the Garden finals! I have to go take a shower and run some errands," I answered while also running away.

As soon as I got home, I took a long hot bath and iced my shoulder and stretched my entire body for an hour. I learned from my gymnastics days the importance of stretching and kept it as part of my daily routine. I didn't want to spend all day inside, so I went out for a walk at lunch time and went shopping for some healthy food options this week. It was a beautiful sunny spring day in April and I was enjoying my walk until I stopped dead in my tracks when I saw one of my sisters pushing a stroller. I froze momentarily, but it had been a few years since I left home and I had absolutely no contact with anyone from my family. I crossed the street and stood right in front of my sister. She didn't hesitate to hug me and said "Meet your niece, she is 6 months old." I had a huge knot in my throat and looked down at the beautiful baby.

I picked her up for a few seconds and gave her a kiss on the forehead. In those few seconds, I was able to see how precious and innocent she was. Something my father had taken from me when I was way too young. I put her down and walked with my sister for the next hour. She told me she was living temporarily at home with my mother until she could save up enough money to get her own place. She told me my mother was doing fairly well and that I should come visit soon.

When it was my turn to share, I briefly told her about the NYC Marathon, the World Championship in Karate and now being a boxer. I also told her about my living situation. We exchanged numbers and promised to stay in touch and hugged before we said our goodbyes.

I was in a bit of a shock going to the supermarket but happy at the same time. It was really good to see one of my sisters after such a long time. I thought about what she said about visiting soon. I wasn't sure how my mother would react. In all my life, she had never said to me "I love you or I am proud of you" and I wasn't even sure she would want to see me, but I missed her. I would need to put that in the back burner until after the Finals.

I purchased lettuce, tomatoes, five cans of chicken broth soup, a dozen eggs and tea. That would be my breakfast lunch and dinner for the next week until Friday. I needed to eat as lightly as possible. NO weight allowances for the Finals! The day went by fast and I felt drained again emotionally. I got home and just had tea-no dinner and went to sleep and thought about my sister and niece.

I woke up with my stomach rumbling of hunger and the smell of bacon and eggs from upstairs. I made myself tea and got ready for another lite run and was planning on going to church. I quietly opened the door and went out running and went towards Queens Boulevard where all my running had started. I wasn't concerned about bumping into anyone anymore.

I ran down all of Queens Boulevard to Forest Hills near the courthouses. It was such a beautiful neighborhood and wished I could live there one day. I had run down too far, but it was worth it. I turned around and increased my pace on the way back. I was cutting it too close for church. "Hey Champ! Do you want to join me and my friend Angel for dinner later," said Adrian from the terrace as I was opening my door. "Thanks so much Adrian, but I would really appreciate if you could not invite me for anything that has to do with food this week. I have to be on weight and don't want to stress," I replied and quickly closed the door.

I made it to church with just one minute to spare and found a seat at the very end of the final row in the back of the church. I always felt safe inside of church as if I was shielded from any harm there. I believed with all my heart that angels were always taking care of me despite having a horrible childhood. I stayed after the service to say a special prayer and then went home.

Monday morning in the office was busy as usual retrieving weekend messages, making sure our supply room was fully stocked and all machines were up and running. This job at Sanctuary for Families had taught me so much about domestic violence, about serving as an interpreter for the legal department, translating documents for the counselors, writing thank you letters to donors and about being a dependable reliable worker. However, I wanted more and I was getting that feeling that it would be time to move on soon.

As soon as it was 5pm, I changed to my workout clothes and ran down to Wall Street Boxing. The members were all asking me how I felt and if I was ready for the finals on Friday. It was a pretty big deal and I was overwhelmed with the attention. Coach came over and said, "Get used to it. You need to come out of your shell. You can't live in your own world when you are trying to become a champion." I knew he was right, but I just didn't know how to come out of my shell.

I was raised with a jealous strict father who didn't allow me to speak to anyone. I had a mom and family who laughed at me. I barely knew anyone who supported me in any way, so being inside my shell was the only thing I knew. "I know Coach. I will work on it soon. That's just the way I was raised." I said. "No, we are going to work on it right now. You are going to go up to someone here that you haven't met yet and introduce yourself and tell them something about yourself. If boxing is important and you want to be a champion, you will do it," said Coach firmly.

There was nothing I wanted more than to be a champion. It was peak time at the gym with people coming from work to get their workouts. I took a deep breath and walked over to a woman who was putting on her wraps and I extended my hand and said, "Hi! My name is Patricia Alcivar. I am a boxer and have made it to the finals of the Golden Gloves on Friday and hope to be a champion someday." The woman smiled and said, "Congratulations Patricia! Thank you for introducing yourself. It is my pleasure to meet you and from watching you train here; I have no doubt you will be champion." I never heard anything like that from my mother or family, but a complete stranger had no problem saying that to me. I went back to Coach and started wrapping my hands.

"You are going to keep doing that every so often. You have to be social. You will thank me some day but for now we are going to work on a plan for this chick Lacy. She is short, stocky and much older than you, so she is going to try and load up with that right hand. You have to stick and move. Now practice that in the ring for 3 rounds." said Coach.

I practiced "cutting the ring" and my slips, weaves, ducks and combinations for 3 rounds. I did that while envisioning my opponent, Lacy who was about 5'1" and in her late 30's from the Suffolk PAL Boxing Club. Her Coach and gym were very well known. She had big arms and looked strong, so Coach was right, I needed to punch and move. After hitting the pads and bag work, Coach sent me home and reminded me to eat lite.

It seemed like anytime I had a big event, I couldn't slow down time. Monday night turned into Thursday night. I had eaten lightly all week, but couldn't help feel anxious about my weight and about this upcoming fight. I got on my knees before I fell asleep and prayed, "God, please help me be strong tomorrow night. Please let me fight to the best of my ability and may it be your will whatever the outcome may be. Amen."

I remembered drifting into a deep sleep and having an awful nightmare. I dreamt that I was back at home in a dark room and a red light was shining in my face and a presence was trying to squeeze me tight. I opened my eyes and my room was dark. "Our Father who are in heaven. GOD PLEASE!" I tried to speak but couldn't. The red light was in my room and after what seemed like hours, I let out a scream and was able to breathe. I jumped out of bed and went to turn on the light.

I took a short nap and then a cold shower, but skipped breakfast. Weigh-ins were at 12 noon at the Madison Square Garden Theatre and I didn't want to take any risks and planned to weigh in on an empty stomach. I took my time getting ready and took the F Train to 34th Street/ Herald Square and walked down a few blocks to meet Coach at the entrance.

"Looking Good Kid!" said Coach when he saw me. I didn't want to tell him what happened last night and instead smiled nervously and said, "I just want to get weighed and not worry about it anymore." Madison Square Garden was New York City's biggest venue where the biggest teams play and world's most famous concerts happen.

It was my first time entering Madison Square Garden and I was overwhelmed. "You got it Kid, let's get you weighed in first and then we'll have a good lunch and you can take a nap at the gym before the fight tonight," said Coach. We walked inside the theatre and I was blown away when I saw the ring shining underneath the lights and the video cameras over the ring. "Is that where I am going to fight tonight?" I asked Coach.

His face brightened up and replied, "Yes Alcivar. I fought here in the finals, but didn't win. I can't fight anymore, so I live through you. You have what it takes to win. You gotta go out there and give it everything you got." I never felt this pressure before. In my Martial Arts days, I didn't care about winning or losing. I just fought hard and that was usually enough.

I walked in the room where the USA Boxing Metro Officials were checking the fighters in. When I came in, they were speaking to my opponent's coach. Lacy had already weighed in and she wanted to stick around to make sure I was on weight. I went in with the women officials and Lacy was allowed to enter but not the coaches.

"ALCIVAR-118.0!" shouted out the official and wrote it down on my boxing passbook and said, "You are all set. You can go eat and rest, but make sure you are back here by 5pm. First bout is at 8pm and you are the 4h bout of the night." I nodded and went back out to see Coach and said, "118.0 and have to be back by 5pm. I am the 4th bout."

Coach gave me a high-five and said, "Okay Kid, NICE! Let's go get something to eat and you can take a nap at the gym." I wasn't even hungry but who can say no to a NYC slice of pizza? My eyes were heavy and I really couldn't wait to take a nap. We arrived at the gym and Coach turned off the lights and locked me in the gym's office. I laid down on the couch in the gym's office and used his coat as a blanket. Even with the music on and the sounds of gym members pounding the bag, I drifted off into a deep sleep.

"Hey yo kid, wake up. It's 3pm," said Coach. I was startled and for a few seconds didn't know where I was or what day it was, but I quickly realized that it was one of the most important days of my life. I was grateful for the nap and felt refreshed. But then the nerves kicked in. I washed my face and got my duffle bag and was ready to leave.

Coach and I hopped on the Number 2 train and got off on 34th Street Penn Station. "Before we go to the Garden, we need to stop somewhere quick," said Coach. I was confused while he pulled the collar of my jacket. "But Coach, it's almost 5pm. We are going to be late," I pleaded. Then, I saw that we were entering St. Francis Church of Assisi. "We just have to say a quick prayer for tonight," said Coach.

I kneeled and closed my eyes and felt tears run down my cheeks. "Please God, help me have courage and strength tonight and may it be your will. Amen." We hurried over to Madison Square Garden and entered through the side entrance. The security guards high-fived Coach and said "Good Luck Champ!" I didn't feel like a champion, but it felt nice to hear it.

I checked in and was directed to the yellow corner dressing rooms. I settled into my dressing room which had lights, a sofa, chairs and my own bathroom. I went in and changed into my black and gold trim trunks, yellow tank top and boots.

It was already 7:30 p.m. and the officials had given me the head guard and gloves to put on. I could hear the crowd already from my dressing room. I went to the bathroom one last time and then I had my hands wrapped in gauze and tape and then my gloves went on right after.

Coach held the pads. "One, two and hook to the body and hook to the head, slip, slip and move," said Coach over and over until I was warmed up. The 1st bout was in the ring already and I heard the crowd go crazy cheering and screaming. The 1st bout was over in the 1st round. Two more bouts and it was my turn. It was only three 2-minute rounds with one-minute rest in between rounds, so I would be entering the ring soon. Coach kept me moving around to stay warm and soon enough we heard "ALCIVAR ON DECK!" and they announced her first, "In the blue corner from Suffolk Boxing PAL, EILEEN LACY" and "in the yellow corner from Wall Street Boxing. PATRICIA ALCIVAR." We stepped in the middle of the ring for final instructions and then the official bell rang, "BOX!"

Lacy and I both came out swinging furiously and the crowd was on their feet during round one. In the exchange, Lacy landed a big right hand that made the referee jump in and give me a standing eight count, "ONE, TWO, THREE," yelled out the referee while holding his fingers up visibly but I had put up both my hands up immediately from the 1st count to let him know I was fine. It was a good solid punch, but I was not hurt in any way. The bell rang for the end of the first round and I went to my corner. "You have to move Alcivar! Stick and move. This chick is strong and careless and comes in with her head down so throw that uppercut," said Coach while he gave me water.

Round 2 started and I was on a mission to pay her back. We started again at the same furious pace and I was now landing the more significant punches and I looked for the opportunity to throw that uppercut and sure enough, she came in with her head down and I threw the hardest uppercut I could and the referee jumped in and now gave her a standing eight count, "ONE, TWO, THREE, FOUR," he yelled over the roaring crowd. Lacy put her hands up on the fifth count and then the bell rang. I went to my corner and Coach pulled out the stool, "Have a seat Alcivar! Now you have to go out there and stay away from her. She is coming to get even. STICK & MOVE!"

3rd and final round, we came to the center of the ring and tapped gloves. I was taller than Lacy at 5'4" to her 5'1" and I kept tagging her with my jab as she came in. I was jabbing and moving and we got into one final exchange which I got the better of when the final bell rang. I threw my hands up on the air and could hear the announcer, Gil Clancy say, "WOW! WHAT A FIGHT! I give the fight to Alcivar based on that final round."

Coach high-fived me and took my head guard off and I went back to the center of the ring next to the referee and Lacy was on his other side. Then the announcer said, "Let's have a big round of applause for these two women! After 3 exciting rounds, we have a split decision.... The winner is... from the BLUE CORNER!"

My heart ached and I felt myself go numb. I didn't want to even look at Coach. I went over and shook Lacy's hand and congratulated her. It was the right thing to do. I did hear the crowd "BOO" the decision but there was nothing to do. I came out of the ring and straight to the dressing room. Coach put his hands on my shoulder and said, "Listen to me Alcivar, YOU WON that fight! It was politics. She had the more popular coach and it sucks, but we are not giving up. You are the Champion in my eyes and in the eyes of that crowd." I could only say, "I am sorry Coach. I shouldn't have made it close. I will do better next time." Coach hugged me and we sneaked out the back door.

We walked to Gray's Papaya which was a popular hot dog place. Coach ordered about 6 hot dogs and ate them within a few minutes. "I eat when I am upset and tonight, I really thought you won Kid. I take the blame. This won't happen again." was Coach's final words before he put me in a cab home.

CHAPTER 5

Chapter Five - Round 5

THE USA NATIONALS

"The purpose of life is to live it. To taste the experience to the utmost. To reach out eagerly and without fear for newer and richer experience," Eleanor Roosevelt

It was midnight when I arrived home after my Golden Gloves tournament. I tried to stay strong and not cry in front of Coach, but now I was all alone in my room and I broke down crying. I fought my hardest and I didn't win. Perhaps my mother was right and I was not good for anything, I thought to myself through tears. "God, I guess it was your will. Please help me understand and accept it. Please help me be strong and see things with clarity," I sobbed and then fell asleep on the floor.

At 8am, the next morning Coach called me on my new cell phone but I didn't answer. I didn't want to talk to anyone and instead, I packed a small backpack and took the train to Central Park. I walked to the New York Road Runners Club first to leave my belongings before I went on a run. I asked the front desk if Mr. Allan Steinfeld was available not realizing it was Saturday. "Oh, I am sorry honey, but it is Saturday and he is not in today. You can leave him a message if you'd like," said the receptionist.

I wrote a note saying, "Hi Mr. Allan Steinfeld, its Patricia, the girl you helped with an entry to the NYC Marathon last year. I would like to run it again this year. Here is my email and cell phone number. Running the NYC Marathon changed my life and helped me feel alive. I just lost my Golden Gloves fight last night and running is the only thing that helps me take away the pain. I hope you are well. Thank you. Patricia."

It was a chilly, grey and damp April morning, but I felt soothed running in Central Park. I ran 2 full loops which was 12 miles and I was finally able to breathe. As I was walking back to change, my phone rang from a number I didn't recognize. I decided to answer it and a man's voice said, "Hello Patricia, my name is David Gonzalez and I would like to interview you for a story in the New York Times about your Golden Gloves fight."

I hesitated, but replied, "Hello Mr. Gonzalez, Thank you so much, but I lost my fight yesterday. Why would you want to interview me?" He chuckled and said, "I watched your fight and Gil Clancy, the crowd and I thought you won that fight. Are you available to meet today for a quick interview? I can meet you anywhere for coffee or lunch." I hesitated, but replied, "Well, I just finished running, but if you'd like, I can meet you soon either here near Central Park or in Queens."

I went back to New York Road Runners and washed my face in the restroom and changed my sweaty clothes. I took my time walking back to Central Park where I would meet Mr. Gonzalez for my first ever interview. As I walked over, a tall thin man with glasses called out, "Ms. Alcivar!" I remembered what Coach had taught me about coming out of my shell and not being so shy. I extended my hand and said, "Nice to meet you Mr. Gonzalez." We crossed the street and sat on a bench inside Central Park. He had a very gentle demeanor and I felt comfortable throughout the entire conversation and for the first time outside of Coach, I told Mr. Gonzalez about being on my own since I was 15, about running the NYC Marathon, about working for Sanctuary for Families and about my dream of becoming a Champion.

He smiled and said to me, "Ms. Alcivar, you may not realize this right now, but surviving on your own, graduating High School with honors and being who you are has already made you a Champion in life." I knew my face and ears were red. He stood up and shook my hand and said he would be calling Coach and Mrs. Laurie Guilfoyle, the Executive Director of Sanctuary for Families and that the story would be featured in the New York Times on Monday morning.

I took the train home and his words kept echoing in my mind. As I walked home, I saw Adrian waiting outside, "Congratulations Champ! You were robbed! We were all there cheering for you. I would like to take you out to celebrate," he said. I felt nauseated and replied before I closed the door, "I really appreciate it, but right now, all I want to do is be alone and rest."

When I entered my bedroom, I saw a new stereo with flowers and a note that said, "Congratulations Champ, love Adrian." I was angry that again he was in my room without my permission. I did not want to go back upstairs and deal with him. I just wanted to rest. Between the fight on Friday and running 12 miles today, I was ready to crash and passed out without even taking a shower.

I woke up early and I took a long hot shower and replayed the events of the past 2 days. I called my sister and asked her if she wanted to join me for the afternoon church service and then have dinner afterwards. She agreed and I felt better right away. I felt alone at times and hearing her voice made me feel better.

My sister met me at church and brought my niece along in her stroller. Seeing my niece reminded me of painful feelings I had as a child. I remember saying out loud to my mother once during an argument that I would never have children and make them go through the torture I was living. Now, my sister was a young mom and she asked if I wanted to carry my niece who was barely a year old. I nervously extended my arms. I remember being overwhelmed with emotions. She was precious, innocent and beautiful. I put her back in her stroller and we listened to the church service. We went afterwards to Georgia Diner, a local eatery that would become one of our favorite places to dine. I told her everything that had occurred in the past couple of days and she shared what was going on with her life. It was a nice Sunday.

As I was hurrying up to catch the train to work, Adrian shouted out, "Congratulations on the New York Times article! I picked up a few copies." I thanked him and took the newspaper as I hurried away to the train station. It was the main story in the Metro Section and it read "A Kind Face, But Her Fists Are Fierce."

The Metro Section

The New York Times

DAVID GONZALEZ

About New York

A Kind Face, But Her Fists Are Fierce

MARTIN SNOW knew that Patricia Alcivar was different when the slender, raven-haired woman took his breath away. Actually, she knocked the wind out of him with a shot to the gut.

She was a student in his boxing-for-fitness class at the New School last year. She wanted to improve her karate punching skills but wound up becoming his fighter, training with the mugs and pugs at Gleason's Gym in Brooklyn.

She's different, and not just because she's a woman. Every day, before she joins the Rocky types at Gleason's, she works as the receptionist at Sanctuary for Families, an agency that helps battered women. She is often the first comforting face seen by the women and children who go there in search of legal advice, a safe bed or a caring heart.

It takes a real mental switch when she steps into the ring against other women, lest distracting moments of contradiction sneak up on her.

"In my job, I try to help women as much as I can," she said, after a sweaty workout at Gleason's. "This is a sport. I don't think of it as beating up other women. I look at it as a challenge."

She still has to bridge the gap between her compassionate, professional side, and the take-no-prisoners attitude her sport demands. Like the time last year she broke her opponent's nose.

"I saw her nose bleeding all over," she said. "At first I felt sorry and stopped punching. Then I said to myself, 'What's wrong with me?'"

DESPITE her doubts, the 20-year-old Woodside resident has already proved her mettle where it counts, in life. Her mother moved back to Colombia when Ms. Alcivar was 15, leaving her alone to work her way through school, balancing jobs with homework. She's now studying to be a paralegal so she can help the lawyers who represent battered women.

She has always been athletic. She went from a childhood obsession with gymnastics to karate, marathon running and boxing.

Mr. Snow, her trainer, said her drive and self-sufficiency were as impressive as any flurry of punches he has ever seen her throw. And while he appreciates the irony of her dual lives, he said the boxing ring represented equality for women and a chance for them to prove themselves alongside champs.

"It's not like she's talking about women's rights or feminism," he said. "She's doing it. So many talk a good game, but she's doing it."

Although she lost in the finals of the women's 119-pound division at the Golden Gloves, Mr. Snow says that she's good enough to turn professional. She has character, skills and smarts, he said. Not a bad combination.

Laurie Guilfoyle, the executive director of Sanctuary for Families, expresses a certain bewilderment with her receptionist's newfound passion. After all, her office is the ultimate violence-free zone.

"A lot of the women here have been knocked down a lot, and not just in the metaphorical sense," she said. "For a feminist, it makes us reflect on what feminism is. Where do you draw the line? There's been a whole line of things that women were told they shouldn't do because they're women. What's exhilarating is that Patricia has an ability to do it and do it well. But, oh my God, I'd never hit anybody except in defense of my life."

She's glad Ms. Alcivar has goals. She's also glad she's not her mother.

WITH a few bouts under her belt (a regular one, not the championship kind), Ms. Alcivar looks at her boxing as a way to build confidence. That kind of self-assurance, she said, was probably the most important thing she could tell any of the women who come to her office.

"I get mad when I hear women get beat up by their husbands," she said. "I wish they would learn boxing or self defense. But it's not only about that. It's about self-esteem."

She suspects that her co-workers, who cheered for her during her Golden Gloves bouts, probably don't relate to what she's doing. And when she looks at her two lives, she goes to the neutral corner when asked if she's a feminist.

"I work with a counseling agency and I believe strongly in what we do," she said. "A lot of things that women go through are unfair. So is a lot of what goes on in New York City.

"I'm not a feminist. I just know the difference between right and wrong."

And right and left hooks, too.

I carefully read the story on the train. Mr. David Gonzalez summarized our conversation very eloquently and apparently had also spoke with Coach and the Executive Director at Sanctuary for Families. He wrote the same phrase he told me on how I had already earned a championship medal in life by having survived living on my own at such a young age. Now, my story was out there and I felt less afraid. Unknowingly, the more I spoke about my past, the less power it had over me.

I arrived at work and tried to catch up on messages and act normal, but it only took a few minutes before Laurie, the Executive Director walked in the front door with the paper in her hands. She took a long look at me and then extended her hand to shake mine.

"Congratulations Young Lady. You are one tough cookie," she said and smiled which she rarely did and then she walked straight back into the copy room. She made a bunch of copies of the article herself and then started going inside every employee's office and leaving the article on their desks.

The phone rang on the private line and it was Coach, "Hey Alcivar! Nice article in the paper today! How are you feeling? I want you to pass by the gym today. I want to take you out for a pizza or something." I took a deep breath and said, "Coach, I didn't win. I don't deserve a celebration meal. I just want to train again for next year." I knew he didn't like what I said, but it was truly how I was feeling.

"The USA Boxing Metro Officials called me and told me that next year; they are holding the 1st ever USA Women's Amateur Boxing National Championships. This is our new goal. Get back in here tomorrow and we will go down to Gleason's to spar." I could feel myself come back to life as I listened to Coach. I had learned at a young age that life was more meaningful when you had something to strive for. "National Championships," sounded incredible and that would be my new goal without forgetting about the New York City Golden Gloves.

Before Coach hung up the phone, he gave me the name and address of a counselor he wanted me to see, Father Joe from St. Francis of Assisi Church on 32nd Street near Madison Square Garden where we had stopped before my Golden Gloves fight. Growing up, I didn't have anyone to speak to about my feelings. I wasn't allowed to say much, but I had to change that as well and this was the opportunity to do it.

I learned through the reading material at Sanctuary for Families that I or anyone in abusive situations had the power of breaking the cycle of abuse with counseling, knowledge and the desire to change. I fought every day to not be like anyone in my family, so this was my chance to make sense of so many things that I had kept a secret for such a long time. I waited until lunch time to call the number Coach had given me.

A soft voice answered, "Hello, how can I help you" and I nervously replied, "Hi, my name is Patricia and my boxing Coach gave me your number. I had abusive parents and have been living by myself since I was 15. I suffer from nightmares and sadness at times. He said you can help me." There was a long pause, but he said, "Patricia, if you are free today at 5pm, I can see you. I am located right across from Madison Square Garden at St. Frances of Assisi Church. "I know exactly where it is Father Joe. I was there recently praying right before my fight. I will be there at 5pm today."

Madison Square Garden was only 15 minutes on the express train from work, so I left a few minutes early and rushed to meet Father Joe. I got there at 4:59 p.m. and as I approached St. Frances of Assisi Church, a medium build, 5'8", short salt and pepper hair 50-ish old man smiled at me and extended his hand and said, "You must be Patricia."

I sat down on a comfortable old sofa and started telling Father Joe my story from the time I was a baby. He listened patiently. "Have you ever taken the anti-depressant, Prozac Patricia?" he asked. "No Father Joe. I don't feel or have never been depressed. Running and boxing make me feel alive and good about myself," I replied. Then Father Joe continued to say something that I still hold close to my heart, "You have been through a-lot at your young age Patricia and the fact that you are the way you are makes you an anomaly. You don't have much street smarts, but you do have God-given instincts! Listen to them. They will not fail you. I would like to see you once a week, so you can heal properly and work through some things so they don't become issues in the future. How does that sound?" I smiled and nodded and shook his hand and agreed to see him once a week.

As I was ready to take the train home, I saw that I had a voicemail and it was from Allan Steinfeld. "Patricia! Congratulations on the wonderful article in the New York Times! I really enjoyed reading it and of course you may run the NYC Marathon again this year and anytime you want. I will have my assistant mail you a special application with the fee waived. Please keep in touch." I was thrilled! Allan Steinfeld would become one of the rare people in my life that was genuinely kind to me from the moment he met me without expecting anything in return.

Working at Sanctuary for Families had become a routine and I knew that for me, that was not a good sign. If something wasn't challenging me or helping me grow somehow, I felt the need to move on. I kept that thought while I enjoyed my breakfast and started my workday returning phone calls, making referrals, translating a few documents, ordering supplies and restocking the food pantry. The day was gone and I was rushing to catch the Number 2 Express train to Brooklyn.

As soon as I got to Gleason's, Coach hurried over and said, "Yo Kid, get changed quick because I have to run back to Wall Street. I have a couple of private clients to train." So, I got changed as fast as possible, wrapped my hands and jumped rope for 3 rounds. When Coach was putting on my gloves, I said "I need tape! My wrists have been sore since the Golden Gloves." Coach looked annoyed, but at himself because he forgot to bring tape. "We are only sparring 3 rounds quick with Judah, so don't worry about it," said Coach. I got really nervous when he said that. Judah was one of the top Male Amateur Boxers in the United States about to turn Professional.

Judah didn't feel the need to wear a headguard and kept dancing around the ring with a smirk on his face which made angry. He threw a hard jab that landed flush on my nose and made my eyes water up. I instinctively threw the hardest right hand that landed on top of his head. He smiled which meant he felt it, however, I felt the impact on my hand even more. Since he didn't have a headguard, I felt like I had just pounded on a rock. We ended the 3 rounds and I landed some nice body punches and for the most part sparred really well. Judah would hug me at the end and shake Coach's hand and say, "You got a talented boxer there."

Coach took off my gloves and headguard and I ran into the locker room to change. My right hand was shaking and it felt really weird. I couldn't even hold my water bottle but I changed and when I came out, Coach had left. Judah came over and said that Coach told him to tell me that he had to leave but to call him when I got home. He also offered to walk me to the subway station, but I was too shy for that and told him I would be okay.

When I got home, my hand would not stop shaking. I called Coach and said, "My hand will not stop shaking Coach! It really hurts and I cannot hold anything on my right hand." He told me to call in sick for work tomorrow and he would take me to St. Luke's Hospital on 59th Street. I hardly slept from the pain. I met Coach at the boxing gym and we took the train to the hospital. I remember what he had told me after the Golden Gloves that he hated to see girls cry, so I kept trying to hold back tears. We got to the hospital and a handsome doctor examined my hand. "Let's have you take an x-ray and make sure it's not broken," said the Doctor.

The Doctor came back with the x-ray results and said, "I am sorry Patricia, you have a hairline fracture of the distal radial bone on your right wrist. This will require you to wear a cast from your fingers past your elbow for 10-12 weeks to completely immobilize that wrist and ensure it heals properly. You cannot get the cast wet, so you can wear a bag over it while you shower. I will need you to check in with me every couple of weeks and let me know how you are doing."

Now, I couldn't help it anymore and I burst out crying! "Doctor, are you sure?" said Coach. He showed the x-ray to Coach and pointed out exactly where the fracture was and then they spoke in a separate room while I dug my face in my hands and sobbed. I cried the entire time they were putting the cast on my right arm. Coach came back out and put his hand on my shoulder and we walked out. "Don't worry kid. It will all be okay. You know who has the best jab in Boxing History? Joe Frazier! The same thing happened to him. You are going to take the rest of this week off from the gym and then get back next week and all we are going to do is work on your left hand. You Got it?"

I started crying even more. "I'm sorry Coach. I know you don't like to see girls cry. I am just sad right now, but I will be okay, I just need some time alone to get it all out of my system, but I will be back in the gym and work on my left hand like you said."

I came home with a cast and with swollen eyes from all the crying. I looked in the mirror and did not like feeling so helpless and sad. I was better than that and started praying, "God, help me be strong, brave and to have courage. This is happening for a good reason that I do not see at the moment. Please help me be patient and keep moving forward. Amen." I fell asleep on the carpet and dreamed that I was at the National Boxing Competition and it was the end of the bout and the referee was about to raise my hand as the winner and all of a sudden, the dream ended when I woke up abruptly to a knock on my door. "Hey Champ! I picked up an extra chicken salad from Boston Market for you. I am going to just leave it here for you. Talk later," said Adrian. I had not eaten anything the entire day and I felt guilty, but I slowly opened the door and grabbed the chicken salad.

I ate my chicken salad slowly and thought about the prayer and dream. The nap had done me good and I felt better. "No more crying and no more feeling sorry," I said to myself. I started visualizing on what I wanted to do. Tomorrow, I will get up early and go for a run and then to work and then shop for disposable plates and utensils. I will learn how to do everything with my left hand. Being born right-handed will present a challenge but I was not going to let being in a cast stop me from the things I loved doing.

Without my alarm going off my eyes opened at 5 a.m. and everything from getting dressed, tying my shoes, brushing my teeth and even going to the bathroom was tougher and took much longer to do with one hand. It was a typical summer morning in New York City which meant hot and humid and within 5 minutes of running, I was drenched in sweat. The cast felt hot and heavy but it felt good to be out running. I ended up running for a full hour and headed back home.

Just as I was approaching my front door I heard, "Hey Champ! What happened to your arm? Are you okay?" I cringed but managed to stay calm and say, "Hey Adrian. Thanks for the salad last night. I appreciate it. I broke my wrist in boxing, but I will be ok in a couple of months. I have to shower and get to work." I waived with my left hand and ran inside.

I took off my clothes and wrapped a plastic bag around my cast. Washing my hair and body with one hand was trying but I managed. On my train ride to work, I thought about how we take our bodies for granted. I was grateful that this cast and inconvenience would be temporary. People on the train offered me a seat because of my cast, so I took it. I welcomed the opportunity to sit and close my eyes and meditate for the next 45 minutes until I got to my stop.

I arrived at the office right at 9am. I sat down at my desk and the phone rang immediately. Picking up the phone with my left hand was awkward and then trying to type with one hand was even worse. Carla opened her eyes when she saw my cast and said "Oh My Gosh Patricia! Are you okay?" I calmly replied, "I broke my wrist a couple of days ago while boxing, but I am fine. The cast will come off in a couple of months. I am 100% okay to work, so please don't worry Carla." I would have to repeat this very same thing over 20 times to each staff member.

It was nice that at least they cared, but I also disliked anyone feeling sorry for me. I always told Father Joe that I don't consider myself a victim of anything and instead a survivor and a fighter. That day, I worked on learning how to type with my left hand and doing my job as normal and as efficiently as possible. My arm would itch and get really hot, but it got easier and I felt ready to return to the Boxing Gym after a week of adjusting. I was anxious going to the Boxing Gym mostly because I did not want to explain the entire story to anyone. When I arrived, Coach gave me a high five with my left and he said, "Nice to see you Kid! Get changed and get on the treadmill and then we'll get to work." I whispered in his ear, "Coach, please don't make me talk to anyone. I don't want to explain anything to anyone. I don't want anyone to feel sorry for me."

It was a warm and humid July summer day in New York City where even the mirrors and windows fogged up in the Boxing Gym. I was always self-conscious of the way I looked and what I wore.

I hated people staring at me. As a Latina, I tended to be curvy and although petite at 5'4", 120 pounds, my weight was mostly in my rear end and legs, but it was so hot and humid that I wore shorts and a sports bra while I warmed up on the treadmill.

I came off the treadmill 20 minutes later drenched in sweat. I wrapped my left hand only and started shadow boxing in the mirror throwing combinations using the jab, uppercut to the body and left hook to the head. Then I started to mix it up and throw three consecutive left hooks to the head then left hook to the head, left uppercut to the body and finish with a left hook to the head. Then I threw a jab and left hook to the head. "That's exactly what I want you to do on the heavy bag but you are going to move around more and add in your slips, ducks, weaves with those combinations. I want you to do 8 rounds on the bag like that and then that's it for today. Tomorrow, we'll do pads."

I had always loved hitting the heavy bag. It was where I got to practice everything I learned, but it was also an outlet. I started moving side-to-side and throwing jabs, ducking, slipping, weaving and then started throwing hard left combinations. I was focused and remembered what Coach had said about Joe Frazier having the best jab in boxing. Having one arm for the next 10+ weeks during the summer would be challenging, but I was going to make the best out of it and I also remembered that my goal of becoming National Champion.

4 weeks had gone by and I learned to do just about everything with my left hand. I signed up for the Police Chase 5k in Flushing Meadows

Park which took place on a Friday evening after work in the dead heat of the New York City summer. A tall former police officer in charge of the event yelled out brief instructions through a bullhorn and then sounded the siren and off we went! I only knew one speed, so I took off and was running with the lead pack of women. "What a trooper!" yelled out a spectator. It was a 2-loop course and he said it again as I ran by and pointed at me. I appreciated the compliment and ran faster. I placed in the top 5 women! I didn't hang around for the awards ceremony. I was happy knowing that I was able to race even with my arm in a cast.

That weekend, there was an article in the NY Daily Newspaper Sports section announcing that the Inaugural U.S.A. Women's National Boxing Championships would be held in Augusta, Georgia next summer! I took a deep breath and closed my eyes and prayed. "National Champion," that would be amazing. I called my sister and we had lunch with my niece at our favorite, Georgia Diner and I told her all about it. She also took the opportunity to ask me to be my niece's Godmother! What an honor and I didn't hesitate to say "YES!" I never thought of myself as a mom, but having a god daughter would probably be the closest I would get.

When I went to the Boxing Gym that Monday, Coach had a copy of the newspaper. "I read all about it Coach. It is what I want more than anything," I said. "Let's work harder than ever and lets get the freaking cast off soon," he replied before I changed and I got in the ring to do pads. My left hand improved significantly. I lost count of how many rounds of pads we did, but it felt like a hundred.

I worked the entire summer at Sanctuary, at the gym and running on the roads. It had been a challenging hot summer and now we were getting ready for fall. 12 full weeks in a cast and I was looking forward to getting the cast off at my appointment at the hospital. Coach met me at the doctor's office. I went in for a final x-ray and burst out in tears when the doctor said that he wanted me to be in a cast for another 4 weeks. "I am just not sure your wrist has fully healed. Although the x-rays don't show a fracture, there is a slight shadow which is inconclusive," said the doctor.

I ran out of the hospital and didn't wait for Coach. I walked to Central Park and walked an entire 6-mile loop and then went home. I powered off my phone and closed my eyes. I didn't want to speak to anyone. I woke up at 5am and forced myself to go out for a run and I was glad I did. The crisp fall air felt on my face while running was cleansing and helped distract me from yesterday's events.

When I got home, I turned on my phone and had 10 missed calls and 3 voicemails. Coach wanted me to come into the gym right after work today. I knew I had to go into the gym and was prepared to get yelled at for running out the way I did and then turning off my phone. I didn't think of Coach as a Father even though he always referred to me as "his kid". Coach was old enough to be my father and I respected him, but he wasn't my father and I was old enough to do what I felt was right. I packed my gym bag and planned to go to the gym after work.

I felt my stomach turn as I walked to the gym after work. When I walked in, Coach yelled from the office, "Hey Yo Kid! Get in this office Right Now!" I pictured my mother pulling my ear when I did something she didn't like. "Sorry Coach for running off yesterday and for turning off my phone. I was very upset and sad." I said. He had a hammer and saw on the desk and said, "12 weeks in a cast is enough. I've had enough of this quack. I think he just wants to see you longer and keep you in that cast forever. I am going to remove that cast. I need you to put your arm on that desk and don't move a muscle."

I was ready to be rid of that cast too! I did exactly as Coach instructed. It took him nearly an hour to fully remove my cast using a hammer, screw driver and a saw. My right arm looked so pale and thin. I stared at my arm and fingers and it felt so weird to not feel the weight of that cast. "You are NOT going to hit anything with that right hand. You can shadow box with it and jump rope, but NO pounding yet. We have to ease that hand into it or you WILL break it again. Do you hear me

ALCIVAR?" I heard him, but was still staring at my arm. "Yes Coach, I understand," I replied.

I changed, wrapped both my hands and started jumping rope for the first time in over 3 months. I inevitably started smiling watching myself jump rope in the mirror. Prior to the wrist fracture, I usually would jump three 3-minute rounds, but today I jumped 6 just because I missed it so much and then I shadow boxed another 6 rounds with both my hands. I saw Coach through the mirror also smile slightly watching me shadow box.

He put both gloves on just so my hand got used to feeling the glove on again. I hit the heavy bag for another 6 rounds but just with the left. "We are going to slowly get that right hand going again. From now on, every time you finish your boxing workout, we are going to hit the weight room and start lifting, doing push-ups, pull-ups and core work. You need to lose that baby fat and be strong for those Nationals Alcivar!" I felt insulted that he said I had baby fat and felt my face turn red, but I marched straight into that weight room.

We started with push-ups and I did 3 sets of 10 chest-to-floor push-ups and then 3 rounds of squats with just the bar on my back followed by 3 rounds of sit-ups and then Coach spotted me on the pull-up bar. "When do you think I can do a pull-up on my own Coach?" I asked. Coach had a smirk on his face and replied, "Well, Alcivar, pull-ups are very hard and you have to be really strong to do them, but if you are dedicated, perhaps in a year or so you can do them on your own." I smirked back at him and thought to myself, "I will do them on my own way before that punk."

As I was riding the subway home, I could feel my legs and arms shaking from exhaustion which meant it was a productive training session. Perhaps, I would fall asleep without my mind racing. My mind would think about everything at bed time from my childhood, to my counseling sessions, my goals, my living situation, my sister, my niece and my future. Prayer always helped and I was hoping to just pass out.

I arrived home quietly and took a warm shower and thankfully fell asleep without having dinner. My routine for the next few months consisted of running 3 times a week, working at the office 5 days a week and boxing 5 days a week. I would have weekends to myself in which I spent mostly running, going to the movies, going to church or hanging out with my sister and niece. I had avoided Adrian at all costs. I had to hang on until I was in a better financial situation. After the Nationals, I needed to find a better paying job, so that I could move.

My favorite time of the year was here-November! I completed another New York City Marathon and cut almost 45 minutes off my previous time. I cried at the finish line from knowing I kept my promise to myself to complete my yearly marathon. Even through the soreness, I took comfort in my achievement. "Thank You God for the strength and courage," I said in a low voice as I limped to get my belongings. When I got home, Adrian had left a note saying to join him and the Track Team for a celebration at a nearby restaurant. That was the absolute last thing I wanted to do. Instead, I took a long hot bath and called for a General Tso's Chinese Chicken delivery with two Coca-Colas!

As I awaited my dinner delivery, I called Allan Steinfeld and left him this message "Hi Allan! Its Patricia! I finished my 2nd New York City Marathon in 4:36 almost 45 minutes less than my first one. Thank you so much for all your kindness! I can't wait to run again next year. In the meantime, I have to recover and get back to boxing training. I have to be ready for next year's Nationals! God Bless you Allan!"

My dinner arrived and I ate slowly remembering another 26.2 miles in my voyage of life. I was eating alone, but I was in peace. Somehow that also made me cry. I would tell Father Joe all about it a few days later. He would say that being melancholic was perfectly normal and the most important thing was acknowledging and accepting these feelings. Talking to Father Joe helped me speak my mind out loud which I rarely got to do.

The New Year had arrived soon after and I spent it running in Central Park at the New York Road Runner's Midnight Run. At the stroke of midnight, there was a beautiful display of fireworks by Zambelli Fireworks, the same company that produces the Famous 4th of July Macy's Fireworks. The sky lit up with breathtaking fireworks as you brought in the New Year running 4 miles. In my family, it was very traditional to get drunk while also eating 12 grapes and cry remembering all the painful stuff. I cried, but it was a feeling of gratitude and hope that the New Year was going to be special. It was now January 1997 and the Nationals would be 6 months away.

I continued to train and get stronger and leaner and one day on February 19th, which was my mother's birthday. I got on that pull-up bar after my boxing workout and did my first ever pull-up! I ran around the gym and said, "Coach! I DID IT! I did a pull-up by MYSELF!" I saw a few people roll their eyes, but that was okay. Coach said, "Let me see it Alcivar." I ran back to the weight room. I pulled from my core and focused on the things that fueled me and all at once, I pulled up again. It took me 3 months of dedication and believing that I could. I needed to continue to apply this to everything in my life.

Coach looked surprised and patted me on the head. "Good job Kid. Gotta keep working hard. Next week, we are going to start sparring again and I am going to enter you into the Metro Games or a local show as a tune-up to the Nationals. I had started to throw my right hand, but was cautious and never threw it at 100% force. My right hand didn't feel as strong, but my left did. I was afraid of breaking it again. The following week, Coach called "Tito" who was an experienced boxer and also getting ready for his tournaments and he worked as a florist in the flower boutique across the street from the gym. Tito agreed to spar with me and go easy on me since it was the first time sparring since I broke my wrist over 6 months ago.

I got to the gym right after work on a Monday wintery afternoon. I warmed up quickly and was ready to spar. Tito danced around the ring and then stood right in front of me. I threw jabs and ducked right after thinking he was going to throw something at me. We went the entire first round not really doing much except moving. During the one-minute break in between rounds, Coach yelled out, "Tito, you have to throw something at this kid. She's gotta work. We are getting ready for the Nationals. Come 'on man!" Then Coach turned to me and said, "I know this is your first time sparring in a while, but we are here to work. Show me something more this round Alcivar."

Next round, I was more aggressive and threw a jab/left hook combination that snapped his head back. Tito looked at me in disbelief and countered with a stiff left jab that snapped my head back which made me look back at him in disbelief. Coach yelled out, "Good Tito! You got caught Alcivar because you stood there after punching. MOVE after you throw! DEFEENSE!" He was right and after getting hit hard, I made sure I was slipping or moving after I threw the jab or any combinations.

Second round was over and I went back to my corner. "Better Alcivar but why are you not throwing any right hands? Does it hurt?" I did not want to tell Coach that I was afraid to throw my right hand and break it again and then the bell rang for final round. As soon as Tito came out, I ducked and threw a right hand straight in the middle of his stomach which was soft. I knew that would not hurt my hand, but it hurt him. Tito spit his mouth piece out and said, "Nice shot!"

I glanced at Coach and then back at Tito. "There I threw the right hand," I thought to myself. Then the bell rang. I hugged Tito after the final round and thanked him for working with me. Everyone knew that Tito could break me into pieces if he unleashed his full power on me. He was a 160-pound man. Tito became my regular sparring partner and was instrumental in getting me ready for the Nationals. We would both meet at lunch time a few times a week to get in a few rounds of sparring and I would come back after work to finish my work out on the bags, floor and weight room. Tito knew exactly the right amount of power to release. I would sometimes see stars from getting clocked, but it taught me to not get careless after I punch.

We were now a month away from the Nationals and I had been consistent with my training and working harder than I've ever worked in my life. I will never forget one hot Saturday I was stretching after an insanely challenging sparring session and workout. I was looking forward to the only day off I had on Sunday and I had made plans to see my sister for Mother's Day. I had changed out of my sweaty clothes and waved good-bye to Coach while he was working with a client. Coach yelled at me "See you tomorrow at 10am!"

My eyes nearly popped out and I said, "Coach, tomorrow is Sunday! It's Mother's Day and I have plans with my sister!" He said something to his client and jumped out of the ring and walked over to me. He grabbed my shoulder and pulled me in and said, "Listen to me right now. We are down to the final weeks! We have to work. I want you in here 7 days a week. While your opponents are sipping margaritas at the beach, you are going to be in here working. You can see you sister in the afternoon. I just want to work on a few things on the floor and pads. You'll be out of here in an hour."

Coach knew I was upset. My face was red and my eyes were filled with tears, but I didn't say anything and walked away. My whole body was sore, but most of all I just needed a mental break and wanted that Sunday to go to church and spend time with my sister and niece. I called her and told her I had to be in the gym in the morning and she was understanding and said we would just meet in the afternoon for brunch. I picked up a chicken Cesar salad from Boston Market and quietly came home and watched television while I ate my dinner and fell asleep.

The dull ache in my stomach awakened me at 5 a.m. and I discovered I had my period just to add insult to injury. The first 2 days of my cycle was always pure torture. I wanted to call Coach and tell him, but he would think I was making it up. I was dreading taking the long subway ride to the gym. I took a cold shower to help shake me out of the foul mood. On my way to the train station, I brought myself a strong Dunkin Doughnuts coffee. I got to the gym and I didn't even want to look at Coach. "Hey Yo Kid! Come in the office," he yelled out the second I stepped inside. "Have a seat Alcivar. I know you are mad that you are here on a Sunday. You will thank me some day. I am not going to kill you today. Repetition is the mother of all skill. I want everything we practice to be fresh in your head," said Coach.

I went to the bathroom and had to change immediately. My maxi-pad was completely drenched in blood already. I had tried using tampons in the past, but they made me get an instant headache and nauseous. Those symptoms meant that I was a good candidate for TSS (Toxic Shock Syndrome), so I stayed away from tampons.

My head was pounding and the stomach cramps were rough, but I had to get through this workout. I had to suck it up for the next 3 weeks. I changed into the baggiest longest shorts and t-shirt I had. I felt so bloated and really didn't care what I looked like.

I came out and wrapped my hands and started to jump rope for just 3 rounds and then shadow box. Coach had a big smirk and said, "What's with the outfit? You're gonna go play b-ball in Harlem or something?" I was doing my best to have a good face and attitude for this Sunday workout, but he was not making it easy. Mostly everything to Coach was a joke. I loved to laugh but I was not laughing today. "I have a stomach ache Coach and didn't want anything pressing against my stomach," I replied without looking at him.

"Okay Kid, let's go into the ring and practice cutting the ring and your defense for a few rounds. No pads or bags today just ring and foot work," said Coach. I breathed a big sigh of relief. I moved inside the ring, side-to-side, front and back and tried to practice cutting off the ring which was used to corner your opponents. Usually, my opponents ran straight at me and I stood right in front and traded punch for punch, but Coach's strategy for me was to enhance my footwork, defense and boxing skills.

Ever since I started boxing, I watched the pros spar at Gleason's and watched Sugar Ray Leonard videos. I tried to take the best in and had developed exceptional foot work and defense skills. We worked for about 10 rounds and then my period came right through my shorts. Coach noticed the big red circle in my butt. "Alcivar, I think that's enough for today. You should've told me that your Aunt Flow was in town." I was relieved once again. I didn't punk out. I did the work I was supposed to do today. We finished right at the hour. "I just got it this morning Coach," I said before rushing to the bathroom.

My red best friend had gone all over my legs. I stayed in the shower for a while scrubbing everything clean. Coach knocked on the door and said, "I gotta run Kid! Close the door shut when you leave and take tomorrow off. I'll see you on Tuesday and we'll spar with Tito. Enjoy dinner with your sister." I smiled to myself and appreciated the day off from boxing tomorrow. Sucking it up today was rewarding in many ways. I was looking forward to seeing my sister and niece even though I wasn't feeling that great.

I fell asleep on the train back to Queens and spontaneously woke up right on my stop an hour later. I was starving as all I had was that Dunkin Doughnuts coffee in the morning. My sister was arriving with my niece as I was walking towards Georgia Diner. "Happy Mother's Day!" I said and hugged her. The diner was crowded with families celebrating as well. It was so good to catch up and see my niece who was growing up so fast. My sister was teaching my niece to say my name and when she saw me, she pointed at me and said, "Witcha!" Hearing that made me smile so big and I would remember that always. My niece is in her early 20's now and still calls me "Witcha"!

I told my sister about getting my period today and being in agony at the gym. "Do you count your days?" she asked. I had no idea what she was talking about. Ever since I started running and boxing, I never knew when my period was due. According to my sister, I needed to count 28 days from the first day of my cycle and that would indicate when it would arrive again. If that was true, I would have it BEFORE the Nationals which would be wonderful and something less to worry about. Since I didn't win the NYC Golden Gloves, I had to pay my own way to Augusta, Georgia and because of that, I was going to be late paying my rent and I I was dreading telling Adrian that.

When I got to the office early the next day on Monday, one of the older staff members who was a paralegal was there already. She came out and said, "Good Morning Patricia! You know, you are so young and should keep moving up. I don't think Sanctuary offers enough growth for you." I was surprised hearing that first thing in the morning. In some ways she was right, but it was still strange coming from her. She was never friendly to me, so it caught me off guard. "Thank you! I love Sanctuary and it has been an amazing place for me to learn so much. I am focused right now on my upcoming National Tournament and I am sure I will have a clearer vision of what I want to do in the future," I replied.

During my lunch break, I filled out my "Request for Time Off" form and put it in Carla's mailbox. I would be gone a full week and needed 5 days off which I definitely had accumulated and I was giving 3 weeks advance notice. When I got back from lunch Carla walked over and said, "Hi Patricia! I approved your time off. Are you going anywhere special?"

Nervously, I replied, "Actually yes! I am going to Augusta, Georgia to compete in the 1st USA National Women's Boxing Championships!" Carla's eyes got even bigger behind her glasses. "Wow Patricia! That is INCREDIBLE! Good Luck!" she replied and then walked out for her lunch break. My sister and Carla knew about the Nationals and now I had to take care of telling Adrian soon. After church last night and some thought, I decided that I would leave a note for Adrian the day I left to Augusta. I did not want the extra stress of him knowing my business nor did I want any gifts or extra food on my door prior to the Nationals. All I had to do was avoid running into him for the next few weeks.

For the next 3 weeks, I trained my butt off sparring, weight training and running. I didn't even have to worry about my weight. I was walking around at 119 pounds without trying from all the training. 28 days since my last cycle had also gone by and I had not gotten my period. "Perhaps, it will skip this month like it has many times," I thought to myself as I jumped rope. It was Friday evening and it would be my last sparring session before the Nationals. We would be leaving on Monday morning to Augusta, Georgia.

"Okay Alcivar, Final 3 rounds before Nationals. I want you to practice everything we have worked on. Tito, make her work," said Coach before the bell rang. Instead of running out, I waited for him to come to me and I caught him with 2 hard jabs and then I slipped and moved out before he threw. "NICE Kid! Keep doing that!" yelled Coach from the corner. Tito would not catch me in that round. The next 2 rounds, I did more of the same, but Tito did catch me a few times. When the final round was over, Tito hugged me and said, "You are going to win the Nationals! No doubt." That choked me up. I gave him a small gift card from Modells Sporting Store.

Coach stuck his hand out to shake my hand and said, "I'm proud of you Kid. You did everything I said and worked harder than anyone I know. Go stretch and call me tomorrow afternoon." I didn't know how to answer and just smiled and said, "Thank you Coach. I'll call you tomorrow." I felt melancholic and didn't want the hard training to end. As I stretched, I played back the final sparring session in my head and Tito's words "You are going to win the Nationals...No Doubt."

I was able to get a seat on the train ride home and I remembered that Carla had given me a card on behalf of the entire office. I took it out to read it and got goosebumps when I opened it. They had taken up a small collection and it read, "You are already a Champion to us. Good Luck in Augusta!" along with everyone's signatures and cash! I did not have to be late with the rent anymore. I closed my eyes and said a gratitude prayer.

When I got home, I felt myself get overwhelmed, so I called Father Joe and thankfully he picked up right away. "Hello Patricia. Are you okay?" he said in a worried tone. "I am fine Father Joe. I leave to Augusta on Monday. I am so nervous," I said. "Of course, you are nervous Patricia! But I know you worked hard and sacrificed more than anyone out there. All you need to do is give it 100% as you always do. I will say a prayer for you," he replied. I took a deep breath and said, "I know you are right Father Joe and just needed to hear that. I appreciate the prayers. I'll see you when I get back. Good night."

I finished my tuna salad and managed to relax and laugh watching "I Love Lucy" reruns on T.V. When I was growing up, my sisters and I used to watch "The Honeymooners" and "I Love Lucy" reruns and it never failed to make us laugh. Over the weekend, I packed a large duffle bag. In the Nationals, you could potentially fight four consecutive days if there were enough competitors in your weight division. It consisted of: The Preliminaries, The Quarter Finals, Semi-Finals and Finals. Coach told me to be prepared and pack to fight all four days because that's just the way it was for me. I only owned 2 pair of boxing trunks and would need to recycle. I packed my trunks, 4 sports bras, 4 tank tops, my boots, mouthpiece, chest protector, head guard, tape and a change of clothes for each day.

The tentative schedule that USA Boxing sent us was:
-Monday morning arrival: Check-in & Weigh-in at 6pm
-Tuesday afternoon/evening: Preliminary bouts
-Wednesday afternoon/evening: Quarterfinal bouts
-Thursday afternoon/evening: Semifinal bouts
-Friday: OFF
-Saturday: Championship bouts
-Sunday- Depart home

I was done packing and triple checked that I was not missing anything. I also had the note ready for Adrian with the rent money that I will leave under his door early Monday morning before leaving to the airport. "Hi Adrian, here is the rent for the month of June. I will be gone for the next few days competing in the USA Nationals. Thanks, Patricia."

Lastly, it was time to call my sister and get her blessing before I left, so I called her and we chatted briefly. I realized I am terrible at goodbyes. I got most of the stressful things to do out of the way and felt it had been a productive evening and was ready to get a good night's rest.

Like clockwork, my eyes opened at 5 a.m. without an alarm. I have not really needed an alarm ever since I was 13 years old where I had to get up around that same time to get ready to pick up the Daily Newspaper and deliver them. I had gotten into the habit of praying the minute I was conscious and it always set me up in the right mindset. So that is what I did before I dressed up and laced up my sneakers to go for my run.

As I put on my shorts, I noticed that my clothes fit super loose. I didn't own a scale, but the way my clothes felt indicated what I thought my weight could be which was not the best idea before such a big tournament. I just didn't have the money to purchase a scale. Coach had weighed me at the gym a few weeks ago and I was exactly 119 pounds. I was sure I was about the same weight.

I headed out the door and even though the air was thick, I was happy to be out running. It didn't take much for me to break a sweat and within a few minutes felt the droplets on my forehead and nose. I started thinking about the Nationals and how much I wanted to be a Champion.

I know what it felt like to have my hands raised at the end of a bout and I craved that feeling. I also started thinking about my mother and wondered if she would finally love me if I became champion. I ended up running almost 8 miles. Coach would kill me if he found out. I was supposed to take it easy and just run 3 miles.

I took a long shower and got ready for church. It was the one place I felt safe and never failed to bring me relief. I spoke to the Pastor afterwards and asked for his blessing. He took both his hands and put them on my head and prayed and then said to me, "You can do all things through Christ who strengthens you ".

I called Coach when I got home later that day and we made the plan to meet at LaGuardia Airport at the Delta terminal at 6am. Our flight was at 8am. I rushed him off the phone as I didn't want to tell him about the length of my run. I cleaned the apartment and although I knew I would wake up before the alarm, I set it anyway for 4 a.m.

I woke up promptly before the alarm and made myself instant coffee. I was ready by 5 a.m. and took my large duffle bag and purse and closed the door behind me quietly. I left the note under Adrian's door and left quickly to hail a yellow cab. Living in New York City, there was a never a shortage of cabs and I barely waited 5 minutes before I got one. "LaGuardia airport, Delta Domestic Flights Terminal please," I said to the driver.

When I arrived, Coach was already there and gave me a high-five when he saw me and said his usual line "What's Shaking Kid?" I never knew how to reply to that and instead just looked at him and half smiled. We checked in and had less than an hour before we took off. Thankfully, we were not seated together. I was nervous and was not in the mood to talk. The flight was only 2 hours and before we knew it, we were landing. We got our bags and we took a cab to the Hyatt Hotel which was also the host hotel and where fighters needed to check in at 3 p.m.

When we arrived, I saw my friend Denise and we hugged. For a small moment, I felt like I was hugging my sister. It felt so good to see a familiar face that actually liked me. Throughout the years, Coach said many things to me that stuck and one of those things was, "Being a Champion is a lonely road. When you are losing, everyone wants to be your friend, but when you are winning, no one really likes you. Misery loves company, remember that Alcivar".

Denise and I made a pact to stick together and keep each other motivated. Even though we were in different weight classes-Denise was 139 pounds and I was 119 pounds, we had the best sparring sessions. I was so hungry but did not want to eat a big meal before the weigh-ins and Denise was nervous about her weight as well.

We all checked into our rooms and Coach said I should take a nap. I unpacked and didn't realize how exhausted I was and passed out for a good hour. "Hey Yo Alcivar! Wake Up," said Coach while knocking on my door. It was 2:30 p.m. and I had to get ready to check in at the hotel's Ballroom. "Okay Coach! Give me 5 minutes," I replied. My mouth was dry, but I didn't want to drink water which could add any unnecessary weight. The rules were the same as in the Golden Gloves as far as the weight allowances: Prelims- 3lbs, Quarter finals -2 lbs., Semifinals-1 lb., Finals- No weight allowance.

When I got out of my room, Coach and Denise were waiting and we went down together. There were so many women already waiting and staring at any one that walked in. There were reporters, cameras, photographers and so many people. A reporter came over to me and asked, "How do you feel to be competing in the 1st ever National Women's Boxing Championships?"

I took a deep breath and remembered what Coach had taught me. "As a Latina from Queens, New York City, I feel proud and grateful to be here. My Coach and I have worked very hard and this is a dream come true to be participating in such an event," I said with a smile. The reporter wrote down my name and quoted me and then took a picture.

I saw that the team from New York City were also present. The women's boxing community in New York was small and mostly boxed at Gleason's, so I saw many familiar faces. "119-pound Women need to weigh in now in Ballroom A," yelled Mercedes from USA Boxing. Coach couldn't go in and patted me on the back, "You got this Kid. I'll be right here," said Coach. My weight division was one of the most crowded- 17 fighters to be exact which meant that if we all made weight, I would fight in the Prelims starting tomorrow!

Everyone looked so big and mean. There was one woman in particular who kept looking at me from head to toe in a nasty way. I tried to ignore her and looked the other way, but it was bothering me. Some women stripped completely naked to make weight. One woman was 8 pounds heavy and had to be moved to the 125-pound division, so now there were 16 of us. When it was my turn to weigh in, I left my sports bra and panties on and held my breath. "Alcivar, 117 pounds!" yelled out Denny, from USA Boxing.

I was so relieved and that also gave me some room to actually have a decent dinner! "Okay Ladies! Go have some dinner and the bout sheets will be posted in the Ballroom tonight by 8 p.m. If you are fighting tomorrow in the Prelims, you need to be down here again by 10 a.m. Bouts start at noon!" said Denny again.

When I came out, it was nice to see Denise and Coach waiting. "What was the weight Kid?" asked Coach. I said, "117!" Coach opened his eyes. "Whoa Kid! That's all that hard work. Now, we can go have dinner and not worry," said Coach. Denise had won the Golden Gloves and her hotel and flights and daily meals were paid for. She went to have dinner with the New York City Team. Coach and I went to the "Waffle House" which we discovered was a big chain in the South. I ordered a bland chicken salad which I didn't finish and Coach had a burger and fries.

When I am stressed, my appetite disappears. I was too worried about who I was boxing tomorrow. I was hoping that it was not the woman who was giving me the nasty looks. We got back to the hotel at 8 p.m. and rushed to the ballroom.

The Coaches and fighters were hanging out and talking about the bouts tomorrow. I walked over with Coach and found the 119 Division Bout Sheet and it read, "12 Noon 119 Bouts: Alcivar, NYC vs O'Sullivan, NYC". I knew O'Sullivan. She was an Irish red head who boxed both at Gleasons and at Wall Street. She had about the same experience as I did. I had seen her box before and was not impressed, but you could never under estimate anyone in boxing or in general, so I remained focused.

"Okay Kid, we know what we are up against. This chick is going to run at you and try to take it from you. You are going to stick and move and make her pay each time she misses. You hear me?" said Coach. The joking was over now. "Yes Coach. I'm going to do exactly how we trained at the gym," I replied. Denise came over and was relieved that she had gotten a bye for tomorrow. "I'm gonna be there cheering you on!" she said. I was exhausted and wanted to go to my room and sleep. Coach was talking to the officials and to some of the other coaches he knew, but came over soon after and walked me up to my room. "Get a good night's rest Kid. We are going to be fighting for 4 days. I'll pick you up at 8am for breakfast," said Coach before I closed the door.

I stood at the edge of my bed and got on my knees and prayed, "God, please help me be brave and fight to the best of my ability. May it be your will. Amen." I surprisingly fell asleep pretty quickly, but woke up in the middle of the night after having a horrible nightmare. I dreamed that I saw my father in the audience and he was laughing in an evil way. I woke up breathing heavily and sweating. "It's just an awful dream," I whispered to myself and dosed off again but would not forget the dream.

I woke up at 6am. I prayed and took a shower and read my Eleanor Roosevelt book that the nurse had given me at the hospital that one time. It was a book that meant the world to me. Although I had memorized almost every quote in that book, reading it helped me feel strong when I needed it the most. The quote I would keep in mind for today would be, "The purpose of life is to live it. To taste the experience to the utmost. To reach out eagerly and without fear for newer and richer experience," Eleanor Roosevelt.

At 8am sharp, Coach knocked on my door. I was ready and opened the door and Coach said, "How you doing Kid? Sleep good?" I didn't look at Coach and just said, "Slept okay Coach. Just want to have breakfast. I am hungry." I wasn't really hungry, but didn't want to get into talking about my nightmares. We went to the restaurant inside the hotel where they were serving breakfast. I had 2 hardboiled eggs and coffee while Coach had pancakes, eggs and the works. When Coach gets anxious the opposite happens and he eats. It was already passed 9am, so we hurried back to our rooms.

I changed into my boxing trunks, sports bra and tank top and packed a small duffle bag with my boxing boots, chest protector, head guard, mouth piece, water bottle and book. I said one last prayer and met Coach outside my room. Coach was dressed in his usual jeans, plaid shirt and baseball cap but also had a spit bucket, gauze, tape and a towel. Coach gave me a high five and we took the elevator down.

There were coaches and their fighters already down in the ballroom waiting and I saw O'Sullivan and looked the other way. I had the opposite reaction when I saw my opponents. I did not want to look or be anywhere near them until we got in the ring. At 10 a.m. they called us into a separate room and a doctor took our blood pressure and vital signs. We checked in with USA Boxing right after. I was the 3rd bout which meant I would fight by or before 12:30 p.m.

One of the worst parts about boxing in general for all fighters was the waiting. I had 2 hours before my bout and couldn't go anywhere, so I read my book, stretched and closed my eyes. At 11:30 a.m., I put on my boxing shoes and chest protector. Coach starting wrapping my hands in gauze and tape which always took him a good 30 minutes. At 12 p.m. one of the officials gave me the 10 oz. gloves to put on and Coach held the pads for me so I could start getting warmed up. "One-Two, Slip Slip," said Coach. We practiced a few combinations for the next 20 minutes before we heard "ALCIVAR/O'SULLIVAN on deck".

"Okay Alcivar, you know what to do so DO IT!" said Coach as we were making our way into the ring. O'Sullivan was already inside the ring and she was throwing punches in the air and staring straight at me. "Okay Mama! Time to be Courageous," I mentally said to myself remembering the words from the Eleanor Roosevelt book. They announced our names and we came into the center of the ring, tapped gloves and then the bell rang.

O'Sullivan charged at me and started winging but I slipped, ducked and weaved every punch. Then it was my turn and I threw the hardest left hook right hand combination I could that made her head snap back. I was amazed for a quick second of how strong my left hook was. Training all those hot summer months just working on my left paid off as Coach had said. The referee stepped in for an 8-count. The second the referee stopped counting and instructed us to "Box", I charged at her and threw 2 hard left hooks followed by a right hand that landed flush on her nose and drew blood. The referee stepped in again and didn't even count and instead stopped the fight.

"The winner by 1st round stoppage and advancing to the Quarter Finals is.....from the blue corner ALCIVAR," said the announcer. I wasn't sure if I had broken O'Sullivan's nose but I shook her hand and made my way out of the ring. Coach held the ropes apart and said, "Nice work Alcivar, 1 down 3 to go!" There were photographers taking so many pictures and a reporter wanted to talk to me but I had to make my way back into the ballroom to give my passbook to USA Boxing and see the doctor again. "Congratulations Alcivar! Your book will stay with us. Come back at 8 p.m. tonight to see who you are boxing tomorrow," said Denny.

The doctor took my vitals again and asked me if anything was hurt. I smiled and said, "I am fine doctor." He palpated my back, face, and hands feeling for any abnormalities or pain. "Okay Kiddo! You are good to go! Tomorrow, you have to weigh-in at 8am before breakfast and then get checked in again. Bouts start at 3 p.m. tomorrow. I took a deep breath and remembered that I could not celebrate. I had to stay strong and focused.

When I came out, Denise and Coach were waiting for me. Denise was smiling and gave me a big hug. She also had to check in tonight to see if she was fighting tomorrow. Coach told me to go upstairs to take a nap and he would come get me for dinner. He was going to stay and watch the rest of the bouts, but more importantly, he wanted to see my other opponents fight.

I got to my room and laid down on my bed. I was worn out even though the fight lasted one round. I felt my head spin and fell into a deep sleep. All of a sudden, I felt my arms stiffen and my chest heavy as if I was breathing through a straw. I saw the room get red and I wanted to scream out for Coach or anyone to help me, but I couldn't speak. "God, please help me! Our Father who art in heaven..." I started mentally praying and then I was able to move and I sat up immediately and started to cry. I did not know what to think or do. I looked at my watch and it was nearly 5 p.m. and Coach would be knocking on my door soon for dinner. I went to take a shower and shake off what just happened.

"Yo Kid! You Ready?" said Coach behind the door. I had thrown on a pair of jean shorts that felt super baggy, a t-shirt and flip flops and opened the door. "How about the Waffle House again?" asked Coach. I nodded my head and we went to the good ole Waffle House. Coach liked the burger from last time and I was cool having the same chicken salad that I probably wouldn't finish. We sat down and ordered the exact same thing as yesterday. "Did you take a look at the girls I am fighting?" I asked. "Yeah. The girl, Leona from New York won. She is tough. She stopped the girl and started dancing in the ring. Not cool at all. Then there's the girl from Arizona who is tall and has a good reach who won her fight and the last girl is from Hawaii. Good Boxer but you are better than all of them. You can beat them all. You hear me Alcivar?" said Coach.

I knew Coach was serious when he called me Alcivar otherwise it was just Kid. "I know you are nervous Alcivar. Let me do all the worrying. You just fight. They got nothing on you. Trust me. When we finish dinner, we will go back and find out who you are fighting tomorrow," he continued. I wished I believed in me as much as Coach did.

We made it back at 8 p.m. and we were the last ones to check the bout sheets. "119: 5th bout: Alcivar vs Salazar" read the bout sheet. I had not seen her fight but I saw her and her coach staring at me from across the Ballroom. She was taller at about 5'7" and it would be the first time for me fighting someone that much taller than me. I mean, I had sparred with Tito and the guys from Gleason's who were taller than me, but this was a real fight. The anxiety started much earlier this time. "Okay Kid, let's go into the gym. I want to show you a couple of things," said Coach.

We went into the hotel gym and to my surprise found a bunch of girls including Denise working out. Some were jumping rope and others were on the treadmill with sauna suits. I guessed that they wanted to make sure they were on weight for tomorrow's weigh-in. For the Quarter Finals there was only a 2-pound allowance. Coach grabbed me and took me to an empty office. "Listen to me Alcivar. I just want you to be clear on what your strategy should be for tomorrow. This chick is taller than you, so you are going to attack the body. Start with the jab and right/left to the body. You have to be relentless!" said Coach firmly. I nodded my head and shadow boxed his instructions. "That's exactly right Alcivar! Just like that! Do that non-stop tomorrow!" said Coach before we headed back upstairs.

I got back to my room and prayed and went to sleep. The events of the entire day had taken a toll on me and sleep took over. For the first time in a while, I was able to get 8 hours of solid sleep. I woke up at 6am and felt refreshed. I prayed again, stretched and met Coach at 7:30 a.m. "You Ready Kid?" asked Coach. I nodded. I disliked the weigh-ins almost as much as I disliked the waiting before a fight.

At 8am, they started weighing in the competitors by weight class. I weighed in at 116.5. I wasn't sure how I lost a half pound since yesterday. I got checked in by the doctor and received instructions to be back by 1 pm. Coach was always eager to hear how much I weighed. "You're not eating enough Alcivar! Let's go eat a good breakfast," said Coach. We had a routine down and he reminded me of the strategy for the fight during breakfast. I had scrambled eggs this time with my black coffee and Coach had his usual pancakes, eggs, hash browns and orange juice.

I saw the New York City team and other female competitors hang out and chat. I was never fond of hanging out in groups. In school I purposely avoided them partially because I didn't want to talk to anyone about my living situation and the other part was that I felt different from all the other girls. Coach had noticed how from the beginning how the girls had kept me at a distance and he said to me something else that still rings true, "If you had lost your fight yesterday, all those girls would be your friends and trying to comfort you. You are not like them. You are in a class of your own." I would learn to understand what Coach meant throughout my athletic career and life.

We finished breakfast and took a walk to the store to buy Powerade and a few snacks as I would not be able to eat a full lunch before my bout. I got back to my room for a good nap and visualized everything I was supposed to do for this next bout.

"Right and then left hand to the body. Relentless body punches. Punch to the face and come down to the body," I whispered to myself before I fell asleep. It felt good to be alone in my room without worrying about Adrian or work or paying rent. I would rather worry about fighting than those other things.

I woke up by noon. I packed my duffle bag with all my gear and put on my favorite black and yellow boxing trunks. They reminded me of the movie "Rocky 2" when Rocky had a rematch with Apollo Creed. He wore the exact same-colored trunks I was wearing. I wore a black tank top to match and kept my sneakers on. I kneeled down on the end of the bed and said my prayer for today, "God help me fight to the best of my ability. Help me be brave, relentless and have courage in today's fight. Amen."

When I opened my door at 12:45 p.m., Coach was about to knock and said "Looking good Kid" when he saw my outfit. We went straight to the ballroom and I got in line with Denise who was fighting today too. She was the 8th bout and Coach would work her corner after I finished my bout. The same doctor checked me in and now the waiting game begun. Denise was the complete opposite of me and went to chat with other girls from the New York City team. I remained focused by myself and every so often Coach checked in on me, but for the most part, I did the same thing and re-read my book, visualized and stretched.

Coach came to wrap my hands at 2:00 p.m. and the bouts began at 3 p.m., so we started warming up right after I was wrapped. "ALCIVAR and SALAZAR on deck!" yelled out one of the officials. "Remember what we practiced! Head and Body! Relentless!" said Coach in my ear.

My eyes met with Salazar's as I was entering the ring. She was indeed taller than me and had these incredibly long arms. We came to the center of the ring tapped gloves and the bell rang. She threw a hard one-two combo straight to my head. Her reach was significant and stunned me for a second. I responded with an over hand right that landed on her chin and made her stumble back and then the bell rang for the end of round one.

"You are waiting too long Alcivar! If it wasn't for that big right hand, you just landed you would have lost that round. Come On! Don't stop throwing. Get busy in there!" said Coach before the bell rang for the start of the 2nd round. I realized that I had to close the gap which meant not doing my usual boxing and instead, stick to her like glue. I threw an over hand right again and followed up with right-left to the body over and over in the 2nd round that kept landing while she kept punching down at me but couldn't catch me and then the bell rang to end the 2nd round.

"Better round Alcivar! This is the Final round, so keep putting the pressure and don't stop until that bell rings! Relentless!" instructed Coach. Final round started and I came out swinging, but Salazar had the same mission and we started trading punches in the center of the ring. She caught me with 2 hard punches and I quickly remembered to slip, duck and move. I turned it on in the final minute and then the final bell rung to end the round. My face was red and I was nervous. 'Did I do enough to win?" I asked myself. Coach high-fived me and said, "Nice job Alcivar!" and I could see Denise in the audience throwing her hands up in the air which was a good sign and then the announcer spoke in the microphone, "Let's have a round of applause for these 2 great competitors.... AND the winner advancing to the semi-finals is.... From the BLUE CORNER, PATRICIA ALCIVAR!"

"2 down, 2 to go Alcivar" said Coach as he held the ropes apart for me to exit. I smiled a little as I knew I was only half way done. I was nearly blinded by all the photographers snapping pictures, but I hurried in to see the doctor and check in with USA Boxing for further instructions. Coach left to go work Denise's corner as she would soon be boxing.

"Hello again young lady...Congratulations on another win," said the Doctor. I tried to smile but I found it to be difficult. From my Golden

Gloves experience, I knew how it felt to be so close to winning and then not win, so I wanted to stay focused and not celebrate too early.

The Doctor lightly palpated my face, head, neck and hands to make sure nothing was injured. As soon as he gave me the okay, I checked in with the Officials at USA Boxing. 'We will hold on to your passbook as long as you keep winning. You can check back tonight at 8 p.m. to see what bout you are and who you are boxing tomorrow. Weigh-ins are at 8am again and only 1 pound allowance," said the USA Boxing Official. I nodded my head and ran out to see Denise's bout.

She was in the 2nd round when I finally sat down to watch her and she was clearly the stronger boxer. Denise was a teacher and played soccer when she wasn't boxing. She won her bout and I hugged her when she came out. She was so happy. By the time she came back out from the checking in with the Doctor and USA Boxing, it was past 6 p.m. She went to have dinner with the NYC team and Coach and I went to the Waffle House. It had worked for us for the past 2 days so we had a quick dinner there and came back to check the bout sheets before the crowd.

"119: 4th bout: ALCIVAR vs DOMEN" read the bout sheet. Noel Domen was a 17-year-old from Hawaii who was coached by her father. I had seen her shadow box and remember being impressed with her grace and movement. She was young like me and a polished boxer. "Let's find an empty space and practice our strategy. Tomorrow, you are going to use your boxing skills," said Coach. I was relieved that we beat the crowd and most of all, I didn't want to see my opponent. "This chick is your height and she boxes just like you. She is not a winger, so YOU are going to be the aggressive one and come in, throw hard and move. She won't be able to handle it," said Coach.

He had seen her fight when I was getting checked by the Doctor. I took everything Coach said to heart. I shadow boxed Coach's instructions for a good 20-minutes and then headed to my room. I laid in my bed and closed my eyes, "God, thank you for helping me come this far. Tomorrow will be my 3rd consecutive day of fighting. Please help me stay strong and focused. Please protect my sleep tonight and always.

Amen." I was sound asleep by 10 p.m. and was thankful not to have any nightmares. However, an intense stomach pain woke me up at 4 a.m. and I couldn't go back to sleep so I went to take a hot soothing shower.

I visualized my boxing plan for this afternoon while I stretched. My opponent today had her father in her corner and had her community in Hawaii raised over $5,000 to get her and her father to this National competition. I on the other hand, had to work a full-time job and pay my own way here. I had to endure living in a creep's basement apartment in order to save money. I didn't have the support of my parents, family or friends. My strategy was simple. I was going to fight for my dreams and make everything I had to go through to get here count.

I walked out to meet Coach who surprisingly was not standing outside my door. This time I went to get him and knocked on his door. It was nearly 8am and Coach had overslept. He had spent the night watching videos of my opponents. "Hey Kid! How you slept? I overslept but I'm ready. Let's go downstairs," said Coach while we rushed to catch the elevator. As we got in the elevator, one of my potential opponents from the New York City team was there, Leona Brown who was nicknamed "Little Tyson" because she had a muscular build, walked around with the signature cut-off towel shirt and was knocking everyone out.

She looked at me from head to toe and then straight at me. I don't know what came over me, but I stared right back. She was much shorter than me, but Leona had fought Eileen Lacy whom I lost to in the finals of the Golden Gloves and beat her. When the elevator stopped, she brushed up against me before leaving the elevator. Coach put his hand on my shoulder and whispered in my ear, "We will see this clown in the finals. Mark my words."

I saw Denise waiting on line and joined her. She had a big smile and said, "Semi Finals Trish! Can you believe it?" She liked calling me that and I didn't mind. As we were waiting in line, Leona came and planted herself in front of us and was as loud as can be. "Let's see whose turn it is to get knocked out tonight," laughed Leona. Denise and I looked at her in disgust. "Ugh! I hope you fight her in the finals and shut her up" whispered Denise.

I did not want to weigh in so close to her so I walked to the back of the line. I had a feeling that she was going to pick a fight with me and I just wanted to avoid her at all costs. I weighed in at a very slim 115.5. I lost a pound since yesterday. I also had that nagging pressure in the center of my stomach. "It's just nerves," I thought to myself. I went to get Coach and saw him talking to Denise. "Did that chick bother you," asked Coach. I just shrugged my shoulders. "We have to eat now because we have to check back again at 1pm for the fights at 3 p.m." I said trying to ignore Coach's question.

Leona was a bully and reminded me of my oldest sister who used to behave even worse with me when I lived at home. I've dealt with much worse in life and the only way to deal with people like that is to take the higher road and ignore them. It was nice to have Denise join us for breakfast this time. I was amazed at how much she was able to eat. Even though we were the same height, at 139 pounds, she was healthy and strong. My stomach was still hurting but I forced myself to eat my scrambled eggs.

We finished breakfast later than yesterday because we were chatting away and now it was almost 11 a.m. and I really was looking forward to my nap. Coach acted as a bodyguard and walked me straight to my room and said he would pick me up at 12:45 p.m. I was getting used to these mid-day naps and dosed off the minute my head hit the pillow. I must have been in a deep sleep for a good half hour before I felt my chest get incredibly heavy and instinctively, I woke up before the nightmare got me. A half hour of deep sleep was better than nothing and I was relieved to get at least that.

Today, I put on a white tank-top but would wear the same black and yellow striped trunks as yesterday. They were my favorite and they had so much meaning. Besides reminding me of the "Rocky 2" movie, it was also the very first pair of boxing trunks I ever purchased. I had to save up enough money to buy and I wore for my first fight ever in the New York City Golden Gloves.

I looked in the mirror and nodded my head and then got my bag when I heard Coach knocking on my door. "Looking good Kid! What's Shaking?" said Coach and before I even answered he continued to say, "Listen, I want you to ignore this chick, Leona. I heard she has been running her mouth about you. She thinks that because she beat Lacy, that she will beat you if she fights you but we both know that you beat Lacy. I got your back." I just nodded my head as I did not want to keep talking about the same topic. All I wanted was to focus on my next bout.

When I arrived at the Ballroom, my opponent, Domen and her team were already there. I avoided looking at her and let her check in first. Her Father came up to Coach and said, "Good Luck this afternoon. May the best boxer win". Coach and I thought that was strange, but figured he was trying to get inside our heads. When they were finished, the Doctor smiled and said, "How are we feeling Champ?" I smiled back and said, "Not too shabby Doctor" which made him smile even bigger. I had learned that term from Coach. I had spent so much time with him throughout the past years that all of his sayings rubbed off on me.

It was already passed 2 p.m. and I was already hearing crowds come in. People were excited to see the 1st ever Women's USA National Boxing Semi-final Championships! I put on my boxing shoes and Coach started wrapping my hands. Since I was the 4th bout, I would definitely be fighting soon after the first bout went on. Denise was the 6th bout, so Coach would assist in her corner again. Today, the waiting wasn't as brutal. I started shadow boxing and then I was called in to get gloved up. The 2nd bout which was Leona's was already in the ring. She stopped the girl in the 2nd round and the 3rd bout started shortly after.

"ALCIVAR/DOMEN on Deck!" said one of the USA Boxing Officials. "Remember what we practiced. You are the better boxer. You got this Alcivar!" said Coach as we waited. In Women's Amateur boxing, it was three 2-minute rounds, so the bouts went by very quickly. The 3rd

bout ended and now we were walking towards the ring. I wondered if Coach could hear how fast my heart was beating.

I entered the ring and so did Domen on the opposite end as our names were being announced. Soon after we walked to the center of the ring. She looked straight at me and I reciprocated. "You are not going to take my dream away" was my last thought before the bell rang and I came out aggressively and threw a right-hand left hook combination that landed and I immediately came down and landed two body punches that stunned her and then I moved out of the way. She kept her guard up high, so I kept punching to the body. The bell rang to end the first round.

"Nice Alcivar! Keep coming in on her. Close the gap and don't hold back" said Coach while I sat on the stool in my corner. After a quick sip of water, the bell rang for the 2nd round. Domen tried to keep me away with her jabs. Because I was used to feeling punches from bigger boxers like Tito and Denise, her punches didn't sting at all. But in Amateur Boxing, if the punches land, they scored. Although her punches were not hurting, she managed to score and she had a better round in the 2nd.

"Alcivar, you gotta move after you punch! Don't let her keep tagging you. She is gonna take it away from you!" said Coach. The bell rang for the start of the 3rd round. I charged at her with furious flurries of combinations that landed and overwhelmed her. The referee stepped in and gave her a standing 8-count, "ONE, TWO, THREE, FOUR...." Yelled out the referee, but Domen had her hands high when the referee counted at Four. "BOX," yelled the Referee. Now we both stood to-to-toe and traded punches until the final bell rang.

I went to my corner and Coach removed my head guard and said, "3 down, 1 more to go." I walked to the center of the ring and waited for the announcer who said, "Moving on to the 1st Ever Women's National Boxing Finals on Saturday is.... from the BLUE Corner, PATRICIA ALCIVAR!"

The Referee raised my hand high and I managed to smile for the cameras. Coach was holding the ropes apart and waited for me to exit the ring. "Good job Kid! Go check in with Doctor and USA Boxing and then come watch Denise fight." I realized that my hands were trembling a bit as I was walking towards the Doctor and the USA Boxing Officials room.

"Congratulations Young Lady! You are in the finals!" said the smiling Doctor. And then I heard Denny say, "It's gonna be two New Yorkers in the Finals!" My smile faded away almost immediately when I realized who the other New Yorker was. The Doctor asked me if anything hurt or if I was injured. I shook my head and then he did his routine of checking my vitals and for any abnormalities. "Enjoy your day off tomorrow and see you on Saturday for the finals Patricia," said the Doctor. I tried to smile and nodded my head as I went over to see the USA Boxing Officials.

"So, it is you and Leona in the Finals!" said Denny. It was the second time she said that and she was trying to see if she got any reaction from me. "Thanks Denny. Is there anything I need to know before Saturday?" I replied. "Yes! You have tomorrow off, but need to come down in the morning to collect your uniform for the Finals. USA Boxing will provide you with the trunks, tank top, socks and shoes. Weigh-ins are Saturday morning and you MUST be on weight. NO weight Allowances and bouts start at 6 p.m. and will be aired on ESPN!"

That was a-lot of information and I just took it all in and said, "Thanks Denny. I'll see you tomorrow." I ran out to catch the last round of Denise's fight which she won. Now, we were both in the Finals. There were 12 Olympic weight classes and the New York City Team had 6 of the weight classes represented in the finals. I was not considered part of the New York City Team, Leona was. The showdown of the best 119-pound female fighter in the Country would come down to 2 New Yorkers- Me and Leona. That was the talk of the night. I hugged Denise when I saw her, but it was Denise who said, "We made it to the Finals Trish!" I want you to come with us tomorrow. A few girls are going to get together and go to the mall tomorrow and then relax at the pool in the afternoon after we get our uniforms in the morning."

The thought of going to the mall and pool sounded awesome to me. "Yeah! Of course! Thanks so much Denise!" I said smiling from ear-to-ear. She gave me one last hug and said, "I'll see you here tomorrow for the uniform pick-up and then we'll have breakfast at the mall and then go to the pool."

"It's late Kid. Let's get a quick bite here at the hotel," said Coach. It was late indeed. It was almost 8 p.m. and my stomach had started to bother me again, but I had to eat something. We walked to the restaurant inside the hotel and I asked if I could have 3 scrambled eggs.

The waiter smiled and said, "Absolutely! We can certainly take care of preparing that for you. But is that all you are going to have?" I hated to waste food and really wasn't hungry, so even scrambled eggs was pushing it, but I replied, "I don't have much of an appetite right now, but thank you, that will be all for me." However, Coach went ahead and ordered the chicken parmesan with baked ziti entrée.

While we waited for our food to come Coach turned to me and said, "Listen Alcivar, you are not going anywhere with Denise tomorrow. No mall, No pool. You are going to put your feet up in your room and watch television and relax all day tomorrow. You don't need to be walking around in a crowded mall and then baking in the sun. They can do that if they want, but not you." I knew better than to argue with Coach. I remembered the whole incident with having to go in to the gym on Mother's Day. Coach had the last word and I knew he wasn't going to change his mind. It did hurt though. I rarely got to hang out with anyone. I looked down trying to hold back tears and said, "Fine. I'll stay all day in my room."

Our food came out and we barely said a word, but Coach did go ahead and say, "You will thank me later for looking out for you. I don't care if you hate me now, but I'm doing this for your own good." I wasn't sure if the stomach discomfort was from nerves, anger or what, but I just wanted to go to my room. Coach inhaled his food and I finished my scrambled eggs and I was glad to be back in my room.

I was exhausted tonight and was glad to fall asleep right away. We wouldn't have to check in for our uniforms until 10 a.m. I told Coach I would be ordering breakfast in my room and would meet him at 10 a.m. I was still tired when I woke up at 6 a.m. and thought that perhaps it was a good idea that I was resting all day today. I treated myself to a bagel with cream cheese and coffee while I read the local Augusta newspaper that was left in front of my door.

The newspaper had a story about the bouts last night and announced ticket sales for the 1st USA National Women's Amateur Boxing Championship Finals tomorrow night. "This is really happening," I thought as I finished my breakfast and closed my eyes imagining that the referee was raising my hand tomorrow night. I felt my eyes warm, but I stood up and threw on my favorite pair of jean shorts and a t-shirt and met Coach outside my door. "How you doing Kid?" asked Coach. "My stomach has been hurting for past 2 days. I think it could be my period," I replied once I realized that the discomfort I was having felt like menstrual cramps.

My period had not come all month, so there was a good chance that was the reason my stomach was bothering me. "I forgot to pack maxi-pads and I need them just in case it does come," I added. "Okay Kid. Let's talk to Denise. Since she is going to the mall later, she can pick some up for you. You will be fine" said Coach as we took the elevator downstairs. The elevator doors opened to Leona standing right in front staring at me. "Don't look at her. She is trying to get inside your head. You do your talking with your fists tomorrow night," said Coach in my ear as went inside avoiding any contact with her.

We saw Denise as we stepped out of the elevator and Coach asked her not to leave me alone once we went inside the room. "Alcivar! Come get your uniform" yelled out Mercedes. I opened up the bag. I was in the blue corner again and had a size small navy-blue tank top, boxing trunks that were royal blue with red and white stripes on the side and royal blue with red and white stripes matching shoes.

They were beautiful! And then I heard a voice behind me say, "You're gonna get beat up tomorrow Alcivar!" I turned around and it was Leona grinning. Denise rushed over and grabbed me and said, "Let's go Trish! Don't listen to that garbage." Denise had seen Leona inching closer to me and knew she wanted to provoke a fight before the finals tomorrow. I had never in my life thrown a punch outside the ring and was not going to start now. I didn't let her words shake me. She was a bully and Coach was right, I will let my fists do the talking in the ring tomorrow night.

"You have to beat her tomorrow, Trish! You have to shut her up!" said Denise as we walked out. I just nodded my head and saw Coach coming over. "What's going on?" said Coach. He saw that Denise's face was red and she was agitated. "Nothing Coach. Leona was just trying to get to me. That's all" I calmly explained. "Okay Kid, you go upstairs right now and watch television and rest. I have to talk to Denise now, but I'll come pick you up for an early dinner at 4 p.m. understand?" I nodded and left. It was nearly noon and I started to feel that annoying pressure on my stomach, so a nap right around now didn't sound bad.

I walked into my room and laid out my new uniform on the bed and after staring at it for a few minutes, I decided to try it on. My favorite color is blue and I thought it was interesting how I had been in the blue corner throughout the entire tournament and now for the finals again and my uniform was mostly blue. Although the top and bottom were a size small, the uniform was super baggy on me. The shorts came below my knee and the tank-top dropped down below my sports bra.

I tried to use safety pins but I am sure Coach would object to that. I was drowsy and dropped like a sack of rocks on to the bed after I took my uniform off. "Hey Yo Alcivar Open the Door!" was the sound I woke up to along with a nasty pain in my stomach. I felt my pants wet and was horrified to see that my sheets were full of blood. "Oh No God Please!" I screeched. "Yo Alcivar what's Going On?" said Coach again from behind my door. I hurried over and opened the door. "I just woke up Coach and also got my period. I don't have any pads either." I said embarrassed. "I am going to call Denise right now and ask her to buy your stuff. Take a shower and I'll come back in 30 minutes so we can have dinner. It's gonna be okay Kid. I promise" said Coach before he left.

I took a hot bath and let the warm water run down my back and then sat down in the tub. "Don't ever sacrifice your life for anyone. You are too precious and owe it to yourself to live your life to the fullest" was what came to my mind as I tried to not feel sorry for myself. Nothing ever came easy for me and this stupid period was not going to get in the way of my dreams. I got out of that tub quick. I rolled up thick layers of toilet paper and would use that until Denise came with the delivery.

I shook off whatever it was that I was feeling. I have been through worse pain in my life and did not want to experience the pain of losing again. I worked too hard to get here. I have to suck it up for 6 minutes and give it all I have tonight or live with the pain of regret. I walked out the door and waited for Coach who showed up a minute later. "What's shaking kid?" he asked. "I'm okay Coach. Let's go eat." I replied. We went to the hotel restaurant and I had my scrambled eggs and Coach had his burger and fries and afterwards we went for a short walk near the hotel.

"Tomorrow is your night Kid. No excuses. I don't care about any period. You worked through a broken hand, you sweated all summer and spent holidays in the gym when everyone else was at the beach and partying. Make tomorrow count!" said Coach. "Don't worry Coach. I have a-lot to fight for tomorrow. I will give it all I have." I replied.

When we got back, there was a bag hanging on my door. Denise had left the maxi-pads on my door. "Sleep good Kid. I'll see you tomorrow at 7:45 a.m. A 119-pound Champion will be crowned tomorrow night. It's there for you to take," said Coach as he closed my door and left. I kneeled down beside my bed and prayed, "God, please calm the fears and help me fight with courage, clarity and strength tomorrow. May the best fighter win tomorrow night. Amen."

I had stomach cramps throughout the night but managed to get a couple of hours of sleep. I felt bloated and hoped that it would not reflect on the scale. I threw on a pair of comfortable stretchy tights and tank top and put my long curly hair in a bun. I was anxious and couldn't wait so I walked down and sat outside of Coach's room. Coach was startled when he saw me and said, "Hey Alcivar! Why didn't you knock?" I just shrugged my shoulders.

"Smile a little Alcivar. Tonight, is a big night!" said Coach as we took the elevator down. There were 23 women already there waiting to get weighed in and get final instructions and with me it was 24- Two fighters per the 12 Olympic weight divisions. The second I walked in, Leona stood up and started eyeing me and started punching her hand. "You'll take care of that clown tonight," whispered Coach in my ear and then he grabbed me and we went inside where the USA Boxing Officials were.

We saw Denise and Coach handed me over to her before he got kicked out of the room. Denise held on to my arm and smiled. We started stripping down to get ready to get weighed and sure enough we started hearing, "Someone is gonna get knocked out tonight!" I recognized the stupid voice and I didn't bother to turn around. It was my turn to get on the scale, "ALCIVAR: 114.5" yelled out Mercedes. Denise gave me the thumbs up as I got off and she got ready to get on the scale.

As I was getting dressed, Leona came behind me and shoved me and Denise came running over and yelled, "What is wrong with you! Leave her alone!" Leona just smiled and said, "See you tonight Alcivar! No one will protect you in the ring." I just stared back at her and realized some of the other officials also saw what was going on. There was one official in particular named Melanie who everyone knew as "The Grandma of Boxing" because she was as sweet as pie and seemed to be like everyone's grandmother. "You have to teach her a lesson and beat her tonight, Trish!" said Denise. I was thankful to remain calm.

"Don't worry Denise, I'll make her pay tonight," I replied while trying to forget about my menstrual cramps. I never had anyone protect me growing up at home, so Denise sticking up for me was something I would always remember fondly.

"Ladies, first bout starts at 6 p.m. tonight. We want everyone to report by 4.p.m. Order of bouts is up on the wall," yelled out Denny. Denise handed me back to Coach and we went to over to the wall where bouts were posted. "119 Championship Finals: Bout #3: ALCIVAR/BROWN," was printed in big bold letters. "Perfect! You take care of business early Alcivar!" said Coach as we made our way to the hotel restaurant for breakfast.

We sat down and I ordered my scrambled eggs with onions, tomatoes and a side of toast and coffee. "How was the weight Kid?" asked Coach. I was hesitant, but I said, "114.5 even though I have my period." He just nodded his head and then said, "Tonight is the most important night of your life. I don't care about period or nothing. You MUST go out there and fight like your life depended on it because it does. You have to shut all those haters up. Make all the days you've worked your ass off count tonight!"

"I know what I have to do Coach. I will do it. I promise," I said just in time for when our breakfast arrived. I made myself eat everything because I knew it was going to be difficult to have a full meal later. Coach dropped me off in my room by 12 noon. Plan was to take a good nap, order a small lunch/snack by 2.p.m, rest and Coach would pick me up at 3:45 p.m.

A nap was ideal. The full breakfast and my period made me sleepy. I laid in my bed and prayed, "I need your strength and courage more than ever tonight. God, please help me perform to the best of my ability tonight and be brave. We cannot let the bad people win. Amen." I slept deeply for an hour. When I awoke, I felt my legs heavy and thought my period had gone through my pants again. It almost did. I took a quick shower to fully wake me up and then called room service for a fruit platter which would be my final meal before my fight later.

As I started to get dressed, I worried if my period would go through my trunks while I was fighting on television. The flow was extra heavy, but I couldn't keep worrying about. My job tonight was to leave it all in the ring and walk out with no regrets. When I looked in the mirror, I saw my trunks were practically falling off my waist and my tank top looked super baggy and falling off my shoulders and then I heard a knock on my door.

I looked through the peep hole and it was Coach, so I opened the door. Coach had a smirk on his face and said, "You can't box looking like that Alcivar! We gotta fix that." Coach took out some of his white wrapping tape and taped my shoulder straps together behind my back and that made a major difference! Then he used tape around my waist like a belt to keep my trunks from falling.

We took everything and headed down the hall to take the elevator. Before we got in, he said, "Listen Kid, it's gonna be crazy down there. Everything we have sacrificed to get here is on the line. You are the best prepared and skilled fighter here. You are ready. This is YOUR night. Go out there and be the Champion that you are." The elevator doors opened and I looked at Coach and said, "I will do my best Coach".

Everything will go as they should in a couple of hours I thought. As we made our way to check in, Denise came over and hugged me tight. Affection was not big in my family growing up, so it was comforting but strange to get hugged this way. "Are you ready Trish?" said Denise with a huge smile. She was so confident and energetic and I really appreciated that. "I nodded my head, I am ready." I replied. We checked in with USA Boxing and I saw Melanie and a bunch of other big deal people in the ballroom. They announced that the President of the USA Olympic Boxing Committee, Gary Toney was there and Sandy Pino the Director of AIBA for International Boxing Association as well as reporters, photographers and Television crews. I wasn't too nervous before but seeing all those people took my breath away and I felt a dull pain in my lower back and abdominal area.

Mr. Gary Toney came over and shook my hand and said, "Good Luck tonight young lady. He had pepper gray hair like Richard Gere and piercing brown eyes. I felt my face blushing, but managed to reply, "Thanks very much Sir." It was already passed 5:15 p.m. and Coach started wrapping my hands. We could hear the announcer welcoming spectators and the crowds that started to fill the auditorium. Mercedes from USA Boxing Metro came over and handed me my blue and white gloves.

"You need to glove up. First three bouts need to be ready. You can keep those after your bout for making it to the finals," said Mercedes as she walked to check on Bouts one and two. I could see it in her face that she did not think nor expected me to win tonight. It was the same expression I saw throughout my life and throughout that day, but it was all okay. It wouldn't be the first or the last time that I had to prove them wrong.

Coach put on my gloves and wanted me to shadow box. "You know what to do. Don't let her get her way. Just move around and stay loose," said Coach. I did as he instructed and stayed loose until they came to get the first 3 bouts. I could see the lights, cameras, television and audience and television in the waiting area as the girls for the first bout made their way into the ring.

My heart starting beating so fast. "I don't want to see them fight Coach. I just want to focus on what I am going to do," I said as I walked away into a small corner to stretch and move. The 1st bout was in and out of the ring quickly and the 2nd bout was on their 3rd round. The Officials and a camera crew came to get me from the waiting room. "God, please help me have courage. No fear."And just like that, I was entering the ring. Coach didn't need to say much and he just looked me straight into my eyes and high-fived my gloves right before the bell rang to start the 1st round.

Leona came rushing at me winging and loading up with that right hand, but I knew better and stepped back and circled around. She missed with every bomb she threw and then I came back and landed combinations. After one of her big right hands, I stepped to the side and landed my big right hand and sent her back into the ropes. I heard the crowd react and scream as she stumbled back before the end of the 1st round.

I went back to my corner and Coach had the stool out and said "Have a seat Alcivar. Nice round! Don't let her breathe and keep making her pay each time she misses! Get out after you throw!" Round 2, Leona came at me again, but I had her number. I knew she wanted me to stand there and trade with her. I made her chase me and made her pay each time she missed. I caught her with a hard jab that snapped her head back and once again, the audience scream. I saw the look in her eyes change. I saw fear for the first time in her eyes and then the bell rang. "One more round and you will be National Champion Alcivar! Make the final round the best one yet!"

Round 3, Leona had not learned her lesson and rushed at me with a barrage of punches, but they all missed. My mission was for her not to land a single punch and she didn't. I ended the final round with a flurry of combinations that sent her back to the ropes and back to her corner. The final bell to finish this National Title bout rung. I raised my hand and smiled with tears in my eyes looking at Coach. "You DID IT Alcivar!" said Coach as he hugged me.

I walked to the center of the ring on one side of the referee and Leona was on the other side. The referee held my wrist while the announcer said, "Let's hear it for this amazing women's bout!" and the crowd stood and clapped. ESPN2 was in the ring with us as the announcer continued, "Your 1st USA Women's National Champion is.... from the BLUE CORNER! From New York City, PATRICIA ALCIVAR!" My first reaction was to put my face into my hands and cry. I knew there was no crying in boxing, but I couldn't help it. For this moment, I was good enough for something.

As I came down from the ring, Melanie Ley, Gary Fisher and Sandy Pino shook my hand and hugged me. "Congratulations Patricia! Please stay close by. We want a team picture of the National Champions after the final bout," said the President of USA Boxing, Gary Toney. I nodded my head and smiled. Coach had to work Denise's corner soon, so I just went to sit in a corner trying to make sure that this wasn't a dream. I wasn't sure why I was both happy and sad. I cried and silently gave thanks to God for giving me the courage and strength tonight.

Denise was the 8th bout and without any doubt, she won and also became National Champion. I hugged her and was so happy for her. For tonight, good had won over the bad. The reporters took turns interviewing and photographing me and then it was time to take the National Team picture while they played a song I will never forget, "We are the Champions" by Queen.

CHAPTER 6

Chapter Six - Round 6

Redemption
"With the new day comes new strength," Eleanor Roosevelt

I was fearful as the plane was landing at John F. Kennedy Airport. I was afraid to go back to reality, back to a basement apartment where a creep was stalking me, back to being scared at night, back to memories that haunted me. We picked up our luggage and waited for a taxi. "Listen Kid, I want you to take a couple of weeks off from everything. Take some time to relax and let your accomplishment sink in. You are the best Female Champion at 119 lbs. in the Country!" said Coach proudly. My eyes teared up and I shook his hand before he closed the door to the cab.

I fought for 4 consecutive days, won every round, won every fight and became the first United States National Women's Boxing Champion in the 119lbs division. It was an incredible feat, but it wouldn't change anything and all of a sudden, I felt this big emptiness inside. The taxi arrived in front of the house and I got out and hurried up inside and closed the door softly. But then I heard footsteps and then a knock on my door, "Hey Champ! CONGRATULATIONS! National Champion! The story came out in the New York Daily News today!" said Adrian.

I had no choice but to open the door and pretend to smile while my stomach turned inside. "Thanks so much! I just got back and want to rest," I replied. "We have to Celebrate! I want to take you out to one of the best restaurants in New York City," he continued. "I will ask my sister if she can come and then we can figure something out. Thanks again and now I must go rest," I said and quickly closed the door. I would have to convince my sister to join me for this one time. I tried to fall asleep, but my mind kept racing and thinking about so many things.

It was Sunday early afternoon and tomorrow, I would be returning to work. I knew that my time at Sanctuary for Families was coming to an end. I had to keep moving. I didn't like feeling stuck. I also thought about the New York City Golden Gloves. I knew that I had unfinished business there too. I was getting overwhelmed and decided to go to Central Park to run. It was one of my favorite places to be, so I got changed quickly and hopped on the subway. I ended up running one of my fastest 6-mile loops ever in close to 45-minutes! I stopped by the New York Road Runners to use the restroom and saw my dear friend, Mr. Allan Steinfeld!

"I read all about your win in Augusta in the newspaper Patricia! Congratulations!" said Allan Steinfeld as I allowed myself to receive a hug from him. He has always been kind to me and it was awesome to see him. "Thanks very much Mr. Steinfeld! I just got back from Augusta a few hours ago, but needed a run before returning to work tomorrow," I said shyly. "I am very proud of you Patricia. I know how much you love this place, so if you want a job here, I know that the Events Department is looking for an Event Manager to help out with their weekly running events. If you are interested, send me your resume and I will pass it on to the person in charge," said Allan Steinfeld as he shook my hand and walked out the door.

I waved goodbye and said, "I will email you my resume!" I finally felt better and calm enough to call my sister. Without a doubt, she was so happy to hear about the Nationals and also agreed to accompany me to dinner with Adrian. I knew I could count on her. Coach had told me to relax, but after the run, I felt I could breathe easier and I was able to sleep well that night even with the lights on.

As I got ready to go to the office the next day, I prayed silently, "God give me the strength to keep moving forward in every area of my life."

I rode the train into work and thought about working for New York Road Runners. Their office was literally across the street from Central Park. It was time for a change and my priority today was to send Allan Steinfeld my resume at my lunch hour. When I arrived at the office, I found a small bouquet of flowers on my desk with a card that read, "Congratulations Patricia! We are in awe of you." Signed by Carla & Kristen. I felt guilty for wanting to look for another job, but knew that I had to stay strong.

Later that morning, Coach called and said that he wanted me to meet him at a place called "Two Boots" for a quick bite and to talk about what's next. I wanted to fight in the Golden Gloves so I didn't hesitate to agree. The morning went by quickly and at lunch time I sent Allan Steinfeld my resume.

I decided to take a walk during the rest of my lunch hour and looked back at my time with Sanctuary. I was grateful for the opportunity as it was my first office job which I held on tight for the past few years soaking up everything and I also did the best possible job. There was no more room for additional growth, so I was confident that I was making the right decision.

When I returned to the office, I saw a reply from Allan Steinfeld and he mentioned that he forwarded my resume to Jake who was the VP of Events at New York Road Runners and that I should be hearing back soon as they wanted to hire someone as soon as possible. I was sure the salary would be more than I was currently making and that would help me move out of the awful living situation I was in. I had a good feeling that this was all going in a positive direction.

At 5 p.m. I took the train and headed to "Two Boots" to meet Coach. It was unusual for him to ask me to meet him for a bite, but if it was to talk about next steps, so I was all for it. When I arrived, Coach was waiting outside. "Hey Alcivar! Come on in!" he said with a big grin. As we walked in and headed towards the back end of the restaurant, there was a long table with a group from the boxing gym as well as his mom and brother. "Congratulations Champ!" they yelled out.

The purpose of this "bite" was to celebrate my National Championship win AND I was also voted "Athlete of the Year" by the United States Olympic Committee. It was the first time ever a woman was nominated for boxing and I also eventually won this honor making it into the history books. I didn't know how to feel except overwhelmed. It was really nice to see Coach's mom and we took a picture holding my belt. While we all ate pizza, I mentioned to Coach that I wanted to enter and start training for the NYC Golden Gloves soon. "Absolutely Kid! You have to get redemption and win those Gloves!" he said. It was a really nice evening which I would remember for a very long time. I rarely got surprises, so this was pretty cool.

The very next day, I received an email from the VP of Events at New York Road Runners, Jake saying that he received my email and would like for me to come in for an interview with him and some people from JPMorgan Chase Bank that Friday afternoon. Although, I had not even received an offer, I had a good feeling that I would get the job. I replied right away and said I would be there and immediately put in my request to take a half a day off from Sanctuary for Families.

A few weeks later after my interview, I received a message from Jake letting me know that the personnel from JPMorgan Chase and the New York Road Runners would like to offer me the position of Assistant Event Manager and if I accept, they would like me to start in the next 2 weeks. I closed my eyes and thanked God.

I called my sister who helped me remain calm and see things more clearly. I had to do things intelligently. I will talk to Carla tomorrow and give my 2-week notice. The New York City Golden Gloves was only a few months away, so my plan was to save up enough money in the interim and find a new place to live after the Golden Gloves tournament.

That sounded like a solid plan, but I was dreading telling the news to Carla and the rest of the staff. I had outgrown my position at Sanctuary and I went to sleep with a big lump in my throat knowing what I had to do the next day. Growing up at home, I always dreaded saying anything to my parents. The result was always the same where I either got yelled at, laughed at or worse physically punished. That insecure feeling never left me.

When I arrived at the office the next morning, I typed up my resignation letter and as I was printing it out, Carla walked in. "Good morning, Carla! Can I come speak to you in your office for a moment?" I asked. "Sure Patricia. Let's talk while I have my breakfast," she replied. God, I felt so nauseous, but here we go! "Carla, Sanctuary has been one of the most important things in my life and I will always be appreciative of the opportunity to learn so much. I have accepted a job with the New York Road Runners helping manage their key events," I said with a knot in my throat.

To my surprise, Carla smiled softly and said, "Congratulations Patricia! We have been fortunate to have you for the past few years. We will miss you dearly and know that you will do an excellent job wherever you go." I was not expecting that at all. I remembered how upset my boss from the Sneaker store was when I told her I had found a new job. My instinct was to hug Carla as I handed her my 2-week notice resignation letter and walked out of her office.

Later that day, I was finally able to have a session with Father Joe. I told him about my new job and how confused I was about Carla's reaction. "You have been surrounded by unhealthy and dysfunctional people for most of your life Patricia, but the way Carla reacted and handled your news was very appropriate," Father Joe said. It was really good to see and speak to him.

2 weeks flew by and Sanctuary even had a special lunch for me on my final day. I took a few days off before my official start date at New York Road Runners. During my week off, I went to the Boxing gym and was able to catch up with Coach. He told me that we were invited to attend a dinner in the late Fall held by USA Boxing Metro. I was nominated and would also win the "USA Boxing Metro Athlete of the Year" award.

I had made history when I was nominated and won "Athlete of the Year" by the USA Olympic Boxing Committee after winning the 1st ever USA Women's Boxing Nationals, so all this seemed so surreal. Then Coach also told me something even bigger. He told me that he was inspired to open up his own boxing gym and that he had found a place! "I have a few investors and the construction on the new gym has started already and we should be up and running in a few months!" said Coach. This was incredible news and I was going to have to do a-lot of work on my own since Coach would be busy with the new gym opening.

I knew that part of boxing was being in excellent physical shape, so I was going to try out this new outdoor bootcamp class advertised in the New York Daily Newspaper called "Platoon Fitness". They were offering one month free and the class met in Central Park at 5:30 a.m. Waking up early was never a problem for me and I knew that Coach would be preoccupied with the new gym, so I was going to do whatever it took to be in the best shape possible for the Golden Gloves.

That Sunday night before my 1st day at the new job, I packed my bag with my work clothes and my toiletries. My plan was to go to Platoon Fitness in the morning at Central Park and then shower and change at the New York Road Runners since they had a place onsite to do so for staff. I prayed and asked God to protect, guide and bless me in my new job.

I woke up at 4 a.m. and had my coffee, I brushed my teeth, changed and grabbed my pre-packed back pack and was out the door by 4:30 a.m. and arrived at Central Park's Tavern on the Green on West 67th Street promptly at 5:20 a.m. As I was making my way to the meet up spot, some lunatic on a mountain bike sped right beside me and almost hit me!

Across from West 67th Street inside Central Park, there was a big white truck that had a huge "Platoon Fitness" logo on it and standing right in front was the class Instructor, Mike, the company owner, Todd and about a group of 40 people and the lunatic on the bike who I would later learn was named Brian.

We got briefed on the workout plan and were divided in two lines and we jogged side by side about a mile to the volleyball courts inside Central Park. The workout was conducted in "Military Style" where we counted every repetition and lined up in an organized fashion. I really loved it and was exhausted after the 90-minute workout. I couldn't wait to do it again the next day. I saw that guy Brian hang around after class was over and chat with everyone. I was there for the workout and I was focused on getting in better shape for the Golden Gloves, so I picked up my backpack and jogged 3 miles to the New York Road Runners (NYRR).

When I arrived at NYRR at 8 a.m., Coach Joe Kleinerman was just opening the door. It was really nice to see him and I immediately smiled and said, "Good morning, Coach Joe! Today is my first day working at the Event's Department! I just finished working out and going to take a shower." Coach Joe used to be a hardcore runner back in the days and if you wanted to see him smile, all you needed to do was talk about running. Coach Joe lived on the last floor in the NYRR. He blushed and said, "You can have my spare key to the building so you can run and change here whenever you want. Now you go on up and take a shower and make sure you get some breakfast before you start work."

As I took a hot shower, I prayed for this job to work out and for the strength, courage and clarity to do the best job possible. I quickly changed and ran down to the Deli which was conveniently a half a block away. I ordered an extra-large black coffee with 4 table spoons of sugar and two buttered rolls. One for me and one for Coach Joe. As I got back, I handed him his buttered roll and thanked him for the keys.

I was back at my desk by 8:45 a.m. reviewing folders of the events I would be responsible for while I ate my breakfast. I was the only one there momentarily, before Jake, the VP of Events walked in and said, "Well Good Morning Patricia! Take the morning to review those folders and we will meet with the rest of the team later this afternoon, but feel free to ask any of us any questions."

The Event's Team while I was there was comprised of the 4 Event Managers: Jessica, Ed, Ted and myself then came Claudia who was the Senior Event Manager and Jake who was the VP of Events. Everyone introduced themselves as they walked in. It was a different environment than Sanctuary for Families and I had a feeling that this job was not going to be easy at all. The events that I was tasked with to begin with were the Empire State Building Run-Up where there was an application process and only about 500 participants were allowed to run-up 86 flights of stairs. There was also an international component to it as athletes from all over the world applied.

I was also responsible for handling the applications, registration process and some of the logistics for the JPMorgan Chase Corporate Challenge which still is the biggest Corporate Running Event in the World with 2-back-to-back race nights and over 18,000 participants on each day. I would later learn in our afternoon meeting that the New York City Marathon was an "all hands" event, so there was no way for me to run in it anymore. It was a challenging first day at work, but right before I left, I went to visit Mr. Allan Steinfeld on the 5th floor. His smile and warmth were very comforting and he told me that as long as I worked hard, everything would fall into place.

For the next month, my routine consisted of attending the Platoon Fitness classes in the mornings and going straight to work, but then the free morning boot camp classes came to an end. I decided to continue as a paying member. I had learned to love the workouts and it became part of my daily morning routine. I also became workout friends with Brian and seeing him became an extra incentive to attend the morning bootcamp classes.

Coach called me a month later to tell me that we needed to meet at Gleason's Gym at least 3 times a week to train and spar in preparation for the New York City Golden Gloves. My desire had not faded and I had to make it work. My first day back in the boxing gym was rough and I felt rusty. Although I had been working out consistently and felt great physically, my boxing was lacking.

Coach saw it as well and told me right before I took off to the train station, "Listen Kid, my priority right now is opening up this new gym, but we will work enough to get you to the Golden Gloves. You have all that experience from the Nationals and that will help you a-lot." I felt a sense of loyalty to Coach and he was the only person I trusted especially in the shady world of boxing, so I would have to adjust to his new schedule and make it work with my new job as well.

I often felt out of place at the New York Road Runners because the staff was not the warmest nor the friendliest except Ted who would often joke around with me. So, I decided to keep my boxing quiet for now. The only one who knew was Mr. Allan Steinfeld and I didn't have to worry about him at all. I would need to rely on the lessons I learned at the Nationals which I thought of often and would stay with me for a lifetime. I had to remain calm, patient and positive despite the obstacles. I found myself resenting Coach as I was not getting the attention I once received from him.

For the next couple of months as I prepared for the Golden Gloves, I went consistently to the morning boot camp class and ran long and hard on the weekends. I visualized getting my hands raised in Madison Square Garden any time I needed inspiration. I felt alone during this round of preparations for such a big tournament, but the experience was teaching me to be self-reliant.

A couple of weeks before the Golden Gloves finals, Coach had the Grand Opening party for his new gym in the downtown area of Manhattan! It was beautiful and consisted of 2 floors. On one floor, there was a ring, boxing heavy bags, speed bags and an area for shadow-boxing and jumping rope. On the 2nd Floor, there was a place for stretching, weight training and men and women's locker rooms.

This boxing gym was not like the others and would cater to a more upscale clientele like Wall Street Brokers, Lawyers, Doctors and other white-collar professionals. Coach explained to me that this was how the gym would survive by training these professionals to box recreationally and have boxing shows where they would have the opportunity to box in front of an audience.

I was happy for Coach but worried for me. I made it to the finals of the New York Daily News Golden Gloves finals once again. I would be fighting a Muay-Thai fighter named Deborah Stein, who also belonged to a women's boxing team named "Supreme Team". I stayed on track with my weight and checked it regularly at work where there was a scale that I used in the mornings after my workouts and according to that, I was at a comfortable 120 lbs. 1-week before my final's bout. On that Monday morning, I notified Jake and Claudia that I would be taking off that Friday. The only person that knew about my Golden Gloves bout was Mr. Allan Steinfeld and he had purchased tickets to go!

The JPMorgan Chase Corporate Challenge event was in early June and although it was only April, the applications had started to come in at an overwhelming rate. I was extremely busy at work entering all these applications as well as reviewing applications for the Empire State Building Run-Up in addition to my other administrative duties. Being this busy helped distract me from the stress of my upcoming bout.

I worked out at the boot camp class until Wednesday and stayed after class chatting with Brian for a bit. We were fierce competitors in class and always raced each other when we had to complete a timed workout. I told him I would not be working out until next week. "Oh really? Is everything ok?" he asked. "Yes! Everything is cool. I am competing in a special event and just need to take it easy for the next couple of days," I replied.

"That's Awesome! I would love to go and support, but I have a family commitment. Please give me your number so I can find out how it went," said Brian. I felt my face and ears get hot, but I managed to give him my cell phone number before I waved good-bye. Brian was in the textile business with his father and brother and worked out of a store in Downtown, Manhattan.

His fair light complexion reminded me of my mom and he was about 6 feet tall with a muscular build, thick dark hair who had a good resemblance of the actor, Ben Affleck. His mother was Irish-Italian and his father, Persian-Jewish.

I jogged back to the office and tried to get him off my mind and focus on my upcoming fight. I had waited a long time for this day and I had to give it everything I had. When I got to NYRR, I made sure to get on the scale and it read 119.0 on the dot! This was after my workout which meant I had to eat very lite from now until the weigh-ins on Friday morning.

After work, I went to the boxing gym and jumped rope, shadow boxed and did a few rounds on the speed bag. From 5- 8 p.m. was prime time at the gym and Coach was so busy. I barely got to hit the pads with him. "Okay Kid, Big night on Friday! I want you to rest, eat lite and call me tomorrow to let me know how you are doing," said Coach.

I realized that there was nothing that I could possibly improve or work on at this point that would make any difference in the fight. I was tired from boot camp, work and boxing today, so I literally passed out when I got home without eating dinner.

The next day, I tried to relax at work and at lunch time I went to see Allan Steinfeld in his office. He never failed to greet me with kindness and just being in his presence for a few minutes made me feel better. He shook my hand and wished me luck and said he would be cheering me on tomorrow night. On my way home from work, I stopped at the nearest church and I prayed and meditated inside before I finally went home. Not surprisingly, Adrian was standing by his window and as soon as I arrived, he came out. "Hey Champ! Are you ready for tomorrow?" he said loudly.

I had done a great job avoiding him, but now, he was standing guard waiting by the window. "Hi Adrian, I get very focused before a big tournament and just need some peace and quiet. I appreciate you being excited, but I really would like to go downstairs and rest. Thank you so much!" I replied as I avoided any eye contact and made my way downstairs.

While, I heated up my chicken soup for dinner, I had thoughts racing through my head. I knew I had to hang tight a little longer while I saved money and looked for a new place. Tiptoeing in every day was not peace, but for now, this arrangement would have to do. I needed to focus all my energy on giving 100% tomorrow night. I ate half of my soup and laid in bed until I fell asleep.

Friday arrived and as I maintained my eyes closed, I said a prayer, "God, please take away all anxieties and help me fight with a clear mind and courage tonight. Amen." I looked in the mirror and could see my abs completely flat and even my ribs were visible, but I was still nervous about eating anything. The possibility of even being an ounce over weight and seeing Coach's disappointment or seeing my opponent's joy would be enough to keep me from eating any food before the official weigh-ins.

I packed the same duffle bag that I used for the Nationals with my trunks, boots, mouthpiece, chest protector and book. I decided to close my eyes for a few more minutes and I woke up in a panic realizing that it was about to be late. I took my duffle bag and rushed to take the train to the Madison Square Garden Theatre. When I arrived, Coach was already there and grabbed my arm and we rushed inside. My opponent, Debra and her Coach who was this tall black guy named Lee looked at me intensely as I walked in the room. Debra had trouble making weight, but made weight on the 2nd attempt. I stripped quickly down to my bra and bikinis and got on the scale. "Alcivar 118.1" yelled the Woman Official. What a sigh of relief! I was glad that I decided not to eat or drink anything this morning, but now I absolutely needed to eat!

The Officials gave us final instructions for tonight which was to be back by no later than 6 p.m., doors to the public open at 7 p.m. and first bout starts at 8 p.m. I was the 5th bout of the night. All this had taken up a lot of time and it was already past 2 p.m. "Okay Kid, Nice job with the weight. We are going to get your meal from the Deli down the block from the gym, then you take a nap and then we come back. I gotta take the dogs out for a walk and make a few phone calls, but you can take a nap on the couch after you eat," said Coach.

For as long as I could remember, dogs held a special place in my heart. I loved everything about them and they never failed to make me smile. Their innocence and ability to just live in the moment without a care in the world made me love them more. Coach had 2 Japanese Akitas named Brando and Chayanne. Brando was my favorite and it was one of the reasons I loved coming to the gym despite the absurd amount of hair they left everywhere!

When we got to the gym, I ate half of my Philly Cheesesteak Sandwich that we got from the nearby Deli and I secretly gave the other half to Brando and then passed out on the couch while Brando laid next to me. In the past, Coach had offered to let me take Brando home with me, so I could sleep better, but I was afraid I would never give him back. It felt good to drift away into a deep sleep. This nap was probably the most important part of the fight.

"Hey Yo Patty! You ready to kick some ass tonight?" was the sound that woke me up. An overly excited gym member named Declan was yelling through the glass window. I knew that people meant well, but

I could also sense their nervous energy and that made me feel uneasy. I didn't particularly like seeing or talking to anyone before my fights. I smiled and waved and then called Coach on his cell phone. "Yo! Why are you calling me on the cell?" answered Coach. "Declan just woke me up with his yelling outside the office door. Can you please come get him? I just want to get ready and go. I am already nervous," I replied.

Just as I was hanging up the phone Coach came running up and talked to Declan. He came in the office once Declan was gone and said "Okay Alcivar. Get everything ready cause we gotta go now. We are going to be late!" It was already passed 5 p.m. and I was due at the Garden at 6 p.m. I knew we were not going to have time to pass by the church to say a prayer this time, so I went into the locker room and locked the door and kneeled down and said my final prayer in private.

When I came out of the locker room, Coach was waiting for me and grabbed me by my jacket and we ran down to the train station. Thankfully, we caught the Number 2 train right away. On the train ride, Coach leaned over and said, "Listen Kid, I know that the training for these Gloves was not the best. I was very busy opening up my own boxing gym, but you have the experience from the Nationals and you are tough. Go out there and show them who the best fighter in the United States is!"

Everything about going into this tournament was different indeed. I found myself being upset with Coach more often than not. I was mad at him for abandoning me when I needed him the most, but I felt confident that at least my endurance and general physical fitness were at a high level with all the training I did on my own at the boot camp class 5-days a week along with all the running, but most importantly, I did have the experience from the Nationals as well as fighting in the previous Golden Gloves.

I was relieved when we finally arrived at our stop and we rushed over to the Theatre at Madison Square Garden at 6:30 p.m. "You are late young Lady! Get yourself changed and checked in with the T.V. crew who wants to do an interview," said Mercedes from USA Boxing Metro.

I was in the blue corner tonight and I quickly got changed into my blue and yellow trunks and blue tank top and went to talk to the T.V. Crew. Winning the Nationals certainly helped polish my interview skills and I was not nearly as nervous speaking on camera as I once used to be.

Right after I got interviewed, it was 7:30 p.m. and there was already a full house waiting for the bouts to begin. Coach started wrapping my hands while the USA Boxing Metro Officials came in to hand me my blue and white 10 oz gloves. "The whole gym is here for you kid. Don't let her or anyone take away what belongs to you. You hear me?" said Coach firmly. I looked at him and nodded my head. I could hear the crowd roar as the 1st bout was entering the ring and that was my cue to start warming up.

I started shadow boxing in the dressing room and I was envisioning this fight from entering the ring to getting my arms being raised at the end of the bout. I was so focused that the 30 minutes that passed by felt like one and the 4rd bout was already in the ring. Coach came in and we started walking towards the ring as the camera men were following our every move.

The 4th bout ended and then the announcement started, "And now entering the ring in the blue corner is the 1st ever USA Female National Champion, Patrica Alcivar!" The reaction from the sold-out crown in Madison Square Garden's theatre was overwhelming. I could hear people yelling my name! When they announced my opponent, Deborah, I was also surprised that she received a nice welcome cheer. Her Coach was popular and was also her boyfriend and owner of the boxing gym she trained out of as well as the coach of the Supreme Team.

We came to the center of the ring and Deborah stared straight into my eyes with anger. I would never understand that part of boxing. To me, fighting and winning was a way to build the confidence my parents destroyed as a child.

Being an athlete was my own way to rebuild myself into a courageous, hardworking and confident woman and it was mind-blowing how many people I would encounter that would try and take that away from me.

The bell rang to start round one. Deborah charged at me and caught me with a quick 3-punch combination. She had speed in her punches, but I didn't feel any power in her punches. I answered back immediately with a combination of my own which made her stumble and it drew blood from her nose almost immediately. The bell rang to end the 1st round. Coach pulled out the stool, "Good job Alcivar, but don't let her catch you with silly punches. YOU Go First and MOVE. This is your fight!"

As I listened to Coach, I realized that I felt really winded. The lack of boxing specific training was evident, but I needed to push until my arms fell off. I knew I had won the 1st round but now I had 2 more rounds to seal this decision. The bell rang to start the 2nd round and I let Deborah come charging at me because I could see she was winded as well. Although she charged at me, I made her miss and pay with my counters. Right in the middle of the round, I caught her with a hard counter left hook that snapped her head back and the referee jumped in to give her a standing 8-count. Round 2 in the books.

"Nice Alcivar! Don't hold back in this final round! Remember, this is your fight and you have to make every second count!" said Coach as he gave me water and the final bell rang. Debra came at me even stronger. We both wanted this fight bad, but I was not about to let her take it away from me. We exchanged a barrage of punches, but my punches had more pop to them and made more of an impression than hers. The final bell rang and I managed to sneak in the final punch and Debra gave me the dirtiest look ever. I raised my hands as no matter what the decision was, I knew I had given everything and I deserved to win.

Coach gave me a high five and took off my head guard and gloves while the decision cards were collected by the referee. I could hear people from the gym screaming out my name. I smiled nervously as I walked to the center of the ring. The T.V. cameras were zooming in on my face as the announcement was being made, "And your 1998 New York City

Golden Gloves Champion in the Women's 119-pound division is......
from the BLUE CORNER, PATRICIA ALCIVAR!" I put my face in
my hands and tried to hold back tears, but the emotion was far too great.
The referee grabbed my arm and held it high while the crowd cheered.

"I did it! Redemption and New York City Golden Gloves Champion!" I thought to myself as I finally managed to smile in front of the
T.V. cameras and photographers. I tried to shake Debra's hand, but she
and her coach turned their back on me. It would become a common attitude from competitors and people to turn their backs on me once I
achieved something great.

After winning the Golden Gloves, I told Coach that all I wanted to
do was go home and sleep in peace. I was never big into parties or celebrations. My reward was the journey and in the accomplishment. Although everyone at the gym wanted to go out for drinks, it was after 11
p.m. and I was not a drinker and to me, there was no bigger celebration
than knowing that for this day, I was indeed a champion. Coach patted
me on the back and sent me home in a cab.

I called my sister from the cab and told her all about it. As I arrived
home, I saw that Adrian's lights were off which meant he had not come
home from the fights which made me extra happy. I still tiptoed inside the apartment. I laid in bed replaying the fight in my head and the
feeling of winning such a prestigious tournament in Madison Square
Garden, in New York City and then I also realized my phone had been
alerting me of new voicemail messages. I had already spoken to my sister,
but I checked to make sure I didn't miss anything important.

The 1st message was from Adrian. I didn't even finish hearing it and
deleted it right away. The 2nd was from Allan Steinfeld! That made me
smile really big. He had come to watch me fight and he said he was very
proud of me.

3rd message was from Brian which said, "Hey Patricia! I was wondering how your event went tonight. I hope it went well and I look forward
to hearing all about it on Monday at Bootcamp!" I felt my face and body
get warm. I was not expecting to hear that 3rd voicemail message. I was

nervous about telling him that I was a boxer. I would wait until Monday morning. I was drowsy and already had a plan of what I wanted to do tomorrow. I slept like a baby tonight even with the lights on.

I woke up startled to the sound of the upstairs door slamming hard. I heard the garage door opening and Adrian starting up his car. "Good, he is leaving," I thought to myself. I took a shower and got dressed. My plan today was to eat my favorite breakfast at Dunkin Doughnuts, then have a session with Father Joe and then have an early dinner with my sister at Georgia Diner.

When I opened my door to leave, I found roses and a note from Adrian that read, "You Did It! Congratulations on winning the Golden Gloves Last night! You are My Champ! I am taking you and your sister to Le Cirque next Friday! Love, Adrian". I cringed and knew that now my priority absolutely needed to be on getting out of this place!

I purchased the New York Daily Newspaper who was a long-time sponsor of the NYC Golden Gloves and ordered my extra-large black coffee with a cinnamon toasted bagel and cream cheese and sat down to read the paper. The headline in the sports section read, "Woman's National Champion and now New York City Golden Gloves Champion". I had started a scrap book to save all these awesome articles and use them as reminders of what is possible even against the odds.

I took the train to see Father Joe and was always amazed of how crowded the trains can be even on a weekend. I was anxious to catch up with Father Joe and when I saw him, he was smiling and shook my hand and said in a very monotone voice, "Congratulations Patricia". I knew he was my counselor and had to remain somewhat professional, but I was hoping for a bit more of a reaction than that. I told him all about the fight, my feelings on resenting Coach and about this guy Brian. I told him that Brian made me nervous and I was afraid that he wanted to ask me out.

"Why would you be nervous about Brian asking you out Patricia?" asked Father Joe. I had to take a deep breath and be completely honest before I replied, "Well, Father Joe, I haven't really gone out on any dates.

I am afraid of what to tell him about being a boxer and about my family and past." Father Joe could see that I was starting to get upset as I said the last part of the sentence.

"Patricia Dear, you have to take it one step at a time. First, there is nothing wrong with being an athlete and that is what you are. You are a strong beautiful athlete. If this Brian guy has any sense of taste, he will see that and be proud of you. You don't have to spill everything right away. He hasn't even asked you out and you are already worrying way too much. We will cross that bridge when we get to it. For now, just enjoy your accomplishment and don't worry about a thing," he said in the calmest demeanor ever.

I left his office feeling less anxious. Father Joe was right in some ways. The guy had not even asked me out and probably was just being nice to me. I was looking forward to seeing my sister and niece for dinner. I had practically starved all week and felt and looked really thin. I could see my sister with the stroller and my niece as I neared Georgia Diner. My niece was older now and she was talking more and greeted me with a hug and a kiss!

We sat down and I ordered a bison burger with everything on it, onion rings and a Ginger ale! My sister laughed and ordered the exact same thing plus chicken fingers for my niece. "Listen, I need you to do me a big favor...I need to keep things somewhat peaceful with Adrian and he insists on taking me out for dinner especially now that I won the Golden Gloves. He wants to take us to this fancy place named Le Cirque on Friday. You have to come PLEASE!"

Adrian had met my sister and niece briefly so it was no sweat and she agreed. The day had gone well and I was content. I couldn't help feel that awkward emptiness I get at times. I knew it had to do with my mother and family. Now, I was a National Champion and a New York City Golden Gloves Champion, but somehow, I still felt like a nobody. The next day, I ran for 3 miles and felt relieved before going to church. It was a nice weekend but not much different than any other particular weekend.

I felt anxious about going to boot camp the next morning and back to work, but I set my clothes, backpack and alarm before I went to sleep. I found myself battling these episodes of anxiety often, but I knew I had to pray and just keep facing them until they were no longer obstacles. Father Joe had told me that many of these feelings were a result of my abusive past, but I had to keep doing what I was doing and although the feelings would never disappear completely, it would get easier.

I woke up before the alarm and got ready for boot camp. I took the Q60 bus at 4:45 a.m. which left me on 60th Street and 2nd Avenue and then I jogged down a little over a mile to 67th Street inside Central Park. I got to the park at 5:25 a.m. and Brian was already there. "HEY! How did it go? Did you get my message?" he asked.

I wondered if he knew how much I was blushing, but I tried to play it off since I had just jogged over. I tried to swallow my dry saliva and said, "HEY! Thank so much for calling and I am so sorry I didn't call you back. I did very well and won my boxing competition in the 119-pound Women's Division. It was the New York City Golden Gloves Finals at the Madison Square Garden Theatre".

Involuntarily, I looked at the ground as I was saying all that. Brian reached over and softly lifted my chin with his hand and said, "That is absolutely AMAZING Patricia! You should be proud and I am sorry I wasn't there to support you." He pulled away when we heard the group jogging over along with Instructor Steve. We quickly joined in on the jog and went our separate ways. It was an odd but nice moment for me and running and working out right now was going to be perfect in helping me release all the apprehension I was feeling. The workout today was simple in some ways. We were to do a timed individual paced full loop run of Central Park and then finish with calisthenics at the Grinder.

We lined up and were sent off. Some people teamed up, but I took the task seriously and pushed my hardest on that loop. I did not want to think about anything and running sub-7-minute miles helped clear my mind and I was practically running by myself at that pace and as the end was in sight, I finished alone right under 45 minutes.

A few minutes later, Brian stumbled in at 50 minutes and the rest of the group trickled behind him. He came to give me a high-five and said, "You are effing FAST! I hope to run the Chicago Marathon this fall in under 4 hours and would love to have someone like you pace me." I didn't know what to reply and instead replied with a warm smile. I had only run the NYC Marathon a few times and my most recent time was 3 hours and 32 minutes at a solid 8 minutes per mile for 26.2 miles. Although I had never paced anyone, I would welcome the opportunity to pace Brian.

We all jogged to the grinder and finished our workout with 3 rounds of 25 push-ups, 50-squats and 100 sit-ups. Summer season was approaching and I was completely drenched in sweat after the workout. The group walked back to Tavern on the Green while I got ready to jog back another 3 miles back to the office. I heard a bike near as I was huffing and puffing up Cat Hill which got its name because it is one of the steepest hills in Central Park and at almost the top of the hill there is a sculpture of an elegant black cat.

"Aren't you tired?" asked Brian while riding his bike next to me. I was glad to see him again and replied with the same question, "Aren't YOU tired?" He was also catching his breath up Cat Hill and managed to blurt, "Hey, if you are free this Friday around 6 p.m., I would like to take you out to dinner." I could not believe he was asking me out while I looked a mess and sweating profusely! I felt like my head was in an oven, but I replied, "I would really like that, Brian. I should be free, but I will confirm later this week.

I gotta run to work now and I'll see you in class!" Even though I was tired, I sped up and ran as fast as I could. I wasn't sure if my legs felt like jelly because of the workout or because Brian just asked me out. Now, I needed to talk to Father Joe ASAP! I arrived at the office, took a shower and went to get my breakfast and left Father Joe a message that it was urgent that we had our session today after work. As I sat eating breakfast at my desk, Mr. Allan Steinfeld peeked his head in with a big warm smile and said, "Good Morning Champ!" and at the same time Ted was also walking in. "Did you know that this young lady is a Boxing Champion?"

Ted was my favorite co-worker because he didn't mind being silly. He had a ton of Event Management experience yet he was humble and didn't ever try to make me feel less than unlike the others in that office. But, most important of all, he made me laugh when I needed it the most. "What? Boxing? No way! I can't see little Patty here beating up any body!" said Ted in disbelief. "Well, you are looking at the newly crowned New York City 119-pound Female Golden Gloves Champion! She is also the reigning USA National Champion. I saw her win with my own eyes at Madison Square Garden this past weekend." replied Mr. Allan Steinfeld before he went upstairs to his office.

"Well, I'm not going to mess with Patty Boom Boom here," said Ted to me as he chuckled and poked me in the ribs. "Hey! I like that... Patty Boom Boom! If I ever turn pro, I will use it!" I laughed loudly. "As long as I get credit, it's all cool!" said Ted before Jake walked in with his coffee in hand and then all the laughing stopped. I was very careful to not cross any boundaries or even have a normal conversation with Jake out of fear of upsetting Claudia. It seemed she had the hots for Jake as any time Jake came over to explain anything to me, she shot daggers at me with her eyes.

Both Jake and Claudia were at least 10 years my senior and having any sort of inappropriate contact with anyone at work was completely against my moral values, so Claudia had nothing to worry about. However, that didn't stop her from treating me indifferently and coldly. In the time I had been there, I had learned to do my job as best as I could and not say much. The Event's Department with the exception of Ted, was not the warmest group to me.

I appreciated being part of an organization whose mission was to promote health and wellness through running and organizing over 50 running events throughout the year including the World Class New York City Marathon. I also enjoyed working across the street from Central Park and running before work or on my lunch hour as well as my morning conversations with Coach Joe and the support from Mr. Allan Steinfeld.

The good outweighed the bad for now at NYRR, but I had heard a rumor that Mr. Allan Steinfeld was on his way out and taking over would be a woman named Mary Wittenberg who was currently the Vice President. I had hoped with all my heart that didn't happen as I felt she had ice in her veins from my seldom interactions with her. I relied on my God-given instincts when it came to people and they pretty much never failed me when I chose to listen.

Father Joe agreed to see me the next day after work, so I waited patiently knowing that after speaking with him, I would see things more clearly. I decided to stop by church on my way home from work and say a prayer. Besides Father Joe and on occasion my sister, I did not have anyone I trusted enough to share my feelings and talking with God through my prayers always made me feel better.

As I walked to church, I felt a sense of relief knowing that the Golden Gloves was over and I could take a break for a bit. But at the same time, I felt anxious not knowing what was next. I always had an incentive; something to shoot for. I felt somewhat lost which added to the anxiety I was feeling already.

I sat down in church and just took a few deep breaths while I had my eyes closed. Then I kneeled down and prayed, "God, thank you for allowing me to become the New York City Golden Gloves Champion and for my job, my health and for being my friend, father and strength. Please guide me and help me find my purpose. You are all that I have. I need you. Amen."

I was feeling better until I arrived home and Adrian was standing outside, "Hey Champ, so I have reservations to Le Cirque for you and your sister and I this Friday. Are you ready?" Oh Gosh! I had already agreed to see Brian this Friday. I totally forgot about Adrian! UGH! "Hey Adrian. Something came up for this Friday. Can we change it to Saturday or Sunday instead?" I said. His face was red and I could tell he was angry, but he forced himself to put out a fake smile and say, "Sure

Champ. No problem. I'll change it for Saturday at 6 p.m. instead, so be ready by 4:30 p.m. I called my sister before going to sleep and let her know about the change.

She agreed right away and would come meet me at the apartment. That night, I fell asleep deeply until I felt a bright red light shining in my face and tried to wake up and couldn't move. "Please no! God! Our Father who are in Heaven...." I struggled to say underneath my breath. The paralyzing dreams returned tonight. But my instincts would always guide me to pray and that would save me each and every time.

At least today, I will talk to Father Joe and wondered if I should confide in him about these awful dreams. I spent the day at the office processing thousands of applications for the upcoming Corporate Challenge event which would be in a couple of weeks. Being this preoccupied was perfect in not allowing me to think of anything else until it was time to leave. To add to the craziness of the day, it became official after receiving an all staff email that Mr. Allan Steinfeld was "retiring" and Mary Wittenberg would be the new President of New York Road Runners. He would still be around when needed and remain active as a board member. This happened insanely fast and I felt sad that my only real friend at NYRR was leaving. Before I left for the day, I sent him an email thanking him for everything.

After what seemed like an eternity on the subway, I arrived at Father Joe's office. Rush hour in the New York City's subways in the summer was an adventure in itself. The city was filled with tourists and the humidity of the summer made me uncomfortably sweaty as I sat on Father Joe's couch. I forced a smile and said, "Hi Father Joe! I am about to puke from all this anxiety I am feeling! Brian asked me out for this Friday! I said yes, but I am having second thoughts now." He smiled calmly and said, "That's wonderful Patricia. You shouldn't be surprised though. You are a beautiful young woman and you must go and enjoy yourself. If he is the right guy, everything will flow naturally. Just stay calm. This guy sounds like a gentleman and if he isn't you know how to defend yourself." Before I left his office, he took my hand and said a prayer for me to help calm my anxiety.

On the ride back home, I remembered Father Joe's words, "You are a strong and beautiful young woman". I never really thought of myself as beautiful and all throughout my life I struggled with my self-esteem. I struggled to love myself since the most important people in my life didn't show me any.

I was also aware that I had the power within to not be a product of my environment and my past did not determine my future. Through prayer, reading self-help books, attending educational seminars as well as counseling, I knew that I could somehow heal. I knew I had the power to break the vicious cycle. What I didn't know at the time is that although things do get better with time and being proactive, it is a life-long process that takes patience, faith and constant never-ending action.

I stopped at Boston Market for a grilled chicken Caesar salad as I re-membered that my fridge was empty. I listened to a message from Coach as I was eating my dinner. He said that he had an extra ticket to a black-tie dinner event in 2 weeks where there would be famous Celebrity box-ers like Evander Holyfield and the person that was supposed to attend the event with him just cancelled due to a family emergency. He wanted to know if I was free to go. Wow! Evander Holyfield was one of my fa-vorite fighters at the time. He had lost a chunk of his ear during a crazy fight with Mike Tyson and I would love to meet him in person!

I called Coach right away and said, "YES! I'll go to the dinner Coach! I want to meet Holyfield!" I was so excited that I didn't even wait for Coach to say anything, but he replied, "You got it Kid. It is a week from this Saturday. I have another call but call me tomorrow and let me know how you are doing." And before I could say anything else, he hung up. I had 3 big dinners on my agenda: Brian, Adrian and Coach and I had nothing to wear!

I called my sister and we made a date to meet at the Queens Center Mall tomorrow at 6 p.m. My sister had great fashion taste and I felt con-fident she would help me pick the best outfits for the upcoming events.

Before I fell asleep, I said a prayer and remembered what Father Joe had said to me. I needed to relax and enjoy this journey. I went to sleep thinking about Brian and learned what it meant to have "Butterflies in your stomach".

I woke up refreshed and was looking forward to Boot Camp class and a full day of work ahead. As I got off the Q60 Bus and jogged over to Central Park, I welcomed the warm summer breeze softly hitting my face before that first drop of sweat trickled down my forehead and nose. I arrived at Tavern on the Green meet-up spot at my usual time and I was disappointed not to see Brian there.

"Perhaps he is just running late," I whispered to myself. But the members started arriving and at 5:30 a.m., Instructor Steve took us on a warm-up jog to Bethesda Fountain which was one of my favorite spots in Central Park. Bethesda Fountain is located in Bethesda Terrace in Central Park and is one of the largest fountains in New York City featuring a an eight-foot bronze angel known as the Angel of Waters and stands above four small cherubim representing health, purity, temperance and peace. It was no accident that being here made me feel good in every way. I wasn't sure why Brian wasn't in class today, but I was going to release any anxiety during this workout and then focus on all the work I had to get done at the office today.

We performed speed drills on the stairs, followed by hill repeats at the adjacent hills and ended with calisthenics and stretching. It was a great class and I knew I had pushed hard from the trembling in my arms and legs, but I liked that feeling. To me, it meant that I pushed myself past my comfort zone. It was something that I did throughout my entire life. What people didn't understand was that I push against myself and I try my hardest to be better than before and in doing so, I am honoring my higher power for my life and health and in the process releasing any mental or physical toxicity.

It was challenging to jog back to the office, but I managed to do so at a slow pace and I took the time to take in the beauty of Central Park. I felt fortunate to be able to shower and change at the facilities at the office. New York Road Runners at the time was located in an up-scale Manhattan neighborhood in an old 6-story brown stone which was built in 1902. It didn't feel like an office at times. I had taken the liberty to leave a couple of sets of clothes in one of my drawers.

Mary, the new President walked in while I was having my breakfast and looked up and down at me with her cold blue eyes and didn't even say "Good Morning". Unfortunately, that type of behavior was very common in many workplaces and that would get me down sometimes. However, one of the guys that worked maintaining the building came in with a small but beautiful and colorful arrangement of flowers. "Someone thinks you are special," said the young worker while handing me the flowers.

I was perplexed, but I opened up the small envelope that contained the note. It read, "Hello Patricia. I missed working out with you at boot camp class today. I have some work commitments this week and cannot go to boot camp, but I look forward to seeing you on Friday evening at Pomodoro. See you soon, Brian". Reading that note literally took my breath away. It was the first time I had ever received flowers.

I took the wrapping paper off and placed the flowers on my desk which warranted questions from every person that walked in to the Event Department's office. Claudia was especially happy to see those flowers as that would mean that I potentially had someone significant in my life. The comments throughout the day were entertaining and helped the day go by fast before meeting my sister at the Queens Center Mall. When I finally saw her, I of course, told her about the flowers.

"Okay! This is a classy guy and we need to get you something appropriate to wear on Friday," said my sister. We went straight into Macy's Department store to the "Business Wear" section. It was the first time I was in that section and everything looked so expensive! We went into the clearance rack and picked out everything that was available in a size 0 which was not a-lot. I had 3 different dresses to try on. The first one I tried on was a v-cut body-hugging, sleeve less up-to-the knee black dress.

I looked in the mirror and didn't even recognize myself. I looked like a woman- not a little girl and that made me feel weird. I was even nervous to show my sister, but I slowly opened the fitting room door and came out. "OH MY GOSH! That is the Dress for You!" said my sister. The price tag read, "50% off! 59.99 Final Sale down from $119". I could buy this dress, but ONLY this dress. I did not have enough money for 2 more outfits. This dress was so amazing that I could get away with wearing it for all 3 events.

I treated my sister and niece for a pizza dinner. We all loved pizza and I wasn't sure what the highlight of this day was- The surprise flowers, the black dress or pizza for dinner with my sister and niece. I was grateful for this day and anxiously looked forward to Friday evening. That night though, I had the paralyzing dream. Anytime I started to feel somewhat happy, something didn't want to allow me to have that privilege. I did the only thing that has always helped me and that was to pray.

The next day, I decided to skip boot camp and get to the office extra early so I could get as much work done relating to the Corporate Challenge as possible. However, at lunch time, I was itching to get a run in, so I went into my stash of extra clothes in my drawer and went for a few laps of the Reservoir at lunch time. The Central Park Reservoir which was renamed, "The Jaqueline Kennedy Onassis Reservoir" features a 1.58-mile bridle path track hugging the body of water. I indulged in the views of the New York City landscapes and felt relief and gratitude for this lunch time run.

As much as I wanted Friday not to arrive so fast, the day sped by. I was already on the train ride home and felt exhausted from not getting sleep the night before and going on that run. I hoped to have a peaceful sleep tonight and inevitably dosed off on the train. I woke up abruptly when my forehead fell on a stranger's shoulder. Thankfully, it was an older man who didn't mind. Riding the New York City subways was a roll of a dice and you never knew if you would encounter someone kind or someone rude.

When I arrived at the apartment, I was not hungry. Ever since I had to starve to make weight for the New York City Golden Gloves, it was easy to skip dinner at times. So instead, I took advantage of the opportunity of feeling so tired and went to sleep by 7 p.m. I thought it was incredible that I was able to sleep straight through until 6 a.m. the next morning! My body and mind were desperate to get the much-needed rest.

I hoped the swelling from my sleep deprived eyes would go away throughout the day before my big dinner later. I put on the black dress and let my long curly hair fall on my shoulders today instead of the usual bun or ponytail. Most of the staff at the Events Department took a comp day from working an event the weekend before except Ted who decided to tease me, "Awww little Patty Boom Boom has a dress on... And where are we going today?" he teased. I poked him hard in the center of his belly and didn't answer. I think he realized that I was feeling embarrassed and he left me alone for the rest of the day. The Corporate Challenge was the following week on Wednesday and Thursday and I felt accomplished to have everything I needed done for the moment.

At 5 p.m. I took my time and walked the 2 miles to Pomodoro on 60th Street and 2nd Avenue. I had shoes I would change into in my purse when I was a block away. As I came closer to the restaurant at 5:45 p.m., I could see Brian standing in the corner waiting. I quickly changed into my mid-sized heels and walked towards him. "Hi Brian," I said softly when I saw him. He was wearing an elegant white summer button down shirt with dark jeans and black loafers. "You look beautiful Patricia!" he replied. "Haha! Different from the sweaty wear I have on during boot camp huh?" I replied. I didn't remember anyone ever saying I looked beautiful in that tone, so replying with a joke helped me digest that compliment a little better. We went inside the restaurant that had dimmed the lights and had small candles as center pieces on each table.

Pomodoro was a cozy and trendy healthy version of Italian Cuisine restaurant. I ordered a hot chamomile tea with extra honey and lemon and Brian ordered seltzer water with lemon and an order of pita bread with hummus when the waiter came to take our order for appetizers. "Are you feeling okay?" Brian asked when I ordered the chamomile tea.

For some reason, once evening hours hit after 6 p.m., my body temperature had a tendency to drop and I felt an internal chill. "I get chilly at night and always drink tea to help stabilize my body temperature," I replied.

The conversation throughout the night was fun and relaxed while we ate our gluten free chicken parmesan dinners. We talked about running, working out and goals. We both reminisced about our experiences running the New York City Marathon. Brian completed the New York City and Philadelphia Marathons and reminded me of how much he now wanted to run the Chicago Marathon with a goal of anything under 4 hours. So, I reminded him of my best time of 3:32 in my most recent New York City Marathon. Brian was impressed and asked me again if I would help him break 4 hours and offered to fly me out to Chicago to pace him.

We spent over 2 hours in the restaurant and now it was time to leave. He hailed a cab for me and gave me the biggest bear hug ever and kissed me on the forehead before he closed the taxi door. I waved goodbye as the cab drove away. I put my head back in the taxi and closed my eyes and thought what a great night this was. He hugged me and only kissed me on the forehead though and I was not sure what this meant.

I called Father Joe and left a message about tonight totally not expecting a call back until next week, but a couple of minutes after I left him a message my phone rang. "Hello Patricia. This is Father Joe. I just wanted to let you know that this guy Brian is OKAY on my list. He kissed you on the forehead because he respects you. That is a good sign so please go to sleep happy tonight," said Father Joe. I breathed a sigh of relief and replied, "I feel much better hearing that from you Father Joe. Thank so much for calling me back and I hope you have a nice weekend."

When I got home, I laid out my dress nicely on a chair as I would be wearing that same dress tomorrow night and again the following weekend. I fell asleep with a smile on my face. But those feelings never lasted long enough. I woke up early with a queasy feeling in my stomach. I knew it was the feeling of not wanting to go out to dinner with that pervert, but at least my sister would be there. I decided to go for a long run all the way down Queens Boulevard up to the Courthouses and back which would be close to 8 miles.

As I ran down the boulevard and passed Calvary Cemetery, Bally's Fitness Gym, the Queens Center Mall and all the significant monuments along this route, I remembered my first run on this route by myself where I got that awful side stitch and how I kept running further each time despite the lack of experience or resources. They were memories filled with so much emotions. No one in my family supported my dreams, but I went ahead and kept on training and completed dozens of running races and marathons, won a World Championship in Martial Arts and now a Golden Gloves and National Boxing Championship.

My stomach felt better after the run and I felt I could breathe with much more ease. My sister would be meeting me soon so we could stop by church and then change and go to dinner. The hot shower was soothing and as soon as I came out of the shower, I heard the knocking on my door. It was my sister and niece. The first thing she asked me was about my date with Brian. "This Guy sounds like a really nice Guy!" said my sister as we started walking to church. I told her about the Chicago Marathon invite as well.

Although my sister was currently a single mother, she was a good mom to my niece and treated her much differently than how we were brought up. She was very affectionate and never lifted a finger to hit my niece, but instead spoke to her firmly and gave her "time out" whenever my niece needed reinforcement of being respectful to her elders or of rules. I offered to help her out as much as I could and ensured my niece had a good wardrobe, shoes and toys.

The time in church together had an instant calming effect and we walked back quickly to get ready for dinner. While we changed, my sister said that she would help steer the conversation and not let him get too close to me. At 4:30 p.m. sharp, there was a loud knock on my door, "Hey Champ! Are you ready to Go?" said Adrian.My sister opened the door and said, "Dang Adrian! Calm down. We are ready". I was thankful, I didn't even have to ask, but my sister sat in the front seat and I sat in the backseat with my niece. She was very aware of Adrian's intentions, so I was relieved that my sister was taking charge of tonight. An hour later, we arrived at Le Cirque, ranked among the best restaurants in the world featuring exquisite French dishes.

My little black dress was appropriate for this place, but I couldn't help feeling out of place. You could clearly see that the people dining here were very well off financially. Besides last night at Pomodoro Restaurant with Brian, I had never been out to a nice restaurant. The only memory I had of eating out was of the few times my father took us to Tad's Steak on 34th street near Macy's department store. Tad's Steak House was a popular buffet type place where you had a choice of ribs, steak or chicken with a butter loaded baked potato. But now, I was at Le Cirque where the waiters all wore tuxedos as their uniform without a hair out of place.

A tall young attractive dark-haired waiter with a French accent walked over and handed each one of us a menu. I felt as if I was in a steam room. "Hello Madame. Can I bring you white or red wine?" he asked. "Sure, white wine please. Thank you," I replied. I could see Adrian's face was also red but it seemed like he was angry. My sister was focused on practicing what she was going to order, "I would like the Black Angus Steak medium well," she said a few times before the waiter returned.

"Are you all ready to order?" he asked. My sister wanted to get it over with and said, 'I am ready. May I please have the Black Angus **Snake**?" The waiter looked startled and I burst out laughing to the point that tears were coming down my face. My sister corrected herself and said, "I'm so sorry, I meant the Black Angus Steak medium well please." I would have the same and Adrian had the Filet Mignon. Dinner was delicious and then we had the Crème Brule for dessert which was delicious.

It was a wonderful dinner and I was really appreciative, but somehow felt as if I should not have accepted this invite.

My sister made sure that she sat in the middle and never let Adrian get too close. I wasn't sure if accepting this invite was the most intelligent decision, but he wanted to celebrate and this would be the last time I accepted anything like this from him. He drove my sister home and then right before I would go into my room, he hugged me tight and kissed me on my cheek, but close to the corner of my lips. I pushed him off and ran inside. I felt gross and knew he was looking for something more.

I thought about calling my sister, but she did enough for me tonight, so I took a warm shower and tried to go to bed and noticed I had a voicemail. It was from Brian and he said, "Hey! I was just thinking about you tonight. Hope you had a great day. If you are free tomorrow afternoon for lunch, I can pick you up. If not, I am driving in on Monday and can swing by your home and pick you up for boot camp. Just let me know."

This was a sweet surprise and it was only 9 p.m., so I took a deep breath and called him. His cellphone rung a few times before he finally picked up and said, "Hey Patricia! What a nice surprise!" I tried to stay cool and laughed a little before replying, "Your message was a nicer surprise! I am going to church tomorrow in Woodside on 58th Street and Queens Boulevard, but I am free any time after 2 p.m. if that works for you." There was a small pause, but then he said, "That actually works perfectly. I have some people I would like you to meet. Sweet Dreams and I look forward to seeing you tomorrow."

I woke up drenched in sweat and I couldn't remember if I had a nightmare. It was probably my anger with Adrian trying to get too close to me last night. It was Sunday morning and I still had time to go for a good run and shower before church.

Then, I remembered that I had also agreed to see Brian again after church. I had no clue what to wear but I quickly threw on my running clothes and ran out the door. It was only 8 a.m. and the streets were still quiet. I ran the opposite direction down Queens Boulevard towards the Queens Borough Bridge.

The New York City Marathon passes through here at the 16-mile mark heading into Manhattan for a steep and steady incline for 1.5 miles. It is a turning point for many runners where they decide to walk. On this morning, I was drawn into going in that direction. From where I was living at the moment to the Queens Borough Bridge, was about a 5k and then another 1.5 miles over the bridge and back for a total of 9 solid miles. I loved running on the bridge today. I felt stronger and was a different runner than when I first ran on that bridge.

I got back to the apartment nearly at 10 a.m. Running this route today was an awesome idea. It was not planned; I just went with what I was feeling and it felt great. As I showered, I remembered that I had a cute summer dress that I had never worn. It was a sky-blue colored dress that had spaghetti straps, a hugging high waist and then flowed right up to my knees. I had let my mind drift and as I jumped out of the shower, I saw that it was 11 a.m.! I threw on the dress and took out a light black sweater to put on over the dress while I was in church. I had no time to blow dry my hair, so I let my long curly hair air dry as I walked the half-mile to church. I made it precisely at 12 noon and as we were reading the bible, I heard my stomach rumbling from not eating any breakfast.

When church ended nearly at 1:45 p.m., I said an extra prayer to help calm my anxieties. I opened the door to exit the church and I saw Brian parked right outside in a silver Camaro. Surprisingly, I remained calm and managed a smile as Brian came out and opened the car door. "Hey! Nice Wheels!" I said before I sat down and gave him a kiss on the cheek. "You look very pretty Patricia. Are you hungry?" asked Brian. I hoped he couldn't hear my rumbling tummy before I replied, "Absolutely! I ran before church and didn't have time to eat anything."

Brian said, "Perfect! My parents live in Rego Park near Forest Hills, so we are going to have sushi in Forest Hills with my parents'. I wasn't sure what to say or do, but decided to go with the flow, so I said, "Cool! Both sound awesome." I wished I could call Father Joe or my sister, but

I relied on my silent prayers and a few minutes later we were approaching the restaurant. He found parking nearby and quickly got out of the car to open the door for me. Brian was definitely a gentleman.

When we entered the restaurant his parents and his younger brother, Jason were already seated and stood up as we walked over. His mother, Pam was a tall elegant beautiful fair skinned woman with bright hazel eyes and I wasn't sure why she was wearing a wig, but the short blond hair complimented her features well. His father, Danny was a classy older man around 5'8" tall, stocky build, brown toned with white short hair that resembled Giorgio Armani. The younger brother Jason, was a good-looking guy with a mixture of both of his parent's looks who had recently graduated college and was living in a shared Manhattan apartment with 2 roommates. He was only a couple of years younger than Brian, but to me, Brian had a different special quality. Each one of them took turns extending their hands to me and welcomed me to sit.

I immediately felt comfortable with Pam. "You have such pretty curly hair Patricia!" said Pam. "Oh, thank you! I guess we are never satisfied. My oldest sister has straight hair and growing up we wished we had each other's hair," I replied. Pam's next question was worded in a harmless comical way, at least that is how I took it when she said, "And you must have some Latina blood in you with your exotic looks Patricia! What is your background?" Fortunately, I had good practice from all the boxing interviews and the one thing I never denied was my background. Despite all the challenges and lack of support, I was proud to be Latina and of Colombian descent, so I replied, "My mother is from Barranquilla, Colombia but I was born in New York, so I am a proud Latina."

Danny ordered 20 different types of rolls for all of us to share with orders of miso soup, seaweed salad and edamame for the table. I told Brian earlier that I was allergic to shellfish and I overheard him tell his father about it. Danny looked older than Pam and guessed he would be in his late 50's to early 60's.

He was a respected man originally from Iran. He was Persian/Jewish and came to the United States with just a few dollars in his pocket working for many years loading and unloading textiles from a truck as well as keeping inventory. He learned everything about the business until he became the manager and now the owner of the textile company. It was very admirable and inspiring to hear his story.

He reminded me of my mother who also came to this country for a better life. However, she did not make it as well as Danny. My mother stuck to the maintenance field and met a monster who lied to her and killed all her dreams. Danny had a cool demeanor but I could also see that he could be a force to be reckoned with and he would have no problem showing his other side if needed. After finishing the edamame, soup and salad, and sushi rolls came right after. They varied from eel, tuna, salmon, avocado and sweet potato rolls. Brian put 2 avocado rolls and a sweet potato roll on my plate. "If you want more, we can order you more," he whispered in my ear. After eating 2 rolls, I felt really full and Brian helped me finish the third.

Jason joked throughout dinner, but they would soon find out that it didn't take much to make me laugh. Both Jason and Brian worked in their father's textile business and at times talked amongst themselves about work. We kept the conversation light during our tea time. I was thankful that Pam and Danny didn't grill me with personal questions. As we walked out the door, Pam gave me a warm motherly hug and said, "Wonderful to meet you and we hope to do it again very soon!' Danny came over and gave me a kiss on each cheek which was traditional in Middle Eastern countries.

I unconsciously let out a sigh of relief in front of Brian. "Are you okay Patricia? I hope that this didn't make you feel uncomfortable," asked Brian as we walked to his car. "Your Mom is super sweet. I really like her. Thank you for everything this afternoon Brian," I replied. I could see Brian glow as he opened the car door. During the short ride back to the basement apartment, Brian told me that Pam has been in remission from breast cancer for 10 years, but that it had returned and she was undergoing chemotherapy treatments which explained the wig. He loved his mom's courage and fighter's spirit and said that I reminded him of her. I tried to lighten the conversation and told him that "Scooby-Doo" was my favorite cartoon growing up. We looked at each other and started laughing simultaneously.

We pulled in front of the basement apartment and Brian got out of the car and opened my door and as I stood up, our lips finally met for the first time. He pulled me in tightly and I felt safe in his embrace. He gave me his signature big teddy bear hug and said, "I'll see you at boot camp tomorrow. Goodnight Scooby". I hugged him right back and replied, "Goodnight Raggie". Raggie was what Scooby-Doo called his best friend Shaggy in the cartoon. As I walked to my apartment, I saw Adrian peeking out his window and I smiled inside. I am glad he caught the kiss. Perhaps, he would leave me alone now.

I fell back on my bed and all I could think about was the kiss! I felt tingly all over and was smiling from ear to ear until I heard a loud knock on my door that startled me. "Who is it?" I asked firmly. There was a long pause and then it was silent. It was really strange and it shook me up. I was sure it was Adrian, but I had no idea what he could possibly want at this hour. I said my prayers and fell asleep to the thought of Brian. I knew I would see him again tomorrow and that made me happy.

I awoke as usual before the alarm sounded and felt rested. I got ready quickly and made my way out the door. On the bus ride, I kept thinking about how I should greet Brian and that made me nervous. The bus let me off and I started jogging towards the meet up spot and as I got closer, I could see Brian was already there and my heart was pounding. I finally stopped right in front of Brian and before I could say or do anything, he held my face and kissed me on the lips.

"Good morning," I said with a goofy smile. "I am very happy to see you again Patricia," he replied and then Instructor Steve and group members started arriving. I didn't know much, but I did know that Brian had a good head on his shoulders and I would let his actions guide me. The workout today was at another one of my favorite spots in Central Park called Belvedere Castle which is one of the most iconic features in the park. Belvedere Castle is a miniature castle located atop a huge rock dramatic outcrop known as Vista Rock. To get to the castle, there is a quarter mile steep hill followed by 4 sets of stairs.

Our workout today consisted of a dozen hill repeats up to the castle and we ended with drills of calisthenics at the top overlooking the majestic Belvedere Castle. As we were finishing up the stretching portion, Instructor Steve announced that he would be leaving to Upstate, New York to open up his own law firm and that Platoon Fitness was looking for a replacement Instructor. That was sad news to me as Platoon Fitness had become a big part of my daily life, it helped me start my day right and I really enjoyed being part of the group, but most importantly, it was where I met Brian.

After class, Brian stayed behind and wanted to talk with me. "Hey, so now that Steve is leaving, Platoon asked me if I could become one of the instructors. I am a certified trainer and I would love to take it, but I think you would also make a wonderful Instructor," said Brian. I was momentarily stunned and replied, "I think you would be an excellent Instructor Brian! I am not sure I would though. Besides, I am not certified". Then Brian said something that impacted me for the rest of my life, "Listen Patricia, you are an amazing Athlete. You are strong and beautiful and people look up to you including me. I will help you get certified while you teach. I can talk to Platoon and tell them that we can both co-manage the NYC Platoon Fitness class".

I trusted Brian and I nervously agreed. I would take the certification classes on the weekends and teach once or twice a week. Before we each went on about our work day, he kissed me on the lips and hugged me again. I felt as if I had known Brian for years. I had never been this close to anyone and I felt as if I could finally let my guard down and I did.

Things at the New York Road Runners had changed rapidly. With Mary being the new CEO, the management also changed. One day, both Jake and Claudia were gone and the new Director of the Event Production Department would be a guy named Peter. He was very different than Jake in every sense of the word, but I just wanted to continue to do my work the best way I could especially with my recent promotion to Event Manager.

Peter had frequent meetings with the Events Team to ensure that the logistics for the events were flawless. I remember on many occasions I would sleep at the office if the event I was managing was on that weekend. Call time was usually around 3 a.m. anyways. There were many more staff changes that made things extra challenging. Personality conflicts would be something I encountered often in the working world. People just wanting to have the authority but not proactively work towards improvement was a common theme in the workplace.

The week had been filled with so much unexpected events that I had completely forgotten about the Celebrity Boxing Dinner this Saturday! Brian called me during my lunch hour and asked if I was busy over the weekend and I told him about the big dinner where Evander Holyfield would be in attendance, so he invited me to my first Broadway show the next day. He took me to see Phantom of the Opera. After the show during the ride home, Brian asked me if I would be his girlfriend. He said that he wanted to see me exclusively. I didn't hesitate to say "yes", however, I had always been exclusive with him since the day we started talking.

I woke up with my stomach in knots and a heavy feeling in my chest. I felt anxious and didn't understand why. Tonight, is supposed to be a great night of meeting boxing people and I would get to hang out with Coach. Later on in my life, I would come to understand that I needed to listen to the signs my body was sending me as they were a way of guiding me. At the time though, I just wasn't sure if they were feelings of insecurity. I knew a run would help, so out I went for a run on Queens Boulevard.

After hitting 8 miles, I headed back to the apartment and I was feeling better until I saw Adrian standing right outside. My stomach went right back into knots. "Hey Champ, how are you? Looks like you got in a good run. I have been meaning to ask you. Who was that guy who dropped you off the other night? Is that your boyfriend?" asked Adrian. I was creeped out by his tone, look and questions, but I replied, "Hey Adrian. Yes, actually he is my boyfriend and his name is Brian. He is a great guy." Adrian's face was red with anger. He looked crazy and it made me uneasy.

"Well, you should really take things slow and not jump into things. I am here if you need to talk," he said. I did not want to be anywhere near him and replied, "Well thanks Adrian. I really like Brian and I will decide the pace of the relationship. Take care Adrian." I rushed in feeling gross as I hated the way he looked at me. I took a long shower and got ready to meet my sister and niece. She offered to do my hair for the Celebrity Boxing event. Thankfully, she was knocking on my door and we went for a walk on Roosevelt Avenue with my niece in the stroller.

On our walk to our favorite Colombian Bakery on 60th Street and Roosevelt Avenue, I talked my sister's ears off and got her all up to date on Brian and what was happening with Adrian. This Colombian Bakery was always crowded because everything they sold was so delicious! We ordered empanadas and arepas which was a traditional Colombian corn cake with melted cheese.

"Man, you have to get out of that place! I think I may have found a place in Rego Park and should know soon, but I also have to find a better job. Why don't you talk to Brian and maybe he can help you find a place," suggested my sister while she ate her empanada and fed my niece at the same time. I was embarrassed to tell Brian the awful situation I was in, but she was right. When I see him again for boot camp class on Monday, I will share what has been going on with my living situation and ask for his help. Without realizing it, we had overstayed our time at bakery and it was almost 4 o'clock!

We rushed back to the apartment and I quickly put on my black dress and my sister got started on blow drying my hair. She had good hands and was just naturally skilled with everything that had to do with beauty and fashion. I always pictured her as the next Latina Coco Channel. Almost an hour later, she finished my hair and make-up. When she was done, she had a funny smirk on her face and blurted, "Be careful tonight and don't let anyone get fresh with you." I hugged her as we walked out together.

While I was on the train, people were certainly looking at me. Although I looked like a grown woman tonight, it was far from how I felt inside. I felt like a scared little girl. I wondered if this feeling would ever get better. I said a silent prayer and walked out on 34th Street. I did not enjoy walking in heels and preferred my running sneakers, but I would make an exception for the special occasions. It was 7 o'clock sharp and I saw Coach standing a few blocks away from the event site. "Whoa! You look nice Alcivar!" said Coach with a tone I had never heard from him.

Coach was wearing a black tuxedo which I had never seen him in before, but to me, he was Coach. In all the years that I've known him, I had always seen him as a parental figure. I respected him and had grown to trust him. He had always called me his "Kid", so I didn't think anything of his remarks. "We have to walk fast and get our seats, so grab on to my arm and I'll help you walk faster and not fall with those heels," said Coach. So, I grabbed on to his arm and we sped up and arrived at the Ballroom at Manhattan Center.

We checked in and there were name plates at a large round table that seated 12. The Ballroom was elegantly decorated. There were famous boxers everywhere and Coach took me around to shake everyone's hands and take pictures. I even saw Evander Holyfield dancing on the dance floor and he did not hesitate to take a picture with me. The evening went by fast. There were some awards and presentations given, but it was nearly 11 p.m. and I was really tired.

"Hey Coach, I am dead tired. You could stay, but I am going to go get a taxi home," I said. Coach stood up right away and said, "I am good too. I'll walk out with you." I probably should not have run so much today, but I was really happy I got to do this today. As we were walking down the street, Coach put his arm around me which felt weird. "It's very windy, come closer," said Coach. In my mind, I thought we have walked to Gleason's Gym to spar in sub-zero temperatures in the winter and he never put his arm around me.

We stopped at an intersection near Penn Station where I could see yellow cabs passing. As we stood there, Coach all of a sudden put his hands on my shoulder and bent down to kiss me on the lips! I froze as my eyes filled with tears.

I became light headed and I am sure the look on my face prompted Coach to ask, "Are you okay?" I looked at him in disbelief and said, "No. I feel sick and nauseous. How could you?" Thankfully a cab pulled up and said, "Where to?" and without hesitation I jumped in the cab. I told the cab driver my address and then stared out the window in a state of shock. The only person that I had learned to trust betrayed me. He was just like my father and worse. He called me his kid and told me that if he ever had a daughter, he would want her to be like me. Tears streamed down my cheeks. I arrived at the apartment 30 minutes later and collapsed on the bed and started sobbing, "Why God? Why another betrayal?"

I had confided in Coach about what my father had done to me. Coach was at least 15 years my senior and he knew my history. I was hurt and confused. I always treated Coach with respect. I felt myself hyperventilating and gasping for air. The pain was unbearable. That night, I asked God to take me away with him where I wouldn't feel this pain and I felt my vision get all blurry and then I passed out.

I woke up almost 8 hours later still in the black dress with make-up all over my face. I quickly remembered the events that took place and the tears started again. My phone rang and I saw that it was my sister and picked it up, "Hey Patricia! How did it go yesterday? I was waiting for your call! I'm running a bit late, so hold a spot for me at church and I'll see you there!" said my sister before I even said a word and hung up.

I forced myself to take a cold shower and got ready quickly and rushed to church. I would not have gone if it wasn't for my sister calling. I got to church early and saved a spot for her and my niece. I looked and felt like a zombie. A few minutes later, my sister arrived with my niece and I did my best to listen to the sermon which had the topic, "Forgiveness". The topic would be one that I would struggle with all of my life. "How can you forgive and forget all of the pain and betrayal?" was my life long question. It would be a life-long process. The one thing that I remembered at the end of the sermon was when the pastor said, "Trust in God and that there is a purpose for the trials and tribulations you are going through and when you feel weak and vulnerable, pray and keep praying."

I felt better for going to church and I cherished and held on to the last sentence of that sermon. After the church service, we walked towards the Colombian Bakery. "So, how did it go?" asked my sister. I looked down for a few moments and then replied, "Terrible! Well, it started out really awesome and I got to meet many famous fighters but then Coach was acting weird and when he walked me to catch a cab, he tried to kiss me on the lips." My sister's face turned from shocked to angry and then she asked, "Did you punch him in the face? Man, I am sorry Patricia! I know he was like family to you. You should tell Father Joe and see what he says. For now, just pray and take some time for you."

My sister was right and I needed to take some time off from boxing and Coach. I had accomplished a lot in Women's Boxing and was often referred to as a pioneer in the sport from being a 2-time New York City Golden Gloves Champion, A USA National Champion, International Champion, Western States Champion, Metro Boxing Champion and the 1st Female ever to be voted and win "Athlete of the Year" by the USA Olympic Boxing Committee. I had made history already and no one could change that. The only thing missing from my boxing resume was the Olympics, but the Amateur Boxing President at the time, Gary Toney and Sandy Pino told Coach that Women's Boxing would never make it as an Olympic sport and not to waste my time waiting.

I remembered asking Coach about turning professional in boxing, but he brushed me off. I have always known early on that if there is no incentive, I see no use in continuing. Perhaps this incident with Coach was my sign to walk away from boxing although, I consistently felt as

I had unfinished business in the sport. I was disappointed and sad and for now, I would just take a break and do other things that I have been wanting to do like a Triathlon, an Adventure Race and be a girlfriend.

CHAPTER 7

Chapter Seven - Round 7

Love is more than a 4-letter word
"A woman is like a tea bag; you never know how strong it is until it's in hot water," Eleanor Roosevelt

After church, lunch and talking with my sister, I walked for a couple of more hours before I finally went to the apartment. I felt emotionally drained and called Father Joe to leave him a message, "Hi Father Joe. I urgently need to speak to you tomorrow after work please. It is about the Celebrity Boxing Dinner event. Something awful happened afterwards." Just as I was about to fall asleep, Father Joe called me, "Hello Patricia. I can see you tomorrow, but are you okay now?" I took a deep breath and replied, "Hi Father Joe. Yes, I am okay now and I will tell you all about it tomorrow. I don't want to talk about it now. Thanks so much."

I slept deeply and was looking forward to a good boot camp class and seeing Brian. He was teaching today, so I wanted to make sure I was there as a source of support. I was not going to tell him anything about Coach yet until I spoke to Father Joe later. I packed my backpack and made my way out the door. When I arrived at Tavern on the Green, Brian greeted me with a kiss, smile and hug. "Good morning, Beautiful!" he said. I giggled and said, "Have a great class! You will be awesome!" And then the group started to trickle in. Brian led the group to "Dog Hill" today for the brutal workout. Dog Hill also known as

171

"Cedar Hill" is in the upper eastside of Central Park. The steep grassy hill is home to many red cedars that form a line of clumps on its crest.

I loved this location as I would see many dogs going out for their morning walks, however, today we ran hill repeats here which left the class gasping for air at the top. The hill repeats were followed by 10 burpees after each of the 20 hill repeats that were about a quarter mile in length. Brian asked me to lead the stretch as a way to ease me into an instructor role. He was also preparing me to teach the following week.

My personal training courses were coming along and he had also scheduled us to take an outdoor certification course soon. It was a fantastic class and judging from all the sweaty and happy faces, the group thought so as well. As I was leading the stretches, I smiled and tried to engage the members afterwards for a short time. I remembered through all the years in boxing of how important it was to come out of my shell and it all began with a smile. I was thankful to Brian for encouraging me to become a certified trainer, so I had to make a good effort. The workout had distracted me from the pain of the events that occurred over the weekend. I would keep it to myself for the time being.

Once everyone left, Brian picked me up and squeezed me super tight! "Haha! What are you doing Raggie? I asked while laughing. Brian laughed as well and said, "I am just happy that's all. It was a great class and you did great at the end too. Next week, you will start teaching Scooby!" I felt happy too even for those short moments. We agreed to meet again the next day and kissed goodbye.

Jogging slowly to the office, I felt that uneasy feeling in my stomach. I wasn't sure why but I tried to run faster in hopes this feeling would subside. Someone from the office had used up all the hot water and I ended up taking an ice-cold shower which helped clear my head. When I came down the stairs to get my breakfast, I overheard the girls at the front desk saying that there was an opening for a Receptionist/Building Services Coordinator. I immediately thought about my sister and called her on my way out to get breakfast and said, "Hey! There is an opening here at the New York Road Runners for a Receptionist/Building Services Coordinator. I can help update your resume and give it to Lynn, the lady you would report to. What do you say?"

"Hey Patricia, absolutely! I am moving into that new apartment soon, so I need a better job than the supermarket and I am willing to learn. I am nervous, but please go ahead and update my resume and submit it to Lynn. Thanks so much!" replied my sister.

It was only 8:30 a.m. when I got back to the office, so I took the half hour I had before people would start to stroll in to work on my sister's resume. At 9 a.m., I was walking into Lynn's office to personally hand her my sister's resume. Lynn was an older woman in her 60's and the Building Manager. She was also one of the few veteran employees left that had been there for a considerable amount of time. The rumor circulating eluded to her retiring soon. "Hi Lynn! I heard that you had an opening for the front desk and the person would also be assisting you in the building operations," I said in my cheeriest of voices.

Lynn replied, "Yes! I have been looking for a while. Do you have someone in mind?" I think I got a bit too over excited and said, "I have the perfect person for you Lynn! It is my sister who is a hard worker and a fast learner, but most importantly, she is a single mom and really needs this job. Here is her resume." I could see that Lynn was very sympathetic and said, "Well, if she is anything like you, I will hire her right away! I just don't want to make a big fuss around here because you are sisters and although you would be in different departments, we don't want to give the wrong impression to anyone. I can call her now and ask her to come in for an interview as soon as possible."

After speaking with Lynn, I worked on finalizing my logistics for my event in the upcoming weekend which would be the Central Park Conservancy 4-mile run. I had everything in place with the logistics which included the equipment/placement list and specific instructions for the Warehouse Staff, call time and instructions for the Volunteers and Part-time/Event Staff and other specific instructions relating to Marketing and Sponsors.

I spent the morning confirming the vendors for the event which included A Royal Flush for the porta johns, fruit vendor for post finish food and updating the P & L. Peter was big on all these things and I had a meeting with him this afternoon to go over these items. The busier my day was, the faster it went and I would hardly have time to think of anything else. Over the years, I had learned to multi-task which helped me stay focused and worked well with my ADD.

As my work day ended, my sister I saw that my sister had left a message saying she was coming in for an interview the very next day! It was the best news of the day, but as I walked to take the train, I had second thoughts about seeing Father Joe. I have been so used to not talking about anything and internalizing everything that I was afraid to talk to Father Joe about what had happened with Coach. But I felt lost and knew I had to speak with him. He always seemed to have the answers and I always felt better after speaking with him. When my train stop was approaching, I said a silent prayer and just hoped for the best.

"Hello Patricia, nice to see you," said Father Joe as he opened the door to his office. I could not even look at him and had my head down as I walked in and plopped myself on the couch. After a few moments, I just could not help but start crying. "Patricia, please look at me and tell me what has happened," said Father Joe while also passing me a few tissues. I paused the crying and wiped my nose and then started, "Coach was supposed to go with a friend who couldn't go, so he invited me to a big boxing dinner event where famous boxers were present. I trusted Coach and everything was going well until he offered to walk me to get a cab after the event at night. All of a sudden, he grabbed me and tried to kiss me! I feel so sad Father Joe. How could he do this to me?" I could see the shock in Father Joe's eyes and then the crying started all over again.

"I am sorry Patricia. I can understand why you are upset and I am sure he has a good explanation. Have you tried speaking to him?" he asked. "Yes, he tried to call me, but I didn't answer him. He betrayed my trust, Father Joe! He always called me his Kid! I have lost all respect for him," I replied while still crying. Nothing he said made me feel any better this time and he knew that. "Well Patricia, this is what I can do. I can call him and hear what he has to say. I think it is better for you to take some time off boxing. I can see you again next week and hopefully we can find a better solution," said Father Joe to conclude our session. I left his office feeling worse and dreaded going home. I took a much-needed nap on the train and unfortunately, woke up right at my stop.

I wanted to take advantage of the sleepiness feeling and perhaps I could sleep well tonight. As I approached my front door, I saw Adrian waiting with a serious face. "Hello Patricia. It seems someone broke into my house this afternoon. I saw the door was open and I filed a police report. Nothing in my place was missing, but I thought I should let you know and you should see if there is anything missing for you," he said.

I was mortified and ran into the basement apartment. I started to understand the awkward sinking feeling in my stomach all day today. I quickly looked in my drawer and sure enough, my Golden Gloves necklaces were gone! I fell to my knees and started to cry. Nothing in the entire house was missing except for my Golden Gloves necklaces even though Adrian's living room walls displayed expensive art and he also owned expensive jewelry such as multiple Rolex watches and a safe which were untouched. I kept my Golden Gloves necklaces inside socks in the bottom of my drawer and somehow, the "thief" knew to look and take only that from the entire house?

I came back upstairs and told Adrian my Golden Gloves necklaces were missing but I couldn't help to add, "Adrian, it is very strange that nothing from your place was missing even though you have very expensive things. Please return my necklaces! I know that it was you!" The look of guilt on his face confirmed to me that it was him indeed that stole my Golden Gloves, but I also knew that this was his way of getting back at me for rejecting him and for having a boyfriend.

"Patricia, I am sorry this happened. I have nothing to do with it and can call the police tomorrow," he said while looking at the ground. I was disgusted and knew there was no possible way to remain in this awful place. I went downstairs and packed the same duffle bag I had packed when I left my abusive home. I had everything I needed and took a cab to the office. The event I was managing was this weekend, so I had no choice but to plan to stay in the office for at least a couple of nights.

It was 9 p.m. when I arrived at the office. I got my keys and opened the door quietly and used the elevator to go upstairs with my heavy duffle bag. I went into the Events office and locked the door after I got to my desk. I called my sister and told her what happened. She was also horrified and in shock. "OMG Patricia! What an EFFING CREEP! Listen, if all goes well with the job interview tomorrow, I should be moving into that small place in Rego Park in about a week or so. We can share the apartment for as long as you need, "said my sister.

Thankfully, tomorrow was already Friday and then the event was on Saturday, so I would plan to sleep right here for the rest of the weekend while my sister's new place became temporary available, but I would also search for an apartment. I fell asleep on my chair in the Event Department's office for a few hours when a loud knock on the door at 4 a.m. startled me and I jumped out of the chair. Then, I heard "Hello? Who is in there?" asked the male voice behind the door. I realized it was Coach Joe, so I opened the door and said, "Hi Coach Joe, it is me, Patricia. The place where I was living got broken into and my personal things got stolen. I had no other place to go, so I came here, but I will be looking for a new place today," I said. Coach Joe has always been nothing short of kind to me.

He put his hand on my shoulder and said, "That's terrible and sorry this happened to you Kid. I won't say a word to anyone. You stay as long as you need," and then he left. An overwhelming feeling of sadness came over me realizing that I was homeless and I felt so alone. My eyes teared up and I could only do what I knew wouldn't fail me and that was to pray. I closed my eyes and although no words came out, I prayed in silence and had faith that somehow everything would workout. I really wanted to go to bootcamp class, but was embarrassed of my situation. I would instead go out on a hard 6-mile loop run of Central Park. It was early enough that I would not bump into anyone and by 4:30 a.m. The intense run temporarily took the pain away. I ran so hard that I felt as if I was holding my breath the whole time, but for those 45 minutes, I didn't think of anything except the run.

I let the hot water run down my back in the shower for a few minutes letting me be soothed even if for a few seconds. When I got back to my desk, I saw that I had a few missed calls from Brian and a voicemail message from him.

I felt my hand shaking as I dialed to listen to his voicemail, "Hey Scooby! I missed you in class this morning. I hope you are okay. It is Friday and I would really like to see you either today or this weekend if you are not too busy. Either way, please call me back. I just want to know that you are okay," said Brian in his voicemail.

One of the things I loved about Brian was that he wasn't afraid to show his care for me. It was something I had never experienced and I was thankful for that. I closed my eyes and asked for guidance and then I took a deep breath and called Brian hoping he wouldn't answer, but he did right away, "Hey Scooby! I am so glad you called. Are you okay?" he asked. I did my best to stay calm and replied, "Hi Brian! I am sorry I missed you this morning. I am managing the event tomorrow in Central Park and I have so much work and then I have to be onsite by 4 a.m., so I am just going to sleep in the office tonight.

There was a brief pause before he said, "I wouldn't like you to spend the night in the office. How about I pick you up at whatever time you are finished and we can get some dinner and you can sleep at my place and I can drive you into Central Park tomorrow. If you need an extra pair of hands for the event, I can help too." This guy was a dream. How can he be so nice? Another deep breath and I replied, "You are an angel. I am not sure what to say except thank you so much! I think all your suggestions are perfect. I should be finished with everything I have to do here around 6 p.m. We have people that we pay to come help us for our weekend events, so I will make sure to add you to our list. Thank you again and I'll see you later Raggie." And then I quickly hung up the phone still in disbelief.

I got myself together and sent out the event logistics to the staff, warehouse employees, volunteers and part-time weekend staff that also included my sister and now Brian as well. I reconfirmed all the vendors and added the final updates to the event P & L for Peter. A few hours later, my sister called to tell me that the interview with Lynn went well and that she got the job! Lynn made an offer at the end of their interview and she would start that Monday! That was incredible news and I was so happy for her.

The end of the work day came and I was the only one left in the Events office at 5:30 p.m. Brian would be coming to pick me up soon and I felt edgy. I had to be open and tell him what happened with Coach, with Adrian and on top of that, I would be spending the night at his place. "It is all going to be okay. God, I know you are with me. Please guide me and protect me tonight and always," I prayed. At 6 p.m., I packed some clothes in my backpack from my duffle bag and went downstairs and I saw Brian's car parked right across the street. I took a deep breath and walked over. As soon as he saw me, he got out of the car to greet me and open the door. I just hugged him as tight as I could possibly remember hugging anyone and he hugged me right back. "Are you okay Scooby?" he asked.

I held on for a few more seconds and I am sure my face gave it away, but I replied, "I will be okay, but I have to tell you something that happened." Brian held on to my arm before he opened up the car door and said, "You can tell me anything. I will let you decide if you want to go to dinner in Queens or pick something up and eat it back at my place." I got in the car and wasn't sure where to begin, but started with, "I hope that what I am about to tell you doesn't scare you away, but I would rather let you know the truth. I come from a very abusive and dysfunctional family. I have been living on my own since I was 15 years old. Financial difficulty landed me in the place I was living up until last night. The owner of that house stole my Golden Gloves because I rejected any of his advances and he was angry when I told him you were my boyfriend. I packed my stuff and left last night. My sister moves into her new place a week from this Saturday and I can stay with her until I find a new place."

I felt myself start to tremble and once again, Brian held on to my arm and said, "Nothing you tell me will scare me away from you. I am sorry for everything that has happened to you and wish I could take it all away. You can stay with me for the entire week until you move in with your sister or longer if you need." I felt the anxiety and fear dissipate into the air when he said that. We picked up steamed dumplings, rice and beef with vegetables at one of Brian's favorite places in Queens and we brought it back to his place. Brian lived in a spacious and bright 2-bedroom apartment in beautiful Forest Hills which he shared with his roommate Neal. It was more like a bachelor pad and that made me a bit nervous.

We ate our dinners at the dining table while I went over the logistics of the event that he would be working and helping me out at the same time. "Whatever you need me to do, just say the word. I don't mind a little hard work," said Brian. Everything he said put me at ease and I was so grateful for that. It was 9 p.m. and we had to be up by at least 3am so we could be in Central Park by 4am, so I apprehensively asked, "So what will be the sleeping arrangements Raggie? I know 9pm on a Friday night is crazy early for you to be thinking of sleep, but we have to be in the park by 4am." Brian took my arm yet again and said, "I know it has been a stressful time for you and I don't want you to stress at all. It will be your choice. You can sleep in the sofa bed here in the living room, you can sleep in my bed and I can sleep out here in the sofa bed or we can both sleep in my room and can promise you nothing will happen. Whatever you feel most comfortable with Scooby."

I decided that we could both sleep in Brian's room. I went into the bathroom changed into my pajamas, brushed my teeth and got ready for bed. Before he turned off the light, Brian kissed me on the forehead and hugged me tight before we both fell asleep and nothing happened that night just as he had promised. I slept peacefully with the lights off and without any nightmares. This was the first time I felt that I was falling in love.

The alarm sounded at 3 am and we both jumped out of bed and started to get ready and were back in his car driving to Central Park before 3:30 am. "Did you sleep okay Scooby" asked Brian as he drove down Queens Boulevard going towards the Queensboro Bridge. "YES! Thank you so much! I have not slept that well in a while. Not to get into great details, but uninterrupted sleep is usually a challenge for me and I've usually had to sleep with the lights on to avoid the awful nightmares, "I replied.

Brian looked perplexed, but just kept driving and said, "Well, I am glad that we both were able to get good sleep last night. After the event today, my dad asked us to meet him and my mom at London Lenny's for an early dinner if that is okay with you." London Lennie's is one of the oldest family-owned seafood restaurants known for their excellence in fresh and delicious food. "Oh! Of course, I would love to hang out with your parents later!" I replied.

Since it was so early, we found parking right away and hurried over to the Bandshell area inside Central Park where everything for the event today started and ended. The Naumburg Bandshell in Central Park is an original feature of the park and much more than just a classical music arena. It is also a site where historical speeches have been delivered by Martin Luther King, Jr. and a eulogy read for John Lennon. The Central Park Conservancy 4-mile Run would start and end right at the 72nd Street Transverse which was adjacent to the Bandshell.

I introduced Brian to the other part-time staff and volunteers, to Peter and later on my sister who I had also called to work this event. Everyone started setting out the hundreds of barricades on to the finish line and setting up all the signage. I would later see Brian sweeping the start line area. He was a hard worker and took pride in everything he did. It was a quality that attracted me even more to him. Periodically, he would come over and ask if I needed help with anything. And for an extra bonus, he partnered up with my sister and seemed to be working and getting along really well with her.

The Central Park Conservancy Run went off promptly at 8 a.m. on a warm summer morning. Since it was just a 4-mile race, the first and last runners crossed the finish line well before 10 a.m. While the runners enjoyed the post event festivities at the Bandshell, the event's staff broke down the start/finish area and started getting everything cleaned up. It was a flawless event and we were finished and walking back to the car by noon.

Brian offered to drive my sister home. We were all tired but had a fun conversation on the ride back to Queens. After we dropped my sister off, we rushed back to Brian's place. It was already close to 2 p.m. and we were going to meet his parents by 4 p.m. We were both wanting to shower and perhaps take a quick cat nap, but that would not be possible. When we got to his home, his roommate Neal was there and he had to introduce me and they started to chat while I took a shower. I felt self-conscious about staying in Brian's room. I hoped the week would pass by fast.

When Brian returned to his room, he was surprised to see that I had showered and was dressed and ready. "That was fast! I know this has been rough for you, but I want you to feel comfortable. I'll do my best for you not to have to worry about anything for the next week while you are here. We have boot camp class in the mornings and I can swing by and pick you up after work and we can drive back together from Monday until Friday. How does that sound?' he asked as he sat down next to me holding my hand. It was as if he knew what was weighing so heavily on my shoulders. "Thank you Raggie. That sounds just about right," I said.

I closed my eyes while Brian went to shower and passed out deeply for 20 minutes before we hurried out the door and into his car. As we drove to meet his parents, I spontaneously asked, "Hey Raggie, have you ever had reoccurring nightmares? I've had these weird reoccurring nightmares that feel so real where I can't move and kind of gasp for air. I just wanted to give you the heads up in case you see me struggle at night." I couldn't believe I just blurted that out, but felt I needed to.

"Thanks for sharing that Scooby! I know saying this might not help much, but just remember it's just a nightmare and no one can harm you without your permission. Anything I can do to help, just let me know," Brian replied as were pulling into the restaurant's parking lot.

Pam and Danny were already seated in the restaurant and it was really good to see them. Pam had beautiful deep hazel eyes that penetrated through my soul. I could see and feel that she had suffered a great deal with the cancer. Her left arm was in a sling because the nerves were damaged in one of the past surgeries to remove the cancer lymph nodes. I hugged her tightly when I greeted her and she hugged me tighter and she whispered in my ear, "I would love to see my son get married before I die."

I tried to keep my warm smile and hide the stunned reaction from my face as I went to give Danny the double kisses on his cheeks. "Are you guys hungry and ready to order or what?" asked Danny. I was actually starving and I am pretty sure Brian was too. "We have been up since 3 a.m. and I helped Patricia with the event she was managing in Central Park, so we are both starving!" said Brian. Before we shared all about our day, I made sure to alert them that I was allergic to shellfish and I ordered the grilled chicken salad, Pam ordered the fish and chips and Brian and Danny ordered the salmon dish and an order of calamari to start for all of us.

I told Pam and Danny about what my job at the New York Road Runners entailed. Although it was a demanding job, I loved it because running was involved and it challenged me in a different way than any other job I've had in the past. Being an Event Manager helped me be creative, multi-task as well as problem solve and value the staff that many people took for granted like the Volunteers, Part-time and Warehouse staff.

Brian kept pinching Danny on his sides jokingly and then said, "So did you spin this morning, Dad?" Danny's eyes lit up and replied, "Oh man that spin class was so hard, but I did good. The instructor told me I did a good job." Brian had told me that his father was a big fan of spin and made it his business to go on the weekends while Pam got together with her girlfriends. We spent over 2 hours in the restaurant and went back to their house which was just a 10-minute drive away.

Pam was a big fan of the board game Scrabble, so Brian, Pam and I played for a couple of hours. Brian and Pam were fierce competitors and kept challenging each other to look up words in the dictionary to ensure that they were real words. I was not an expert and I was just happy to be playing and not thinking about anything stressful for a change. We finally said our good byes and tentatively agreed to get together soon in the coming weeks with his brother Jason and his girlfriend Jessica.

It was already dark when we got back to Brian's place and there was no one home. "Neal probably went out tonight, so we will have some peace and quiet tonight. Do you want to sleep, watch a movie or something?" asked Brian. I was drowsy and I knew my face was telling him the same, so I said, "Hey Raggie, I am feeling very wiped out and if you don't mind, I would love to just lay down until I fall asleep." Brian didn't hesitate and started getting ready for bed.

It was close to 11 p.m. which was past my bedtime. Brian and I had such different lives growing up. I didn't hold it against him, but I knew it was difficult for him to understand. Although his father, Danny immigrated to the United States, he gave Brian and his brother a completely different life than I had growing up. For the most part, his parents were encouraging and never abused them. They grew up in a beautiful neighborhood until they decided to live on their own and still had a nice relationship with their parents and family. I was already in my pajamas and was pulling the covers over me when Brian came to lay next to me and asked, "What's on your mind Scooby?"

My face always had to give my emotions away and I thought that Brian deserved to know what I was feeling, so even if what I said pushed him away, I had to share. "I really appreciate everything you have done from picking me up, helping at the event, dinner with your parents and letting me stay here Brian. No one has ever been that nice to me. I just had mixed emotions seeing how much love there is with your parents. I never had that and it made me a bit melancholic, so I apologize if I am a bit off. I will be okay." Brian turned off the lights and just hugged me tight until I fell asleep.

At about 2 a.m. I felt my chest heavy and I couldn't move. I saw a dark shadow and tried to call out Brian's name. "In the name of the Father, The Son and the Holy Spirit," I mentally started to pray while gasping for air and then Brian instinctively woke up and started shaking me and yelled, "Scooby are you okay? Wake up!" THANK GOD! I finally was able to move and breath while tears came down my face. "Thank you Raggie. I am okay. It was the nightmare," I replied while catching my breath. Brian hugged me tight once again and we tried to fall back asleep. It was the first time anyone had ever seen me having this awful paralyzing nightmare. At least someone could now see it was real, but I just kept having this feeling that I was scaring this guy away. Thankfully, we both fell asleep soon afterward.

The next day on Sunday morning, Brian took me to Forest Park. He said that his mom used to take him and his brother there when they were kids to explore the trails. Forest Park is a park in Queens with over 500 acres and not as popular as Central Park, Flushing Meadows Park or Prospect Park which is why I had never known of its existence. I was overawed of the beauties of Forest Park which had a running track, a golf course, a bandshell and over 10 miles of trails right here in Queens! We were like two kids in the park and spent all morning and part of the afternoon there without a worry in the world.

At nearly 3 p.m., we were both thirsty and hungry and Brian asked me where I wanted to eat, so I naturally said, "Have you ever been to Georgia Diner here on Queens Boulevard?" He shook his head no and agreed to give it a try. It was only a 10-minute drive and we got seated in a booth right away. I ordered my usual at this diner which was a bison burger with extra lettuce tomatoes and onions and a side salad and Brian ordered a grilled chicken platter with rice and a side order of pita bread and hummus. "Thank you for showing me Forest Park Raggie! I really needed that. I hope last night didn't spook you too much with my nightmare. I tried to give you the heads up. I have been having those nightmares for a long time now. They are so real and it feels like something is after me. I have a counselor named Father Joe who I have told, but I don't think he believes me," I said.

Brian got up from his side of the booth and sat on my side right next to me and held my arm and said, "I believe you Scooby and all I can tell you is that I will be there to protect you anytime I can. If there is anything I can do to help just say the word. I am not going anywhere." I gave Brian a kiss on his cheek and touched his ears softly. "You know my dad used to rub my ears like that when I was a baby to help me fall asleep," he said. I noticed something reflecting the light on the edges of his ears then I realized he had the cutest tiny little fuzzy hairs sticking out that reminded me of my Teddy Bear. In Spanish, "Osito" is the name for Teddy Bear and I shared the whole story about my Teddy Bear and how my father threw it away.

That would be another name I would call Brian- Osito. We had talked for few hours at the diner until it was nearly dark outside. We got back to his place to shower and to get ready for an early morning bootcamp and work. It did not take much for me to fall into a deep sleep in Brian's arms. Tonight, I did not have any nightmares. Before the alarm sounded, I opened my eyes at 3:30 a.m. and went to the bathroom, changed and packed my bag for my day.

I came back and sat next to Brian and watched him sleep so peacefully. I rubbed his ears and kissed him on his forehead and said, "Good morning Raggie. It's 4 a.m. and we need to leave to bootcamp soon." Brian hugged me tight and got up quickly to get ready.

I had recently completed my certification as a personal, group and outdoor instructor and we were teaching the NYC-Platoon Fitness Bootcamp three times a week on Monday, Wednesday and Thursday at 5:30 a.m. and I felt myself improve as a person and as an instructor. I was grateful for Brian's encouragement.

As we got close to Central Park, we saw signs of "No Parking on Friday, Saturday and Sunday for the NYC Triathlon". The NYC Triathlon is an iconic event since 2001 featuring an Olympic Distance Triathlon starting with a 1.5-kilometer swim in the Hudson River, a 40-kilometer bike ride on the West Side Highway and finishing with a 10-kilometer run from the West Side Highway to Central Park.

"Have you ever done a Triathlon Raggie?" I asked enthusiastically. "No, but I would love to. Have you Scooby?" he asked. I hesitated momentarily, but replied, "I don't know how to swim. My father threw me in a lake when I was a child and I nearly drowned. I have been afraid of going into the deep waters ever since, but I would love to participate in a Triathlon someday." As he finished parking the car, he turned to me and said, "Let's do a Triathlon then! We can plan it out properly. It is only June, but I know there is a triathlon in Harriman State Park in September and we can get you ready with lessons while we also train for the Chicago Marathon this October."

I was thankful. I needed this change. I needed the break from boxing, so this was perfect. "Let's do it Raggie. We will talk some more, but I am excited!" I said as we got out and started jogging to meet the group. It was my turn to teach, so I took the class to the beach volleyball courts. After our warm-up jog and stretch, I sent the class on 3 timed laps of the sheep meadow which was a beautiful 15-acre lawn and the perimeter was about 1.25 miles each lap. Then I had them do different plyometric drills inside the sand-filled volleyball courts ranging from frog jumps, short sprints, backwards running and side shuffles. By the end of the work out, everyone was sandy, sweaty and tired which to me meant, a great class!

As soon as the class was over and everyone left, Brian picked me up and hugged me tight. I got lost kissing him against a tree by the volleyball courts. It was a barking dog that startled both of us. "Great class Scooby! You are such an awesome instructor. I will pick you up at the office around 6 p.m.?" I remembered that I had a session with Father Joe today, so I replied, "I have a session with my counselor Father Joe at 5 p.m., but I should be done by 6 p.m. He is right on St. Francis of Assisi church on 32nd Street near Madison Square Garden. I would love to introduce you to him." Brian did not hesitate and said, "Deal! I will pick you up right at 6 p.m. and say hello to Father Joe. Have a great day at work Scooby!"

I started jogging to the office and was inspired to run a few laps of the reservoir to help get any nervous energy out. It was my sister's first day of work at the New York Road Runners and with the new management staff, I felt stressed and the 5-mile run was exactly what I needed. After a quick shower, I started working on the logistics to the next event I was managing which was one of the Marathon Long Training Runs taking place in a couple of weeks where runners who were preparing for a Fall Marathon had the choice of completing anywhere between 1 to 4 loops (6 miles, 12 miles, 18 miles or 24 miles) of Central Park. Although it was not a race, the NYRR provided the water stations, Gatorade, energy gels, porta john's, course signage, timing and support, so it required logistical management as it also attracted over 3,500 participants.

I was so focused on my work that I barely noticed the hours go by until my stomach started rumbling to let me know that it was past lunch time, so I decided to take a walk and find something to eat. When I went downstairs, I saw my sister answering the phones at the front desk. "Hey! How is it going?" I asked as she finished her call. "Are you going to lunch? I am ready to go too! I can meet you outside down the block if you want. I nodded my head and waited for her down the block away from the building. I was not expecting to go out with her on her first day, so this was a nice treat.

When I finally saw my sister, I was jumping up and down like a puppy. "How is your first day going?" I asked. "Calm down... It's going well. I was answering phones for the morning and this afternoon, Lynn will show me procedures on the building, Library and other stuff. So far so good. My co-workers are interesting to say the least, so I will just have to make the best out of it, but I am thankful for this job," replied my sister.

We walked a few blocks to a small eatery called Chirping Chicken that served lunch portions of rotisserie chicken with your choice of salad, potatoes or rice. I got my sister all caught up with my weekend with Brian. "He has been wonderful to me! I just feel awkward staying in his bedroom, but at least it will be for just a few more days. How is everything looking for your move on Saturday?" I asked. "Everything is all set and I can actually move in on Friday if I want. The daycare will be conveniently in Rego Park, so I will just get all of our things and take a cab to the new place after work on Friday and move right in since the place is already mostly furnished," she replied.

Although I was happy for my sister getting a place of her own, I couldn't help think of my mother. Now, she would finally be by herself. Growing up, she always used to say on a daily basis, "I'd rather be by myself in peace" and now she would get her desire. There was no one left. All of my sisters had left the house and had kids of their own. I always wondered what my mother would do if she saw me. Would she say anything to me? Would she hug me? I knew one day I had to put all my feelings aside and just go see her, but I was not in a good place mentally to even think about that now. I had too much pain, resentment and confusion and I had to work through those emotions first.

We finished our lunch and headed back to the office. It was nice to have company for lunch for a change. I have done so many things alone for most of my life that I just got used to it. I usually spent my lunch hour running, walking or working right through lunch. I finished out the remainder of my work day and headed right back out to see Father Joe. I had so much to tell him that when he saw me, he knew it right away. "Hello Patricia! I am very glad to see you. I have been wondering how you were," said Father Joe.

I didn't know where to begin, but started with, "So much has happened in such little time Father Joe! The man where I lived stole my Golden Gloves, so I leave that house immediately. He made up some story that someone had broken in, but nothing in his house was stolen. He was mad that I rejected him and got back at me by stealing something so precious to me. I stayed one night at the office and Brian has let me stay at his place for the past few nights, but I will be moving in with my sister this Saturday temporarily until I find my own place."

"Wow Patricia! That is a lot! It seems like you are handling it well though, so I am happy to see that. How do you feel about staying with Brian and moving in with your sister?" asked Father Joe. "Well, Father Joe, throughout my life, I've always felt like I was going from one crisis to another, but prayer has always helped me stay strong and in the end, all these experiences are helping me become the person God intended me to be. I have been independently living on my own since I was 15 years old, so all this is very nerve-racking to me, but I am doing the best that I can. Brian has been a blessing and helped me so much. He is going to pick me up here at 6 p.m.," I said.

We spoke non-stop until time was up. We discussed so much in what seemed much more than an hour. We even touched on Coach. For now, I was just taking a break from boxing and focusing on my first Triathlon, the Chicago Marathon and discovering new things until I was ready to box again if ever. When we went downstairs, Brian was sitting in the waiting area and came over to shake Father Joe's hand. "Nice to meet you, Father Joe. Patricia speaks very highly of you," said Brian. Father Joe looked at Brian as if he was inspecting him, but then smiled and said, "Likewise Brian. Very good to meet you. Have a safe drive home."

Brian put his hand around my waist and we walked over to his car and before he opened the passenger door, I gave him a big hug. I had missed him throughout the day and was really happy to see him. He hugged me back tightly and opened the car door.

We spoke about our day on the ride to his place and picked up one of the most delicious thin crust pizzas I had ever tasted. It was from a place called Dee's Wood Fired Pizza Kitchen. They had been serving Forest Hills since 1993 and are considered one of the best pizzerias in Queens. Brian rarely cooked and usually picked up dinner somewhere. He always joked that his mom was a terrible cook which made me laugh because I was not any better. We had our pizzas while we watched some television and then made our way to bed, but tonight was different.

I brushed my teeth and changed into my pajamas and Brian took a shower and he was sharing how he had already signed us both up for the Harriman Triathlon in the Fall and purchased airline tickets for Chicago as well. And we would start our swimming lessons this Wednesday after work in midtown with a swim coach. I was not sure if I was dreaming or what! I gave him a super tight hug and we started kissing very passionately and the moment turned into the most intimate experience of my life. Although Brian was a very attractive guy, I had fallen in love with his heart, compassion and generosity.

I didn't ask for anything, yet he encouraged me to become a fitness instructor, helped me at my work events, and now was helping me learn to swim and registered me for my 1st Triathlon and to run the Chicago Marathon with him among other incredibly detailed gestures. That night was a night I would never forget. For the first time in my life, I would sleep without any clothes on and in his embrace for a night I wished would never end.

We did not have to teach bootcamp the next morning, so we were able to sleep in a bit. I woke up to a delicious smell of breakfast and of Brian looking over me. "Good morning Raggie! Are you cooking?" I asked in disbelief. Brian had a smirk and replied, "Good morning, Pretty Woman…Yep! I thought I would try to make you some coffee, eggs and toast before we drive in to the city." Brian knew that "Pretty Woman" was one of my favorite movies and for that moment, I felt special. It was nice to feel that someone put in that type of effort.

I took a shower and got changed and looked forward to eating my breakfast. I felt myself glowing from the inside out. I did not want the feeling to ever go away. Breakfast was great, but the best part was that Brian made it. Brian held me hand as he drove me into work. When we got to the office and he opened the door, he whispered in my ear, "Have a great day Scooby. I will pick you up later. I love you." I did not hesitate to say, "I love you Raggie".

Brian would never know the impact of what he has just said to me. It was the first time in my life anyone had said "I love you" to me and it was the first time I said it as well. Growing up, I never heard those words from anyone in my family. It was not part of their vocabulary. Throughout my life, I would hear people say it to each other and I would get sad inside wondering if I would ever hear it. In church, I would hear the Pastor say that "God loves us" and I would find comfort in that, but today those words were finally said to me and it meant the world to me.

Today, I was not the first one in the office for a change and everyone I encountered had to comment on my glowing face and flowers on my desk! I did feel myself glowing but not for the reasons many people would think. For the first time in my life, I felt loved through the thoughtful details, care and words. But then I remembered my mother's words about men, "Love does not last. He will change. They all do when they get bored."

By lunch time, my glow had turned into anxiety, so I went out for a run on the bridle path and trails in Central Park. At the end of my run, I looked into the Reservoir and prayed. I remembered telling Brian how important faith was to me and asking him about his beliefs. His father, Danny was Jewish and his mom, Pam was Catholic, however, he and his brother were raised in the Judaism religion which was important to his father. They celebrated both holidays and Brian practiced more out of respect for his father, but he was not a true believer of anything. He told me that he respected my religion and beliefs.

Brian picked me up from the office, we picked up sushi for dinner and had another beautiful evening. The week was going by fast and soon our short time living together would come to an end. Brian and I got along very well because it seemed like we enjoyed many of the same things. We both were not good at cooking and liked eating out, we loved watching movies and working out. However, I would learn further down in life that all those qualities were good but not the essence of a long-lasting relationship.

After work, I took the train to mid-town and met Brian at an expensive looking high-rise apartment building. Our swimming lesson would be in an indoor pool on the roof. The instructor, Nicholas who was originally from Greece, met us in front and took us up and showed us the changing area. Brian gave me a kiss on the lips and we went to our separate locker rooms to change. As I changed into my bathing suit, I felt my legs trembling. Brian knew how to swim and was not afraid of the water at all, but he had never competed in a Triathlon and wanted to better his swimming techniques.

Nicholas was already waiting for us in the pool and had us sit on the edge of the pool and was asking us about our swimming experience. I said, "I have zero experience swimming. I almost drowned as a kid and developed fear of the water from the incident, so please be patient with me." He nodded and said, "Okay, thank you. Let me see what you got. Please, both of you put your goggles on and just swim to the other end of the pool."

Brian went first and I was impressed. He needed some work with learning how to take breaths in after every 2-3 strokes and better his stroke efficiency, but he certainly was on a different level than I was. I took a deep breath and tried to swim, but the minute I put my face in the water, I started to hyperventilate. I had never experienced that type of anxiety. I hated to repeat the story of how my father had thrown me in the water when I was a kid and passed out in the water. "Okay, okay, don't worry my dear Patricia, please hold my hand and watch me first and try to do the same thing. We can do together, "said Nicholas. He fully immersed under water and blew bubbles for a few seconds and came back up a few times.

When it was my turn, the hyperventilating and crying started. Brian came over and held my hand and Nicholas held my other hand. At the count of 3, all three of us would go down and blow bubbles for 5 seconds and come back up. We did that for a full hour until I was able to do it on my own and by the end of the hour, I was able to blow bubbles underwater without crying or hyperventilating for 10 seconds. After we changed back into our clothes, Nicholas scheduled us separately on different days as we clearly had different needs.

"I am proud of you Scooby. It takes a lot of courage to get in the water after what you went through as a kid," said Brian. I was embarrassed and said, "I am so sorry Raggie! I had no idea that I would react this way. I have never hyperventilated nor felt like that. Thank you for helping calm me down and showing me how to blow bubbles." The blowing bubbles would become something I did each and every time I got in the water no matter what. It would help get me mentally and physically ready before any swim.

As we drove to Queens, I realized that tomorrow would be our last day together as my sister would now be moving in on Friday after work. "Hey Raggie, I just wanted to thank you again for letting me stay with you all these days. You saved my back from sleeping in the office! Haha! My sister is actually moving in this Friday after work instead of Saturday, so I just want to be there and help her," I said. Brian calmly replied, "Oh, really? Well, it has been my pleasure and there is no rush at all. Whatever you need, I am here for you. I can help if you need, just let me know Scooby."

I was not sure if I was blinded by the love I felt for him, but I could not find any fault in Brian. I got used to sleeping, eating, and working out together and felt incredibly close to him, so when Friday came, I felt very sad to the point of tears when he dropped me off at work with all my things. "Are you okay Scooby?" asked Brian as I was noticeably quiet on the ride in. "Aren't you a little sad Raggie that I am not staying with you anymore?" I asked. When Brian wanted to reassure me of anything, he grabbed my hands as a sign of his sincerity.

So that is what he did and said, "I know you have been through a lot and I just want you to do what you think is best. I am not going anywhere and I am not sad because we will be together and you can spend the night in my place any time you want." We kissed goodbye and I took my duffle bag into the office.

On this day, I felt my insecurities and demons ever so present, haunting me. Brian had a healthy childhood and was loved by his entire family, so his reaction was normal. I on the other hand did not understand at the moment why I felt abandoned and blue. I felt even worse when he called me at lunch time and said he was going to spend time with his friends on the weekend playing basketball and they were going to go out for drinks in the evening. My heart felt completely broken, so I called Father Joe urgently. He told me that I needed to calm down and trust Brian. He repeated a few times, "Let Go, Let God."

That would be a phrase I remembered and told myself throughout my life when things were out of my control and I had to trust in my higher power. I helped my sister move in that Friday and slept on the couch. I didn't feel good about that at all, but would need to hang tight until I found my own place. When I finally saw Brian again that Monday for Bootcamp, I confided in him how heartbroken I was of knowing he was out with his friends and my fear of him being unfaithful. Once again, he grabbed my hand and said, "Scooby, I love you. I am not going to do anything to lose you. I am sorry you felt that way about me going out for drinks with my friends. My friends are important and I love playing basketball, but I understand about the drinking part at a bar. I will try to avoid places like that from now on. This weekend we have dinner and Scrabble with my parents, brother and his girlfriend, okay?"

I never had an issue about him spending time with his friends, it was the bar/drinking that made me uneasy. I knew he was right for the most part and felt silly for telling him how I felt, but that nagging insecurity did not want to leave me. I looked at the sky and nodded, "I trust you Brian and I can't wait to get together with your family this weekend," I said and then I kissed him goodbye.

Even until the present moment as I write this book, I have never been dancing to any clubs and going out for drinks with friends was something I never did nor was it my desire to do so. I felt like I was an alien and not from this world at times, but I did come to realize that is the norm and the way people spend time socializing.

Midweek after work, I went for my swimming lesson with Nicholas. I changed, stretched and slowly got into the pool which was at a perfect room temperature. Nicholas came over and held my hands and said,

"Okay Patrizia, you know what to do…I will be with you this time, but you will do this part by yourself each time before you start your swimming drills or any activity in the water. Remember, this is your chance to relax and get mentally ready for the water." One, two, three…and down under I went blowing bubbles. The first round, I came up gasping for air after 3 seconds and hyperventilating a bit, but I went back down and it got much better after the 5th round. I did this for about 10 rounds. Then Nicholas gave me a swimming board and I did kicking drills up and down the pool for another 10 rounds. I also used fins and swimming paddles on this day. I was wiped out after this lesson, but happy. Anytime I was this tired, I felt accomplished and as if I had earned my right to a restful sleep.

I loved spending time with my sister and my niece, but I also missed my privacy and my alone time. I was so used to being independent and having my space to come home to after a long day, but I tried to make the best out of the situation since it would be temporary. When I got to my sister's apartment, she saved dinner for me which was awesome. Having a home cooked meal warmed my soul in many ways. It was one of the good memories I had of my mother.

Growing up, we were considered just below middle class. We rarely ate out and my mother was a great cook when it wasn't the dreaded soup. My sister learned from the best and I never would say no to anything she cooked. While we ate dinner, we talked about my upcoming Triathlon and Chicago Marathon events. My sister casually mentioned that she wanted to get healthier and lose a few pounds.

Before she even finished her thoughts, I interrupted and said, "You need to have a goal and use that as an incentive to kick you out of bed to work out. I can help you get in shape and you can even come to my boot camp class and we can run at lunch together if you want."

My sister could see how excited I was and she asked, "What kind of incentive? Like an event or something?" My eyes sparkled and I smiled and replied, "How about the New York City Marathon? Since you are staff, you can still get in and this is the perfect time to start training."

My sister is a couple of inches shorter than me and was about 20 pounds over what she should ideally be, but more importantly, I wanted her to experience something beyond special that would change her life the way it did for me.

She agreed and would allow me to help train and guide her for the next 16 weeks. I would put all my knowledge and experience as a runner, instructor and athlete. My plan was for her to work out in boot camp class 1-2 times a week, run at lunch time 2 times a week and get her long runs in on the weekends. Brian called before I went to sleep and I was able to share the details about my swimming lesson and the news about my sister. He was happy for us and agreed to pick us up for bootcamp the next morning. I missed him and was looking forward to seeing him.

The alarm sounded at 4:15 a.m., but I was already up and getting ready. The alarm was more for my sister who was not used to getting up so early. As I made a cup of coffee waiting for my sister, I remembered how much I pleaded with my sisters to run with me when we were younger. I offered to do their chores and even give them part of my small allowance. Anything to not run alone in the dark lonely streets, but no matter how much I begged, no one ever ran with me.

A half hour later, Brian honked the horn to let us know he was waiting. I ran to the car while my sister dropped my niece at the neighbor's apartment. We figured that part out over the weekend. The neighbor was a single mom as well and worked in the evenings, so she got along well with my sister almost immediately. They would exchange favors like that consistently throughout the next few years.

When I saw Brian, I gave him the biggest hug! It felt as if I had not seen him in years. "So, good to see you too Scooby! Are you ok?" he said as he hugged me back tightly. My eyes involuntarily teared up and I nodded my head and replied, "I just missed you Raggie, that's all." Then, my sister got in the car and we took off. Brian liked my sister and niece and admired her for everything she did as a single mom, but that didn't stop him from teasing her. They treated each other like brother and sister and poked at each other at any opportunity they had.

It was my turn to teach today and we began with a 2-mile jog to another amazing spot in Central Park called the Obelisk or Cleopatra's Needle. The Obelisk was created around 1425 BCE in Heliopolis, Egypt. It is located on a rocky hill known as Greywacke Knoll, across from the Metropolitan Museum of Art. Central Park is the third location for this 220-ton monolith, a single piece of stone carved out of granite. In the 1870's, the Egyptian government gave one obelisk to England, and the second obelisk was gifted to the United States. It was installed in Central Park in January 1881.

After our 2-mile warm-up, I had the class do a series of dynamic stretching and then right into our drills that included 3 rounds of 10 different plyometric and calisthenic exercises ranging from stair jumps, star jacks, satan lunges, running back wards, push-ups, dips, bear crawls, buddy carries, squats and planks. We ended class with another 2-mile cool down on the trails followed by static stretching. It was a true full body and cardio work out and judging by their sweaty quiet faces, my mission for today was accomplished.

"Whoa! What a class man! I'm already sore!" said my sister. I burst out laughing from how her annunciation of every word in that statement. Brian laughed as well and agreed with her. "Good! That means I am doing my job. I need you to get your butt out here every week at least 1-2 times to get you prepared for your marathon," I replied. Brian offered to drive her to the fastest train stop so she could go home feed my niece, shower, drop my niece at daycare and get to work.

Platoon Fitness had become more than just a bootcamp class. The NYC program had about 80 members. Half of those members were regulars who attended every class rain or shine. I evolved from being a student to becoming an instructor and it also allowed me to grow as a person in many ways. I felt so much gratitude as I was doing my own run before work. As I ran my laps around the reservoir, I also thought about my mother. I thought of her often.

With the weekend now approaching, I told my sister that I had weekend plans with Brian and was not sure if I would sleep in her apartment.

My sister embraced the weekends to spend quality time with my niece, do her house chores, visit my mother and get her long runs in, so I was glad to not be in the way. I slept at Brian's place from Friday thru Sunday.

On Saturday, he drove us to a park in New Jersey called Wawayanda State Park which has over 60-miles of trails and about 20 of those miles is a section of the popular Appalachian Trail. We ran 16 miles on the gorgeous, but hilly trails. We took a dip in the lake afterwards and laid out on the sand for a much-needed nap. We were starving and, on the drive, back, we stopped at the Cheesecake Factory for dinner. I could not think of a more perfect day than this and again wondered if he would change one day.

The next day on Sunday, we took a hot yoga class together and Brian suffered dearly, but the deep stretches was exactly what he needed for his achy knees. As a teenager, he had a torn meniscus injury from basketball and had a few other injuries that at times came back as nagging aches. I could see his discomfort, but for some reason, he did not voice any of them to me.

On the drive back to his place, we got caught in this incredible traffic because of a motor vehicle accident. It was the first time I saw Brian grind his teeth and it frightened me. "Are you okay Raggie?" I asked. "I really hate this traffic and my knee is bothering me, so I am sorry if I seem upset Scoob," he replied. This was a new side of Brian I had never experienced before and I wasn't sure what to do. I froze and became noticeably quiet. I wanted to give him space but we were meeting his family in a couple of hours and needed to get ready, so having him drop me off at my sister's place wasn't much of an option. At one point, I could see the veins on the side of his neck bulging when the traffic didn't move, but suddenly it opened up and I breathed a sigh of relief. I needed to talk to Father Joe about this.

We got back to his place with just an hour to get ready, but I knew I needed to say something. "Hey Raggie, I know the traffic was stressful for you and your knee is hurting you, so I don't mind if you want to reschedule dinner and visiting with your family. I can always go home to my sister and give you some room to breathe," I said. Brian looked serious and replied, "I love you, Patricia. I am sorry I was angry. It is something I need to work on, but I am fine now and would love if we just forget about it and go have a nice dinner with my family." I nodded and went to take a shower and ready quickly.

Thankfully, there was no traffic to get to his parent's home. It was good to see Pam again and I gave her a big hug when I saw her. Brian's brother Jason was already there with his girlfriend Jessica. Apparently, the relationship with her was on the serious side since he rarely brought any of his girlfriends home to meet his parents. Jessica was a tall slim young woman in her early 20's with dirty blonde hair who had recently graduated college. Her parents would be considered high class as her father was an executive at a well-known toy company, so of course, her education was fully financed by her parents. However, that was not what I found annoying about her.

Although Jessica had graduated college, she had no idea what she wanted to do and was considering furthering her education to obtain a Master's Degree in Teaching, but she would take a break while she made up her mind. She was not employed and lived at home with her parents. She spoke with an entitlement demeanor and her whole attitude rubbed me the wrong way, but I did my very best to not show how I felt about her.

Attending college and having your parents pay for it was a privilege in my eyes and so many people like her took it for granted. I resented that and it was something I would struggle to comprehend and accept. Danny had ordered Persian food for all of us. I helped Pam and Danny bring out the plates and cups and helped set the table. I didn't know how much I would like Persian food. I dug into the Kebab Koobideh which was ground beef as well as the rice while Jessica played around with the rice on her plate. I really enjoyed trying out this new food. We sat around talking for about an hour and then Pam wanted all of us to play Scrabble. It would be Pam, Brian, myself and Jason and Jessica would play as a team.

We played 3 rounds and it was going well until I was winning the last round and Jason was getting upset. He was very competitive with Brian, but I just wasn't sure why he was getting upset that I was winning a silly game of Scrabble. I noticed the tension on Jason's face as Brian told his parents of our plans to run the Chicago Marathon together and how we were training for our first Triathlon and of how well teaching for Platoon Fitness was going for us. I was too naïve at the time to realize that his own brother was jealous, but it was the sad reality.

I would also realize that Brian would give his life to defend his brother, father and family before anything or anyone else and they could do no wrong even if they did. I tried to take in the good and on the drive back asked Brian to drop me off at my sister's place which made Brian worried. He said, "Anything you want Scooby, but is everything okay? I thought you could spend the night at my place so you would teach tomorrow." I was not happy about having to lie, but felt I had no choice and replied, "Thank you Raggie, but I forgot that I have an early meeting that I have to prepare for. I did not get to finish my work on Friday and I have to be at the office extra early, so I am sorry that I just remembered. I can teach on Wednesday instead if that's okay with you."

I just wanted to relax and sleep this day away, so that's what I did. The next day, I ran with my sister at lunch time and told her all about Jason, Jessica and all the nonsense from the day before with his road rage. She thought that I should speak with Brian and tell him my thoughts, but I would decide after my session with Father Joe later that day. Father Joe would not think too much of what I told him. He thought I was overreacting and should calm down and give Brian and his family the benefit of the doubt even though it was also he who told me to always rely on my God-given instincts.

In spite of the challenges, the weeks and months went by and Brian and I did grow closer. I was staying over his place half of the week and the other half at my sister's place and then one day after class, he said to me, "Scooby, I want to find a place for you and I to live together in. We practically already do anyway, so I think we should officially move in together once we find a nice place in Forest Hills. What do you think?" I did not know what to think. I was lost for words. He was right though and we spent so much time together, so it would make sense. This was a leap of faith that I needed to take, so I breathed deeply and said, "Let's do it Raggie! I think we make a great team, so moving in together does make sense." He grabbed me and hugged me extra tight.

We were both task oriented, so that weekend, we got to work on finding an apartment right away. We must have gone to over a dozen open houses, but we found one co-op apartment in Forest Hills that we both really liked. It was only one block away from his current apartment, so the neighborhood was exactly where we felt the most comfortable and we placed a bid. Brian had to go through extensive approval by the board and banks, but within a month we were accepted and planned to move in soon after.

The weekend before we were planning on moving in together, we were preparing to participate in our first triathlon. I had never missed a swimming session in the last 3 months, my running and biking were as good as it could be, so I wasn't sure why I felt so nervous. We woke up at 4 a.m. and were out in the car with our gear and bikes by 4:45 a.m. Harriman was a 75-minute drive and the start was at 7 a.m., so it would give us just enough time to collect our race numbers and set-up our bikes at the transition area. "Are you nervous Raggie?" I asked because I could not tell. Although Brian was a genuinely kind soul, I had a difficult time sometimes reading his emotions.

He didn't have any issues swimming, biking or running, so I guess he really didn't have anything to be nervous about and I was just projecting my feelings on to him. "No Scooby...I am excited for both of us though. You are one of the strongest people I know, so you will be fine, he replied as we made our way to the registration site.

The men's wave would go out first and the women's wave would start 15 minutes after. We warmed up and Brian headed out to Sebago

Lake with the rest of the men's field. I lost sight of Brian in the sea of swimming caps and then the gun went off. There was furious splashing everywhere as they made their way around the big orange buoys to complete the 800-meter swim portion that had a 30-minute cut-off time. I cheered on Brian as he exited the lake and went into the transition center for the bike portion. He looked as cool as a cucumber while my heart was about to come out of my chest as I made my way into the water.

I walked into the lake and it seemed like a good idea at the time to be right in the center. For the first time in my life though, I felt an intense pressure on my chest and then the gun went off! I didn't have time to blow any bubbles to calm down and stuck my face in the dark water where I could not even see my hands nor the bottom of the lake. Elbows were bumping into me and hands were grabbing at my feet. My head came right back up and I couldn't breathe. I was gasping for air and little did I know that I was experiencing a panic attack for the very first time.

A young lifeguard on a kayak made his way to me and yelled, "Are you okay? Do you need to be rescued?" I grabbed on to the side of the kayak momentarily to catch my breath and said, "No, I am okay. I am sorry...this is my first triathlon." I could see the look of concern on the lifeguard's face, but he then said, "If you are okay then you have to let go of the kayak and start swimming before you get disqualified and remember you need to exit the water in under 30-minnutes."

That was all I needed to hear which lit a fire under my butt to get moving. I let go of the kayak and got on my back and started swimming using the backstroke and alternated with a side stroke, doggie paddle and new strokes I invented along the way as long as my face was not in the water. Not being able to see what was below me freaked me out, but the fear of failure was even greater. I was dead last exiting the water in 29:30 with 30 seconds to spare and ran into the transition area to prepare for the bike portion.

I felt my legs shaking as I put on my socks and bike shoes. I strapped on my helmet and jumped on my bike with a mission of making up time. Being the last woman out of the water fueled me to crank my pedals and give it everything I had. I passed over half of the women's field on the steep hills. My legs felt heavy after the 12-mile bike as I ran into the transition area to drop my bike, change shoes and take some water before the final portion which would be a 5k run. I felt as if my ankles had weights on them as I ran quickly out of the transition area, but then I saw that many athletes had the same heavy stride. Some were even limping and some were walking. I was not the only one feeling smoked, so I just needed to push through it. I pushed the pace and tried to put everything I was feeling aside. My breathing was fine, but it was my muscles, joints and back that I was afraid would go into a spasm.

"Come on Scoob! Finish Strong!" I heard as I was approaching the finish line. Brian picked me up and hugged me as I crossed the finish line of my first triathlon. "Congratulations Scooby!" said Brian. "You Too Raggie! Congratulations! You looked so good coming out of the water!" I replied. I finished in the top 5 women in my age group division and top 25 female overall. Considering that I almost got disqualified, was dead last out of the water and had a panic attack, I was so grateful to have completed this triathlon and not be paralyzed by the fear.

This triathlon was symbolic in so many ways. I realized that if I don't face my fears, I will never live my dreams. Just like my past, it would be a process and I had to keep at it until the fear would not be as strong. I would go on to complete over 2 dozen triathlons throughout my life ranging from Sprint, Olympic and up to a Half Ironman. Presently, one of my goals still is complete a full Ironman one day.

Brian was happy and we hung out for a while talking about our experience and then we went to the Cheesecake Factory to celebrate with a good meal. I saw an event flyer for a Team Obstacle Course Trail Race called "The High Rock Challenge" in Staten Island in a few weeks. "Hey Raggie, why don't we enter this team obstacle course trail race?" I asked as we waited for our food. I added, "We can enter the coed team division and call ourselves The Dream Team or something." I could see that Brian was hesitant, but he replied, "We can try Scoob, but my knees have been aching and I don't want you to get your hopes up of winning or placing in the coed division. I just want us to have fun."

"YES! We will have fun but I know we can do really well too Raggie!" I said. What Brian did not understand was that pushing past my comfort zone was a necessity and the need to feel cleansed while overcoming the fears. I had hoped he felt the same way and we could keep experiencing these events together. I thought the High Rock Challenge would also be a great and final tune-up before the Chicago Marathon.

As the server brought out our chicken teriyaki over steamed white rice, it crossed my mind that at this time next week, we will be living together and it prompted me to ask, "Raggie are you nervous about next week when we move in together?" Brian did not hesitate and said, "No Scoob...So far, we get along really well and we like many of the same things and we have been able to get past silly disagreements, so we have to take the next step and see how we do."

I wished he was this calm when it came to the road rage situation, but I had to take in the good with the bad and agreed with him. I had decided to take off that Friday from work to get a head start on the move while Brian was at the office. My sister was supportive of my move in with Brian. I cried in silence as I packed my small possessions from her apartment and then took a cab to the new apartment with all my belongings. The new place in Forest Hills was a bright and spacious 2-bedroom apartment with a marbled floor kitchen, the living room and bathroom had wood floors on the 3rd floor of a 6-story pre-war building complex. It would be the nicest place I had ever lived in.

I got to work right away and started dusting, sweeping and mopping the entire apartment. Brian sent one of his warehouse workers named Sam, who was a big African American middle-aged man with a long white beard who he considered to be one of his best and strongest employees. Sam wasn't big on conversations. He just wanted to get the work done. Since Brian's old apartment was only a block away, we loaded all of the pre-packed boxes on a dolly and hand trucks and wheeled everything over. It took us the entire morning to complete the move.

Then the new sofa and dining room table were delivered while Sam assembled the bedroom furniture. Everything was in place by the time Brian came home around 6:30 p.m. "Wow Scoob! I can't believe you guys did all this today! There is nothing for me to do except take you for a nice dinner at Dee's!" I was exhausted, but I wanted everything to be exactly like this. I took a quick shower in our new apartment and we headed out to Dee's.

The owners of Dee's knew Brian not only because he was a regular customer, but he also ordered the same thing all the time which was a large cheese pizza with hummus and I ordered the tri-colored grilled chicken salad with hummus. Our first night and week in the new apartment could not be more perfect. His family and friends joked often that we were "tied to the hips", but I didn't see anything wrong with that. We trained together, we worked for Platoon Fitness together and we lived together. Brian was my best friend, lover and partner. I prayed daily that he wouldn't get tired of it either.

One day after work, I came home to a delivery of boxes. The boxes contained trail sneakers, leggings, swim wear, jackets, hats and all these wonderful accessories in my size and in all my favorite colors. "Raggie! Oh My Gosh! Thank you! Is it our anniversary or something? What is the special occasion?" I asked. Brian had a funny smirk and replied, "I love bargains and my favorite online store, Sierra Trading Post had a big warehouse sale for the upcoming Labor Day Holiday. I know you needed some gear and I saw a big sale on your sizes so I got them for you."

These selfless acts are what made me fall deeply in love with Brian. I didn't own any expensive brands or quality gear, so it was very appreciative. Growing up at home, everything was so expensive for my mother to buy all 4 of us, so I usually got my older sister's clothes that she had outgrown or we would wear our shoes until there were visible holes in them. I did not remember anyone in my life ever buying me clothes and shoes other than myself and mother, so it was an emotional moment for me that I knew Brian wouldn't understand.

I brought myself back to the present moment and hugged Brian tightly trying to express my gratitude. All the gear would come in handy since we spent so much time outdoors and it was soon time for the High Rock Challenge Trail Obstacle Race event and the Chicago Marathon soon. I knew wearing brand new shoes for a competition was not the best idea, but I was so happy about my gifts that I took the risk. I had to wear my new trail shoes for our first Team competition together! "Good morning Raggie! I got you a juice for breakfast and packed your extra clothes and sandals for after the race," I said as he was walking towards the bathroom. Brian was the first person I had ever heard of not liking coffee or hot drinks for that matter. In the stressful moments of being a first-time mom, Pam did not heat up his milk when he was a baby, so he never got used to or liked hot beverages.

It was a classic "Pam" story that made me laugh often. Brian enjoyed smoothies and protein drinks in the morning for breakfast instead of coffee. He sipped his Naked Juice in the car as we headed to Staten Island. The High Rock Challenge is a 10K trail race with obstacles and mystery challenges that must be completed as a two-member team. We saw many teams stretching and warming up as we arrived at the parking area of the campgrounds.

"Dream Team-Brian & Patricia, we got you... Number 119. You guys start in 30 minutes," said Matthew the Race Director. We pinned our numbers and started warming up immediately after. The co-ed teams were the biggest and most competitive field, so we had our work cut out for us, but I just had a good feeling as we lined up jumping up and down to avoid starting out too stiff. As the 10-second countdown began, Brian gave me a kiss on the lips and said, "Lets have fun Scoob, I love you" and off we went!

I wanted to sprint, but realized we are a team and needed to stay together, so I ran right next to Brian. "Take the lead Scoob and set the pace. I will follow you," yelled out Brian. I nodded and set an ambitiously fast pace right before we got to our first obstacle which had us in a kayak where we had to paddle across a lake before continuing our run on the trails. "Scoob, you paddle right and I paddle left!" yelled Brian.

"Got it Raggie!" I yelled back. We heard teams getting into arguments and even saw a couple fall out of their kayaks. We remained focused and kept going as hard as we could. We completed over a dozen obstacles and crossed the finish line in under 90 minutes. We hugged and kissed elated to have finished in one piece and smiling instead of fighting like so many.

We were filthy, muddy and sweaty, but happy. We sat down on the grass stretching and smiling as the cheers supporting the teams crossing the finish line continued before the awards ceremony. "I don't think we won anything Scoob, but we can stay if you really want," said Brian. I thought we were flawless and ran a very strong race. I knew in my heart we had to have placed in the top 3 in our division. "Well, Raggie, I would love to listen to the times of the winners so we know what to shoot for next year if that's okay with you," I replied.

The Race Director took the microphone and started thanking the spectators, sponsors and participants before he started announcing the top 3 teams in each division which was would first be Male, then Female and lastly, Coed. When he got to the Coed division, I squeezed Brian's hand and then we heard, "The winners for the Coed division are Number 119- the Dream Team, Brian & Patricia!" I jumped up as if I had just heard the winning numbers of the lottery! "I told you Raggie! We did it!" I whispered in Brian's ear. Brian was not expecting to hear our names at all, but we walked to the small platform and received our 1st place medals along with event embroidered running vests for each one of us.

My smile could not get any bigger. I had not felt that sense of satisfaction since the last time I had boxed. Our hard work paid off and I was proud of us. Later that day, we were scheduled to meet his parents for an early dinner and a movie. Jason and Jessica going to be there as well, so we skipped taking a nap on the grass and having lunch as we would barely make it on time. On the drive back, we talked and laughed about the event. One of the challenges was a 3-legged run for about 500 yards where we each had to have one leg tied to each other. With Brian being 6 feet tall to my 5 feet 4 inches height, it was comical.

It was good to come to our little home and take a shower in our bathroom. I did not want this day to end. It was surreal and wished we could just snuggle in bed. I did not mind seeing Pam, but had mixed feelings about everyone else. I laid in bed after my shower while Brian took a shower and I wondered how my mother was doing. I thought about her every day of my life. In spite of everything that happened, she gave me life and I prayed that one day I would see her again. I felt a tear roll down the side of my face and I quickly jumped out of bed and got dressed.

It was nearly 4 p.m. and we were so hungry and hurried out to meet everyone at Nick's pizzeria which was a 10-minute walk for us. Nick's pizzeria was another neighborhood favorite restaurant known for its delicious thin crust pizza, but they also served other signature dishes and salads. Everyone was already there when we arrived and Danny waived us over. Brian and I kissed everyone hello and I made my way to sit next to Pam who looked beautiful as usual.

I noticed that something was different about Pam. She was more hunched over and looked so weary. "Hi Pam, I missed you! How are you?" I asked. Pam looked at me with her big hazel green eyes and squeezed my hand and said, "I missed you too Sweetie. It's so good to see you! You make my Brian happy and that makes me happy. This fucking cancer doesn't want to leave me and is putting me through hell. I've lived a good life though." I squeezed her hand back and whispered in her ear, "I love you Pam. Don't worry about a thing."

Apart from Brian, Pam was only the second person I had ever said "I love you" to. I could see the pain in her eyes and wished I could take it away. Brian came around and gave us both a big hug and said jokingly, "What are my 2 favorite ladies talking so seriously about?" I admired Brian's family for being so affectionate. They constantly hugged and kissed each other. I remember Father Joe telling me that is supposed to be the way healthy families treated each other. My family sadly was toxic in every way, but it was never too late to learn a different way.

Then, Brian and I unintentionally took over the conversation. Pam and Danny wanted to know how the new apartment was going, so we updated them and also told them about our Triathlon debut and our High Rock Challenge win. I usually get overly excited when I talk about anything that I am passionate about. Pam and Danny were laughing hysterically when we told them about running with our legs tied and about my triathlon experience which sparked Jason's curiosity and he said, "I think Jessica and I could do really well in that team event. Jessica is a runner, so we will look into entering next year."

Somehow, I was not surprised by Jason's comment, but I also did not know what to say, so I just stayed quiet. We finished up our meals and walked a few blocks over to the Midway theatre which has been in Forest Hills since 1942. It is a cherished monument amongst locals. Danny had already purchased tickets to see "Panic Room" featuring actress Jodie Foster and actor Forest Whitaker. I enjoyed watching all types of movies, but always appreciated a good watching dramas and thrillers and this movie had it all.

We said out goodbyes after the movie and Brian and I walked home. "Hey Raggie, is Jason always that competitive with you?" I asked. Brian's face changed. He was not angry, but I could tell that he was bothered by my question. I did not pursue the question and instead said, "Never mind Raggie. I don't think I expressed myself correctly. I was just surprised to hear Jason say he was entering the competition with Jessica next year instead of congratulating us." Brian's face relaxed a bit and he replied, "Don't worry about it Scoob. Jason could be a bonehead sometimes, but he means well. The fact that he would even be interested in the same competition is a compliment to us."

That would become one of a plethora of times that Brian made excuses for his brother's behavior. I made the mistake of trying to forget about it. Things like that don't just go away.

As we neared the apartment, the breeze felt different. Summer had turned to Fall and next up was the Chicago Marathon in a few weeks and I wanted to focus on tapering and being ready for that. I was going to pace Brian to break 4 hours, so it was all about helping him accomplish his goal.

A few weeks after the Chicago Marathon, my sister would be running her first marathon ever. Her training had been challenging, but I knew she was going to get through it and I could not wait to see her cross the finish line! We took a day off from our jobs and left to Chicago on a Friday morning. It was our first trip together and I was looking forward to this new experience and visiting a new City! However, I sometimes felt that I overwhelmed Brian with how attached I was to him. It was just part of my personality and thinking that if I was going to love someone or something, I was going to do it 100%. We arrived in Chicago at nearly lunch time and went straight to the Expo Center to retrieve our race numbers and packets.

I loved Marathon Expos as they reminded me of the New York City Marathon. Although my first marathon experience was bittersweet, I cherished the memories and feelings. The experience always reminds me of the beauty of faith, strength and courage. Brian shared my excitement at the Expo and we were both like kids in a candy store looking and wanting everything. Without Brian looking, I picked up 2 pacing bracelets- one for 3:40 and one for 3:50.

Based on my last couple of Marathons where I ran a 3:29 at the New York City Marathon, I knew I could pace Brian to break 4 hours without a problem and the bracelets would help me evaluate where I needed to be. We left the Expo almost 4 hours later and we decided to have an early dinner at P.F. Chang's. We shared an order of their delicious chicken lettuce wraps appetizer and then had the Mongolian Beef with steamed rice dinner entrée. We were full and headed to the hotel which was a good mile and a half walk away and once we checked into the hotel, we took turns taking a shower and then laid out our clothes. The forecast was calling for very chilly conditions in the low 30 degrees

Fahrenheit range which was very cold for October standards and made me nervous. We snuggled closely and slept deeply for a full 7 hours before the alarm sounded at 5 a.m. We were both ready by 5:45 a.m. and went downstairs to grab a lite breakfast before we started walking the mile to the start at Grant Park.

We arrived to our corral at 7 a.m.- one hour before the start of our wave and took turns waiting on line for a porta john, then stretched and warmed up. It was so COLD at 25 degrees Fahrenheit, but I said a prayer while I was hugging Brian to stay warm. As the countdown began, he kissed me on the forehead and said, "I love you Scoob, thank you for being here. Let's have a good race." And then the gun went off! I was a little too excited, but I was also very cold and started way too fast. The first mile was at a 6:30/per mile pace and I could see that Brian was out of breath and he said, "Scoob, you are going too fast!" As soon as I saw the time, I slowed down and replied, "Sorry Raggie, I will slow down. I was just cold, but I am better now."

The course was the flattest course I had ever run, so I had no issues with the pacing. Chicago was a beautiful city, but I discovered on this day the reason they called it "The Windy City". I kept looking over at Brian to make sure he was okay and at my watch to ensure we were on pace. He was a trooper right through mile 20 and that is when his knee started to hurt. He took an Advil and I told him, "Raggie, I know its hard right now, but you have to push through. We are on pace to break 4 hours. You CAN do it!" My sweat had dried up and I was now getting the chills from the attacking wind. I could see the digital temperature displayed on scrolling billboard that read 29 degrees Fahrenheit.

Brian nodded in agreement and kept pushing right behind me for the final 6 miles. As we made our way back into Grant Park, the crowds were screaming in support and the music was blasting. In the final yards before the end, Brian stretched his long arms and grabbed my hand and we crossed the Finish Line together in 3:51! "YOU DID IT RAGGIE! You broke 4 hours!" I said while wiping tears away.

That would be one of many adventures we did together. We participated in over a dozen of marathons, triathlons and in Team Adventure Races, but we would come to realize when it was all said and done that there was only one real adventure worth accomplishing in which only a few succeed.

Chapter Eight - Round 8

The Wedding

"The giving of love is an education in itself." Eleanor Roosevelt

A year later after moving in together on a Monday Spring morning as we arrived into Central Park to teach the bootcamp class, the owners of Platoon Fitness, Todd and Mike were there already waiting for us. I was surprised, but didn't think too much of it. We communicated with them weekly via email to update them on the NYC group, so I was not sure why they just popped in from Philadelphia without mentioning anything. It was my turn to teach, so I took the opportunity to make the class extra challenging. Mike and I had a brother/sister, love/hate relationship, so I would enjoy seeing him struggle during the challenging exercise drills.

Brian requested that we do the cooldown back at the "Grinder" aka volleyball courts which I found odd, but I agreed. The class usually got into their rows at the grinder to get ready for drills and stretching, but today they formed a big circle around me. Brian came into the center of the circle and took my hand and kneeled down on one knee and said, "Patricia, will you do me the honor of marrying me?" while placing a princess cut diamond ring on my ring finger.

I would have never expected what had just occurred. My face was burning hot and I felt my eyes fill up with tears, "Yes Brian, I will marry you," I answered. The class started clapping and cheering for us as if we had just crossed the finish line of the New York City Marathon. Todd and Mike videotaped the whole thing and congratulated us. Now, all the weirdness of the day made sense. This is where Brian and I first met, so it was appropriate for him to share this very special moment in the place that brought us together. Many of the members had also become our close friends, so it was just perfect.

"Are you okay Scoob?" asked Brian as we were about to go our separate ways to go on with our work day. "Of course, Raggie! I am just still in a bit of a shock. You totally surprised me, but I am happy. Are you really ready to make this commitment to us?" Brian smiled and held my hands and said, "Scoob, I have partied and lived my life fully. I am ready. I know you are nervous, but we have lived together for the past year and we make a great team. It can only get better... My mom's time is very limited, so we have about 3 months to plan and make it happen. My mom will call you and you two can discuss everything, but if you get overwhelmed at any point, just let me know okay Scooby?"

I felt light-headed, but kept that to myself and kissed him good-bye. I walked. I didn't run back to the office. I was excited, but I wasn't sure why I wasn't happier and I called Father Joe right after I took a shower and settled at my desk. "Hi Father Joe. Could we change our Wednesday session to today at lunch time today? Brian proposed during our morning bootcamp class and I am feeling overwhelmed," I said. "Hello Patricia. Congratulations! Absolutely! Please come in at 1 p.m. today. See you later," he replied.

As I sipped my sugary black coffee, I was startled when my phone rang. I quickly answered it and it was Pam. "Congratulations Sweetie! Tell me all about this morning!" she said. This was the first time Pam ever called me at the office, but it was really good to hear her voice and I replied, "Hi Pam! It's always so good to hear your voice. Brian proposed at the end of bootcamp class today while the class circled around us!" Pam went on to tell me that she, Danny and Jason knew all about it before it happened. Danny actually wanted Brian to come in a horse into Central Park like a knight in a shining armor.

We had a conversation about costs and planning. She said that Danny and herself would take care of the costs and they would be asking their relative, David, who at the time was the owner of beautiful event catering hall, Capitale, if we could have our wedding there in June- exactly 3 months from now. Capitale, is located in the heart of Downtown, Manhattan and was originally the Bowery Savings Bank built in 1893 and is a national historic landmark. Its interior features tall Corinthian columns, beautifully coved ceilings and an art glass skylight. It is one of New York City's most luxurious and sophisticated event spaces.

Pam had recently been put on supplemental oxygen and her condition had deteriorated significantly, so I understood why this wedding had to be planned as quickly as possible. She asked me to put together my invitation list as soon as possible and mentioned we had a limit of 200 people. I burst out laughing and said, "Pam! I can count on one hand how many people I would want at my wedding! But I will speak to Brian tonight and get you our list soon."

Pam and Danny had many friends and a very big family. I would soon come to realize that this was going to be an extravagant farewell event for Pam and not just my wedding. After the talk with Pam, a stunning bouquet of flowers was delivered and put on my desk. The note read, "We make a great Team! I love you Scoob!" And then my co-worker, Ted walked in the office and noticed my ring and said, "Is that an engagement ring? Is little Patty Boom Boom getting married?" I blushed and nodded my head while looking down. Ted gave me a big hug and I knew that he would be on my invited guest list.

I rushed down the stairs to tell my sister who would be my maid of honor and my niece would be the ring bearer. My sister was jubilant. She had always thought very highly of Brian and thought he was a wonderful guy. I confided in her that I felt nervous, but she thought it was normal. The morning went by quickly as the word around the office got around and people kept stopping by to congratulate me and to see my ring. At 12:30 p.m., I rushed out to see Father Joe and when I arrived at his office, I sat down and cried. "Goodness Patricia, why are you crying?" he asked. I felt relieved to get that out of my system. Crying to me was not a sign of weakness, but instead allowed me to let go of the heaviness.

As soon as I felt ready, I spilled out everything that was making me feel anxious. I told him how I was worried about the guest list and about the whole change of life. "Well Patricia, you guys have been living together for almost a year now. Things would not be so different. What are you really worried about?" I had to be honest and said, "Living together with Brian as boyfriend and girlfriend has been great Father Joe, but he mentioned that if we ever got married, we should have 1 joint bank account and that he would handle our finances. I have been so independent all my life! I am also afraid that he will change. My mother always told me that men change once they get married. I am so scared Father Joe."

I was appreciative of the fact that Father Joe gave me the space I needed to just let it all out. It was unusual for us to go past the hour session, but he made an exception today and we spoke for nearly 2 hours. In this session we even discussed speaking to Coach again and inviting him to the wedding, so I called Coach from his office. I hoped he wouldn't answer the phone, but he did. I took the deepest breath in and said, "Hi Coach. I know it has been a while since we spoke, but I wanted to invite you to my wedding this summer."

There was a momentary pause and then Coach said, "It is great to hear from you Alcivar! You got it Kid! I will be there, but I want you to come in to the gym soon so we can talk. I am very sorry about everything that happened." Although there was not much said after that, it was a lot and it was long overdue. I felt less anxious and better overall, but I would never get rid of that nagging discomfort in the center of my soul. A nagging feeling that in reality was and is guidance from above.

For the next 3 months, our lives would be consumed with planning this wedding. Brian and I picked our wedding song for our first dance as husband and wife, "Con te partiro," by Andrea Bocelli. It was a song on one of the CD's he once gifted me. It was and is still one of my favorite songs of all time. "Con te partiro" means "Time to say goodbye" and at the time, the song to us meant that it was time to say goodbye to our old lives and enter our new lives as a married couple. We also enrolled for ballroom dancing lessons after work.

A week later, Pam, her sister, my sister and I spent a Saturday together looking for my wedding dress. I wanted to be as considerate as possible taking into consideration that Danny and Pam were absorbing the costs, so I suggested "David's Bridal Department Store" in Westbury, Long Island which was a short 20-minute ride from Forest Hills. When we arrived, a woman was immediately assigned to help me.

We picked out 6 dresses to try on. They each had their own style ranging from cute, sexy, sophisticated, precious, elegant and dreamy. I chose "dreamy" which had a heart shaped body-hugging corset for the top and then loosened and flowed on the bottom like Cinderella. It was also the least expensive dress at right under $300. The veil I chose was a "Virgin Mary" type veil that would honor my faith. My whole wedding outfit was complete and we had also chosen the bride's maids dresses which was a simple light sage colored slim fitting knee length dress.

Now, we needed to find Pam a dress, but this was not going to be the place to look for it. We went to several expensive boutiques and found a dress that took our breaths away. Pam's dress would be an elegant satin dark champagne colored dress that featured stones trimming the corset top. It was absolutely gorgeous. This was already along day for Pam and we decided to head back to her home and order food from there and continue with our planning since Brian, his dad and his brother were out getting fitted for their tuxedos and having dinner.

Pam sat at the kitchen table sipping her iced tea while my sister and her sister went to pick up food for everyone. "Do you have your invite list Sweetie?" asked Pam as she took out her personal notebook. I nodded my head as I reached into my purse. Brian had 20 of his personal friends and I had 10 people on my list and we also invited another a small group of our personal clients from bootcamp, so our list had 50 people in total. The remaining 150 people would be Pam and Danny's family and friends.

My sister and my dear boxing friend, Denise would be my maid of honors and I would ask Coach to walk me down the aisle. I had decided to forgive and try to forget about what happened with Coach. This was going to be a new chapter in my life and I wanted to start fresh. We would have a Catholic/Jewish wedding. Father Joe would perform a part of the ceremony and a Rabbi would do the other part. We were 8 weeks out from the wedding date and Pam had already picked out the menu, center pieces for the tables and now that she had the invite list complete, the invitations would be sent out that Monday.

There was still something left that I had never thought of because it was not important to me, but Pam did. "Sweetie, I asked Jessica to plan your bachelorette party with your sister, so that should be happening soon," said Pam. I did my very best not to cringe. I did not have many friends and I thought bachelorette parties were silly even though I had never been to one. "Thank you so much Pam, but I think I will be fine if I don't have a bachelorette party and hate to bother anyone with that," I replied just as our sisters returned with burgers and fries for everyone.

"It has already been planned and it is happening next week, so don't make plans to compete in any races," Pam said while looking at my sister for confirmation. My sister giggled and said, "Well, I wanted it to be a surprise but yes, some of the girls from your bootcamp class, Jessica and I have already planned to take you out to Caroline's the Comedy Club for dinner and drinks and then out dancing. It will be about 8 of us altogether, so it should be a fun night." I had never been out drinking or to a comedy club or to a dancing club, so this would be an interesting night for sure. I was glad that at least my sister would be there. That was really all I needed.

The boys arrived soon after and it was late, so we headed home. "Hey Raggie, are you having a Bachelor Party?" I asked as we drove home. Brian knew that it could potentially be a long night when the "going out with your friends" topic came up. Although Brian was trustworthy,

I needed his reassurance and, in the beginning, he had no problem providing it. "Yes, Scoob! The guys and I are going to play paintball and then have dinner and drinks. I'll probably be back home before you. I told the guys that I don't want any strippers or anything like that. I promise you that you have nothing to worry about. I love you and I am not going to do anything to jeopardize us," he replied while holding my hand tightly.

I sighed in relief. There was nowhere else to go with the topic. I just hugged and thanked him. Even though I functioned fairly well for a person with my past trauma, one of the things I constantly struggled with was mistrust, doubts, insecurities and fears. I worked on these issues on a daily basis through prayer, faith, counseling, self-reflection and exercise.

Some days were good and some days not so good and battling inner demons was ongoing battle that I hoped to win some day. I was my biggest project, a never-ending work in progress that would require faith, courage and always being pro-active.

On the day of our bachelor and bachelorette parties, I was still very edgy. As Brian walked out the door to meet his friends for the drive to Long Island for their paintball game that afternoon, he comforted me with his promise to not engage in any behavior that would risk our relationship. I believed him and got dressed to go out for a run by myself in the trails of Forest Park. I ran hard even though I was tempted to stop a few times to pet the cute dogs I saw along the way. 6 miles in under an hour was what I needed to clear my head.

When I got back home from my run, I called my sister and made a plan to meet her at the Roosevelt Avenue Train Station by 7 p.m. We were all meeting at Caroline's Comedy Club that used to be located in the heart of Times Square and had featured legendary comics such as Jerry Seinfeld, Billy Crystal, Rosie O'Donnell and Jay Leno among others. We had a table reserved until 10 p.m. for dinner, drinks and a few stand-up shows before we headed to one of NYC's most famous nightclubs called Roseland.

Right before I jumped in the shower, my phone rang and I was surprised to see that it was Brian. "Hi Raggie! Are you okay?" I asked. He whispered, "I'm good Scoob, I just wanted to call you quickly and wish you a great night tonight. Have fun and don't worry about a thing... I love you." Between the run, Brian calling, the shower and a prayer, I felt like I was good to go. I put on my black skinny jeans and a sheer black button-down top accompanied by high heel ankle boots.

As I walked to the train station, I heard a few whistles from cars passing by and wondered if I had overdone it with my wardrobe. I hurried to take the train and could not wait to see my sister. I hoped that she would be on time for at least tonight. She was notoriously late for just about everything and it drove me crazy at times, but tonight, she arrived promptly at 7 p.m. and I hugged her tight when I saw her. She giggled and said, "Dang, you look good!" We both started laughing out loud.

On the train ride to Times Square, we were able to catch up on her fitness, work and my niece. With a few minutes to spare, we walked around Times Square and then got to Caroline's right at 8 p.m. where all the girls were waiting already and clapped as we walked in. It was Mary, Bonnie, Denise, Kimberly, Jessica, Melissa, my sister and myself. I was seated immediately in the center after I hugged everyone hello. The waiter came to take our drink orders. I had no clue what to order, but everyone knew what a crazy sweet tooth I had, so they ordered me a sour apple martini. "Yum! This tastes just like one of my favorite candies-Sour Patch Kids!" I said as I sipped my sour apple martini a bit too fast. Kimberly, one of the regular bootcamp class members chuckled and ordered me another one and kept refilling my drinks for the next couple of hours.

The comics were great and I was laughing pretty hard, but probably from the sour apple martinis and not the jokes. At 10 p.m., it was time to start heading to the club. We started to get up and my knees buckled and I fell right back in my seat. "Whoa! I am having trouble standing up," I said to my sister. My sister and Bonnie looked at each other and then Bonnie said, "It was probably all those sour apple martinis she drank. I think we should take a cab and get her some coffee. She should be okay soon." I stood up again, but this time my sister was on one side and Bonnie was on the other side helping me walk out. A cab pulled up and I plopped myself inside. I was in the middle of Bonnie and my sister and then all of a sudden, everything turned black and I passed out.

"Oh My God! She is Not Breathing! We have to take her to the Emergency Room!" yelled out Bonnie to my sister. The cab dropped us off at the New York Hospital Emergency Room. I was completely disoriented when I woke up and I saw a man standing over me grabbing my arm, so I instinctively punched him in the face! "Tranquilize Her!" the doctor yelled and then I felt a sharp pain in my thigh before I passed out again. The next time I woke up, I was being wheeled out in a wheelchair out of the hospital by Brian. He collected the outpatient report that read in big letters, "NO DRINKING AT THE WEDDING!"

The doctor explained to him that although rare, I had suffered alcohol poisoning and drinking anything more than a glass of alcohol could be fatal to me. I would later reflect on the irony of my alcohol sensitivity even though I was the daughter, granddaughter, niece and cousin to alcoholics. Theoretically and statistically, I was supposed to follow in the tradition.

I was groggy, nauseous and had a nasty pounding headache as I started to vaguely remember bits and pieces from the prior night. "Scooby, I am taking you home so you can rest, okay?" I nodded while holding my right thigh that was sore from that tranquilizer shot. The bright side was that I slept deeply until the early afternoon. It was a night that I would never forget for sure and every time I tell the story, I do manage to laugh.

The night before our wedding, Brian slept over his parent's home. Pam thought it would be nice for us to be separated and give ourselves space to get ready before the big moment. Before living with Brian, I spent years living alone and relished in my alone time, so I welcomed the opportunity. I watched a movie at home while I ate sorbet, spoke to my sister, prayed and went to sleep.

My sister rang the doorbell at 10 a.m. My sister, niece and I had an appointment to get our hair and make-up done at Spectrym Hair Salon on Austin Street, a high-end modern beauty salon and a long-time neighborhood business. As we chatted on the 15-minute walk down to the salon, I thought about how good it was to have my sister and niece be with me on this day. The hairdresser took a look at my "Virgin Mary" veil and suggested an elegant "Audrey Hepburn" pulled back hairdo. I never imagined being able to pull that off but I agreed and I decided to just go with the flow. I relaxed as she washed, blow dried and used the hair iron to smooth out any frizz. It was a hot and humid NYC summer day in June after all.

She asked me not to look in the mirror until everything was complete. The make-up artist worked for another hour or so and went for the natural soft look. The hair dresser put my veil on before I could finally stand up and look in the mirror. My sister was smiling very big and then I almost cried when I saw my reflection in the mirror. I didn't look exactly like a bride. I was reminded of when I did my first communion, but I didn't mind. I looked like a more mature elegant version. My sister and I loved it.

It was nearly 3 p.m. now and we were due at Capitale in 1 hour. The wedding ceremony started at 6 p.m., so we rushed home trying not to sweat and picked up our dresses and called a cab. NYC traffic on a Saturday summer afternoon as expected was ridiculous and we were lucky to arrive 75 minutes later. The outside of Capitale had two imposing looking lions and a long red carpet as you walked up the stairs. Inside, there was a lovely silk chuppah which is a Jewish wedding canopy with four open sides. The Rabbi would perform the ceremony inside the chuppah.

Adjacent to where the chuppah was placed was a separate open space that had a gorgeous spiral staircase where Brian and I would be coming down after the wedding ceremony to dance our first dance as husband and wife. The whole set-up was a dream and all through the weeks up until now, I could not shake off that uncomfortable sinking feeling in my gut. "There you are Sweetie! Let's get you dressed!" said Pam as her sister transported her in the wheelchair over to where I was standing. Pam was already dressed in her gorgeous gown. I felt her eyes infiltrate my soul. I looked back into them and could feel her melancholy. I did not want to weep, so I kissed her on the forehead as the feeling was mutual.

After my sister and niece got dressed, my sister helped me slip into my dress. "How are you feeling Patricia," she asked in a concerned way. My face was probably giving my true feelings away, so it was useless to tell a white lie, so I replied, "It is probably just nerves, but I have been having an awful feeling in my stomach and chest. I am sure it will go away after, so don't worry." Soon after, my friend Denise, Coach and Father Joe walked in. I had never seen Father Joe in his priest attire. He was a monk priest, so he wore a robe. "Looking good Alcivar," said Coach as both him and Denise came over to hug me from each side.

The ceremony was about to start and everyone went to take their places. The wedding processional song begun and my heart fluttered off beat. The Rabbi and Father Joe walked out first followed by Brian's groomsmen. Then Brian walked down with Pam and Danny on each side followed by my niece holding the rings and then Denise and my sister and finally it was my turn.

Coach held out his arm and said, "Come on Kid, it's showtime!" I quickly wiped away a tear that streamed down the side of my cheek as I saw an image of my mother in my head. I took one big deep breath and we started walking out. During the most overwhelming times in my life, my mind and body had involuntarily learned to disassociate. It is a survival mechanism especially for those who suffered from intense trauma which explained why many things in my life seemed like a blur.

I only remembered taking the deep breath and everything went blank after that. However, with modern technology, everything was captured on video, cellphones and pictures to help me remember every moment of my wedding day.

After Father Joe performed his part of the ceremony, then the Rabbi took over and did his part and during the final part of the ceremony, he presented me with a ketubah, which is a Jewish marriage contract and Father Joe then did the ring exchange part and Brian broke the glass with his feet which signifies "As this glass shatters, so may your marriage never break" to finalize the wedding ceremony. Brian and I kissed and the loud sounds of "Zaghrouta" or ululation by the women drowned out the applause.

Everyone quickly went to the adjacent room and Brian and I were hurried to the top of the spiral stairs as we heard the start of "Con te partiro". Brian kissed me on the lips and we walked down the spiral stair case and met in the center of the dance floor. He grabbed my hand and kissed it before we started our choreographed dance to Andrea Bocelli. There was not a dry eye in the room as we finished our dance with Brian picking me up and then finishing with a dip for the grand finale.

The image that I would never forget is when I glanced over and Pam was sitting in her wheelchair breathing with supplemental oxygen, but during our dance, she was at peace. It was an incredibly emotional, but beautiful wedding and now we were husband and wife. We would not go on a honeymoon as we were uncertain of Pam's health and did not want to be away in case of an emergency.

Pam passed away of complications developed from breast cancer a month later. She was in her mid-50's and gone too soon. We barely had time to enjoy being newlyweds and went straight into mourning, but I was grateful that we gave her the opportunity to be with all her loved ones in style the way she had wished.

For the moment, married life was not much different from our previous life as we had lived together for almost a year prior except that we did get a joint account where both of our paychecks went and Brian managed our finances. I was in charge of maintaining our home. I made the bed every morning and kept the apartment tidy and clean throughout the week as well as did the laundry and cooked whenever possible. For the next few months, I tried my best to be supportive to Brian after Pam passed away. Although, I was not a good cook, I asked my sister for easy recipes that I could follow. My rice always came out way too soggy, but to my surprise, Brian loved it. He used to joke that it looked like "slop", but tasted so good. We still taught our morning bootcamp class, worked our jobs, raced in events such as Adventure Races, Triathlons and various distances running races and went to the movies on the weekends.

Life for the most part was good, but I missed having specific goals; something meaningful to strive for. I missed the cleansing feeling of overcoming and achieving. I just had a feeling that I had so much more to do than be a housewife. One evening during our dinner, I mentioned that I still had unfinished business in boxing.

Many people including Brian thought that I had already accomplished enough in Women's Boxing from being a 2-time NYC Golden Gloves, National and International Champion and the 1st Woman to be voted and win "Athlete of the Year" in boxing. The only thing missing was the Olympics, but Coach said that everyone he asked said that Women's Boxing would never be an Olympic Sport, so the next step would be to turn professional which would be a huge step and something Coach never did.

There are many differences between the Amateurs and Pros. In Amateur Boxing, you use a headguard, you fight with gloves that are between 10 -12 ounces, the rounds are usually 3 to 4 rounds and you do not receive any financial compensation. In Professional Boxing, the headguard comes off, the gloves are 8 ounces, you fight anywhere from 4 to 12 rounds and you get paid to fight. I wanted to go all the way. Brian wasn't against the idea, but he was not jumping for joy either. He knew that my relationship with Coach was strained and that it would be a world he knew nothing about.

He also took the opportunity to mention that his father Danny would be retiring soon and that he and his brother Jason would take over the business. I didn't think much of it as Brian and Jason have been running the day-to-day operations already. Danny did most of the traveling to meet clients and develop new business, show sample textiles and sell, so Brian would have to take over that part which I wasn't too fond about. But what did get my attention up very high was when Brian mentioned that the NYC rents kept rising and affecting their profits and they would need to eventually move the business out of New York and that they already had a place in mind in- North Carolina.

"North Carolina? Raggie are you serious?" I asked. By the look on his face and his whole demeanor, it was obvious that he had been planning this with his brother and father for a while. "Scoob, we have no choice. My business cannot survive paying these high rents. We are not going to renew our lease which is up next summer in August. The space in Asheville, North Carolina is 3 times bigger for a quarter of the rent we pay now which means more money in our pockets and just a better life overall," he reasoned.

We had been married for just a few months and it was now January which meant he wanted us to move to a whole new State in 6 months. "Raggie, but my job, my sister, my niece, boxing and everything I know is here in New York. What will I do in North Carolina? I don't even drive!" I pleaded. "I know I am asking a lot Scooby. I don't know what to say. The only thing that comes to mind is having a long-distance marriage. We can take turns visiting each other, but I would prefer if we are together," he answered. I felt my stomach twisting and that awful feeling in my chest. "This cannot be happening," I thought to myself.

"Raggie, I don't think a long-distance relationship would work. I wish I knew this before we got married. Everything I know is here in New York. I have goals and one of them being that I want to eventually see and talk to my own mother again who lives here," I said through tears. I put on my sneakers and ran out the door and into the trails of Forest Park. I was sad, angry, confused and I let it all out on the trails. I ran for 2 hours non-stop and would have kept going if it wasn't turning dark and had work the next day.

When I got back home, Brian had fallen asleep on the couch and stayed asleep as I took a shower. I decided to leave him there and I went to bed. "God, you are in charge of my destiny. Please protect me and help me be strong and see things clearly," I prayed as I laid in bed with tears streaming down my face. That night, the paralyzing dream came back soon after falling asleep. "Our Father who art in heaven...." I said mentally before I could finally move again.

I woke up at 5 a.m. and made a smoothie for Brian and then woke him up with a gentle kiss on his forehead and said, "Good morning Raggie, it's time to get up." Brian was startled for a moment and then realized he had fallen asleep on the couch. "Whoa! Sorry Scoob! I didn't even realize I fell asleep on the couch when you went for a run. I know all this about moving is very difficult for you and I appreciate you trying to be open minded about it for us. I owe you big time," he said. I felt myself starting to get emotional and took a deep breath and replied, "This is a lot to take in Raggie, but I am going to do my best for this marriage. I am going to tell my sister and Father Joe today and my job soon after.

We also have to break the news to Platoon Fitness so they can start finding a replacement for our morning bootcamp soon. I am going to go ahead and take the train to work and I'll see you later after work." I kissed him on the forehead and left.

It was a Friday morning, but I called Father Joe and made an urgent appointment to see him at lunch time. He agreed and said he had something important to tell me as well. Everything seemed to be taking a wild turn in my life and I needed to be strong. As I walked down to get breakfast, I saw my sister and told her the news about moving to North Carolina in 6 months.

She was momentarily shaken by the news, but said, "Your marriage is your priority and you have to do everything to make it work. Just make sure you visit us often!" There was no question about it and I would make it my business to visit often, but my thoughts were about seeing my mother again, so I asked, "Do you think mother would want to see me again? I would like to see her before I move even though I will be visiting often." My sister's face lit up and said, "Of course she would love to see you! She always asks about you, but you know how she is.... Her pride gets in the way, but you should absolutely see her. She is going to retire from her job after 45 years next month, so she will have a lot of free time on her hands."

I was somewhat relieved to get that off my chest and tell my sister. Later that day, I saw Father Joe and broke the news. He thought that change was good and that I should give North Carolina a solid try for the sake of my marriage. He also thought that I could still move forward with my boxing goals, but find new people, a coach and gym there. "Patricia, my time in this location has come to an end as well. They are moving me to Paramus, New Jersey, so this will be our last session," said Father Joe in his calmest demeanor. That was the last thing I expected to come out of his mouth and found myself upset at how he blurted that out without any emotion.

"You too Father Joe? I am having a very hard time with all these changes. I am not going to say goodbye to you. I am just not," I said as I ran out the door crying. Father Joe's office was inside a church, so I went into the church and kneeled down praying and crying. I remembered Father Joe saying to me that challenges and changes in life are meant to help us grow into the person God intended us to be.

Brian picked me up from work later that day and told me that he told Platoon Fitness about our move in the late summer. They were in shock, but understood and would start coordinating instructor tryouts with us for the next few months. And just when things couldn't get any more interesting, Brian said that his father wanted to get together with us and Jason and his girlfriend for dinner that Sunday so we could meet his new girlfriend!

I was in complete disbelief! "Raggie, are you joking? It has only been a few months since your mom passed away! How are you this calm? Do you really expect us to go meet his new girlfriend over dinner?" I asked. I know that unless it was traffic, Brian rarely showed any real emotion, but this was crazy! "Scooby, we need to show respect for my father. He helped take care of my mother for many years. He deserves to find happiness. I find nothing wrong with what he is doing," said Brian.

Prior to being married, we were rarely on opposite ends of anything and now it seemed we couldn't agree on anything. I felt something inside of me start to change involuntarily. A major reason why I had been so attracted to and fell in love with him besides his affection and attention to beautiful details was the fact that I felt we were a team and had each other's back. This was in big jeopardy and I felt scared.

I remembered Brian always taking his brother and father's side when we were dating and remembered how his demeanor changed when anything remotely negative was said about them. I had noticed it and it concerned me, but I didn't fully address it. I had hoped things would improve, but now, the same issues were back, but much bigger.

That Sunday, we all met at a steakhouse in the city. When Brian and I arrived, Jason and Jessica were already there as well Danny and his new girlfriend. I could not hide my disgust. The new girlfriend was younger than all of us in her early 20's!

She was just as tall as Brian at nearly 6 feet tall, blonde and Canadian. I have never been any good at lying or pretending. Brian poked me in the ribs as we walked over and said, "Scooby, I know this is hard, but please smile and try to have a good time."

I extended my hand and said, "Very nice to meet you Elise" while forcing a half smile. Apparently, she and Danny had met at a bar a few months ago. She came from a wealthy family who currently lived in Florida, so supposedly, she was not with Danny for his money I would hear later from Brian as I zoned out when she spoke. My attention came back when Jason announced that he had proposed to Jessica and that they would be getting married in Buffalo where Jessica is from originally and where her parents lived. They would get married there before we all moved to North Carolina.

I felt myself go numb. Before all these impacting announcements, Brian and I had a great intimate relationship, but it was starting to show signs of trouble because my mind, heart and soul all felt disconnected. I gave of myself because I had felt a spiritual connection with Brian, but the fact that I was being forced to make painful decisions such as move and leave everything behind as well as accept Pam's replacement and tolerate pretentiousness from Jessica was now compromising my moral values. I just couldn't pretend that everything inside of me was fine because it wasn't.

In the months that followed, I told Peter, my boss at New York Road Runners that I had no choice but to resign due to my move to Asheville, North Carolina. "Patricia, are you sure about this move? I have big plans for you in this department. In my evaluation of your performance, I said you were a "Diamond in the ruff" because I truly believe you are. Please think about this decision," he said. I had worked so hard to obtain the knowledge and experience as an Event Manager and was excelling in my position, but my hands were literally tied.

All this was truly painful and I found myself resenting Brian. He was making this move and would have his brother and sister-in-law, his job in a new office, a traffic-free city and peace. I on the other hand would have nothing. No job, no friends or family, no transportation and no church. All this prompted me to finally go see my mother. I took a Friday off of work and I just showed up in the same old apartment in Woodside, Queens where my painful past lived.

My mother is a creature of habit and rarely changed. Her maintenance job started at 5 p.m., so she usually started cooking at 2 p.m., ate by 3 p.m. and left by 4 p.m. Nothing changed since we were kids, so I stopped by the Colombian Bakery and got her Colombian cheese bread right before I started walking towards the apartment. My hands were sweating and I felt short of breath before I knocked on the door. I had flashbacks of the blasting music my father would play on every weekend that made the entire apartment shake.

I rang the bell at 12 noon. I heard her look through the peephole and after a small pause, she opened the door. "Hi Mami, como esta? (How are you)" I said holding back tears and kissed her on the cheek. She didn't hug me, but she did put her hand on my shoulder and kissed me back on the check and said, "Bien gracias, Patricia (Good, thank you)," she replied and invited me to come in. We sat in the dining table and had coffee and the cheese bread and talked for a couple of hours. My mother always did an excellent job of hiding her emotions.

I told her all about my recent marriage, future move and my sports. It was the most I had ever said to my mother, but it felt good. She told me about her retiring soon from her job and complained about people we mutually knew, so she had not changed at all. After I left her home, I called my sister and told her we needed to arrange a retirement party asap and I would take the opportunity to introduce her to Brian. My sister thought it was a fantastic idea and we would start working on it right away! She contacted my mother's friends and some family members. I found and paid for the rental space, flowers and cake as well as helped collect pictures for a poster collage.

I experienced a roller coaster of emotions throughout all these events which I internalized since I didn't have Father Joe to speak to any more. I didn't trust Coach with anything anymore and Brian was no longer my best friend. I prayed more than ever. I felt myself drift further and further apart from Brian emotionally as this move got closer.

I applied to the Asheville School of Massage & Yoga which was an 18-month certificate program that I hoped to use to find work upon graduation and support my continuing education in Health and Wellness at the University of North Carolina in Asheville. At least, that was the plan I envisioned.

Asheville is a city in western North Carolina's Blue Ridge Mountains. It was voted the happiest city in the United States for 5 consecutive years and it is known for a vibrant arts scene and historic architectures, the vast 19th century Biltmore estate which displays artwork by masters like Renoir. It is paradise for active people who are into rock climbing, hiking and rafting and Asheville is also known for its breathtaking views, magical waterfalls and fresh clean air.

It is the mecca of holistic health, massage and yoga. Brian agreed to me going back to school, but I suspected he would agree to just about anything I suggested in order to keep what was left of our peace. In the next few months, Brian travelled to Asheville often to supervise some of the construction of the new office space as well as to find our temporary apartment. He wanted to rent while we looked for a permanent house to purchase. Jason and Jessica got married. She was more pretentious than ever. Her parents would gift her and Jason a brand-new home in Asheville as a wedding gift and she would become pregnant soon after their wedding.

A month before our move to Asheville, my sister and I surprised my mother with her retirement party. She kind of knew and had her hair done and wore a beautiful new pink outfit. After working for the same maintenance company for over 40 years, she deserved to get all dolled up and a party. It was not an easy job and the upper management was not kind to her. I remember my mother being constantly stressed and in a bad mood because of that job, but she had no choice. She had to pay rent and feed her children.

About 50 people altogether showed up. There were family members in attendance that I had not seen since I was a kid and I met a few of my mother's co-workers. My mother also had the chance to finally meet Brian. Although Brian knew the whole family history, he didn't hold anything against anyone and he was a gentleman with my mother which I appreciated. My mother liked him immediately. She got to dance, mingle and enjoy the night which made us happy. She did not have much of a vision upon retirement except relax and that would become a very big problem down the line.

Platoon Fitness did not have any success in finding instructors to replace us for the NYC morning bootcamp class. They had about a dozen different instructors try out, but either the clients did not like them or they could not commit to the early morning 3-day per week schedule, so they were forced to shut down the NYC program. The bigger news however was that Danny and his girlfriend, Elise got married and she was expecting.

Danny was 63 years old and about 40 years older than his new bride with a baby on the way. They had purchased a big brand-new house on a golf course in the Fort Lauderdale area which is where they would be living now. He was officially retired now and Brian and Jason were fully in charge of the business, but Danny would still get a monthly "pension" from the business.

Even though it seemed like everyone around us was having babies, it was the last thing I wanted. I knew from a very young age that children were not in my future. I thought it was just a phase that would pass, but the desire not to have children only strengthened with time. I didn't think it was fair to anyone to bring a child into this world that could possibly suffer. An innocent child deserves better. It was probably something Brian and I should have spoken about before getting married, but the topic never came up.

My last day working at the New York Road Runners was disappointing. After nearly 7 years of hard work, there was not even a farewell lunch or a sincere hug from anyone. Father Joe used to tell me to just stop expecting things and I would be much less disappointed throughout life. Brian had put out multiple "moving sale" ads for our final weekend in New York City and we sold just about everything we had in the apartment.

It was nearly the fall season and I purposely did not make any special farewell dinner plans with my sister or mother because I knew I would be back soon to visit. I told Brian that I needed to come back within the next 3 months and he agreed. Despite the fact that I would be visiting, I wept as we packed the van with our remaining belongings and throughout the 13-hour drive from New York City to Asheville, North Carolina. "Good bye for now New York City...I will be back," I whispered to myself.

Chapter Nine - Round 9

Asheville, North Carolina
"If you lose money, you lose much. If you lose friends, you lose more. If you lose faith, you lose all," Eleanor Roosevelt

Faith, prayers and church have and will always be an important part of my life and they are essential to my overall well-being. It has been the single constant in my life and I would never have been able to survive without it. We had almost everything from school, visiting family and temporary living arrangements figured out except church. In New York City, I attended a special Christian church named Iglesia de Dios Ministerial de Jesucristo Internacional (IDMJI, Church of God Ministry of Jesus Christ International) which was founded by a woman named, Maria Luisa Piraquive in 1972. The church has over 500 locations worldwide and also offers audio/interpretation services in English and other languages.

As Brian focused on driving, I searched for the nearest IDMJI Church in North Carolina and I got excited when I saw that they had a location in Charlotte, North Carolina. "Raggie! How far is Charlotte from where we will be living?" I asked. Brian looked confused, but replied, "Charlotte is about a 2-hour drive from Asheville. Why Scooby? What is in Charlotte?" My excitement quickly turned back to gloom. I knew that Brian disliked anything that involved prolonged driving and he was not going to be driving me over 4-hours back and forth to church on a weekly basis. "Raggie, that is where the nearest IDMJI church is located. I know you hate driving for long periods of time, but if we can even make it there once a month, I would really appreciate it and maybe you can stay for a service," I said.

"Scoob, there are other nearby churches in Asheville. I actually found one that is non-denominational called "New Life" that we can both go to. There is no need to drive all the way to Charlotte. We can give it a try next weekend if you'd like," he replied. This would be another big issue that would drive a wedge in our relationship. I had invited Brian a few times to the IDMJI church I attended in New York, but there was always an excuse. Whenever he invited me to temple or any of his family's religious gatherings, I went with an open mind and heart even though my church was not in favor of us attending any other religious gatherings outside of our belief. I needed to figure something out quick and it dawned on me that I had to learn how to drive ASAP!

"I understand that I am asking a lot for you to drive me to Charlotte for church Raggie. I would love to drive myself eventually, so I just need you to teach me to drive since it seems like public transportation is not an option where we will be living" I requested as if I was asking one of my parents. I felt uncomfortable with the fact that for the moment, I would be fully dependent on Brian for just about everything from transportation, companionship, money and all-around support. I literally had nothing except my faith and even that was in jeopardy because I had no means of getting to my church. Brian looked frustrated and with much hesitation replied, "Scoob, I am not a driving instructor, but I agree and you need to learn how to drive. I can start you out with a few lessons in a nearby parking lot and then we can take it from there."

I had my work cut out for me and decided I would apply for a permit immediately upon our arrival to Asheville. This would be the start to get back my independence. After almost 12 hours, we finally arrived to our new spacious 2-bedroom apartment in Asheville. The place was in a great location near the famed Biltmore Estates and fully furnished for the most part as we would be there temporarily. We unpacked the van and went straight to bed. I hardly slept one wink while Brian snored the night away.

The next morning, Brian woke up and had a full schedule at work while I had no planned agenda. Massage School would not start for a few weeks. When Brian left to his office, I ventured out for a run and discovered that we lived right by a section of the beautiful "Mountain to Sea" trail which stretches 1175 miles from the Great Smoky Mountains to the Outer Banks. The 7-mile trail run was comforting and helped motivate me to schedule an exam for my driver's permit at the Department of motor vehicles in Asheville the following week. I downloaded the permit handbook and started studying it right away. I cleaned the entire apartment, did laundry and cooked dinner by the early afternoon.

I wanted to walk down the street and get a coffee, snack or anything, but couldn't. Asheville did not have a corner deli, bodega or any type of store that you could just take a stroll to. Everything was a short ride away. The nearest store was a 30-minute walk to "Ingles Supermarket", so I decided to take the walk there. Asheville is a big supporter of local businesses and did not welcome chain business easily. I also stuck out as an olive-skinned Latina with long curly hair with a NYC and Spanish accent that prompted the male cashier to say in a heavy southern accent, "You ain't from around here are ya?"

Although that comment should have bothered me, it made me burst out laughing and I spontaneously replied as I paid for my groceries, "I heard Asheville was voted the Friendliest and Happiest City in the United States for 5 consecutive years by Outside Magazine, so I just moved here from New York City." My forearms were burning from carrying two bags of groceries all the way home, but I felt as if I had done something useful for the day.

I spent the afternoon setting up my computer and had a list of things to search out and I started with the nearest boxing gym. In my search, I found that Asheville didn't have any boxing specific gyms. They had MMA and CrossFit gyms that had boxing punching bags for training, but the nearest boxing specific gym would be Dyme Boxing in Charlotte, NC, White Rock Boxing in South Carolina and Decatur Boxing in Atlanta, GA. It was time to put my big girl pants on and train myself here in Asheville for a few months while I learned to drive and once, I learned to drive, I would contact the boxing gyms for sparring and perhaps enter the North Carolina Gloves tournament before turning pro.

This move to Asheville made me realize more than ever that I had unfinished business in boxing and in life. It was almost 5 p.m. and Brian should have been on his way home, but instead he called and said that he wouldn't be home until much later and that he also had to make travel arrangements for the next few days to a textile show in Texas. I put my head down on my computer and started to cry and then my phone rang. It was my sister and I picked up the phone right away, "I am so glad you called!" I said through tears. "I felt a poking sensation to call you Patricia... are you okay?" asked my sister.

I hated to make her worry, but I could not hide my sadness. I wiped my tears away and through sniffles replied, "I am okay, you just caught me at a bad time. I feel very lonely out here. Brian was supposed to be home and will be working late and traveling for the next few days. There is no public transportation and Brian doesn't have the patience to teach me to drive and I have no job, no friends or anyone and the nearest church is over 2 hours away and Brian will not drive me there." There was a long silent pause, but my sister replied, "I think this would be a perfect time to get a dog! You have always loved dogs and you said you eventually wanted to be a dog mom. It will all be okay though. Just stay strong and pray. God is using all this to make you the fighter you have always been. Try to get a good night's rest and stay positive."

My sister was right in everything she said. The only way I was going to survive this was to pray and stay strong and positive. I also took a moment to register on Petfinder.com and be notified when a small breed young male puppy needed to be rescued. We both would be doing each other a big service by rescuing each other at this point. I had always loved dogs and throughout the years watched "The Dog Whisperer" as well as read all of Cesar Millan's books and felt that I had the tools to be a good dog mom.

My highlight for the next few days while Brian was away in Texas was receiving a call from my former boss from the JPMorgan Chase Corporate Challenge event series, Dan Brannen. I always respected him not only as my supervisor, but as a person and an athlete. He took pride in hard work and owned his own event company, DJB Event Consultants, Inc.

Dan was also a Hall of Fame Ultra Marathoner and Adventure Racer whom I had previously bumped into in an adventure race in New Jersey while in neck deep muck before my move to Asheville. "Hey Patricia! How is Asheville treating you so far? I am calling you because I am helping put on a cancer walk/run event near you and was wondering if you want to work it and also go for a hike?"

This was the best news I had heard for a while and I am sure he had no idea how happy his call made me. "Hi Dan! It is so good to hear from you! Absolutely! I am not as busy here as I once was in New York City, so I would love to work your event and go for a hike.

I have an extra bedroom in the apartment and you are welcomed to stay with us for however long you need." We agreed and Dan would be arriving in a few weeks which was peak foliage in the area, so I was looking forward to my first ever hike even though at the time, I had a misconstrued idea that hiking was for old timers.

Dan mentioned that he would arrive a couple of days before his event so we could hike and attempt a summit of Mount Mitchell, so I searched it and found out that Mount Mitchell is the highest peak in eastern North America and considered a challenging 12-mile hike with an elevation of 6,684 feet and usually takes about 7-8 hours to complete. I was confused as I couldn't picture grandparents hiking something like this. I shrugged my shoulders and couldn't wait to work and see a familiar face again.

I developed a routine while Brian was away of waking up, going for my trail run, studying for my driving permit and maintaining the apartment spotless while also keeping my eye out for any part-time jobs in the fields that I was familiar with. I saw an opening for a part-time/freelance job as a Spanish Interpreter for the Buncombe County Board of Education, but I was not sure if it was an error when I saw the pay rate of $10/per hour.

I was making double that per hour when I left New York City, so I was pretty sure that it was a typo. I decided to call the number listed. "Hello, I am interested in the part-time Spanish Interpreter position but I saw that the pay rate was $10/per hour and wanted to get clarification on that," I said. "Yes Dear, the pay rate starts at $10/per hour and increases to $12/per hour after a year. I'd be happy to give you the exact email address of where to send your resume whenever you are ready," she replied. I took the email address, thanked her and I was relieved she could not see the expression on my face. I could not understand how this rate was possible though.

I had worked so hard for so many years and it pained and humbled me at the same time to have to go back to what I was making 10 years back when I first started working at Sanctuary for Families. When Brian was finally back on a Friday evening, I updated him on the news of Dan coming to visit us in a few weeks and taking us on a hike to Mount Mitchell, his work offers for both of us.

I also bombarded him with a task list of things that were on my priority list from driving lessons on the weekend, taking the driving permit exam that Monday, visiting workout gyms and the desire to adopt a dog. "Wow Scoob! That's a lot of info to absorb right now. I am exhausted from the travel and work from the show. Do you think I could relax a bit and we can talk about everything tomorrow? We can plan to spend the day tomorrow with a lite run, looking at new homes and movies in the afternoon. Is that okay?" Brian used to never be too tired for me, but I had to be understanding. Besides, he was in fact the sole bread winner for now. I fought back tears and nodded my head and kissed him goodnight.

That night would be a night I would never ever forget. For a moment while I was sleeping, I thought I was having the paralyzing dream because I felt the bed shaking. I opened my eyes slightly only to painfully discover that it was Brian self-gratifying himself with me right next to him! Did he think I wouldn't know? Tears rolled down the side of my cheeks as I struggled to remain silent. It had been over 6 months since we were intimate and I guess he had immediate needs despite being so "tired" from his trip. I didn't know it at the time, but that was really the beginning of the end. Between the disagreements over his family, the forced move to Asheville, his reluctance to give my church a chance, it all had taken a toll on our connection and things would inevitably get worse.

The next morning, I tried to act as normal as possible and woke him up with a kiss on his forehead and said, "Good morning Raggie! Do you want a smoothie before our run? I am all ready to go for whenever you are..." He stretched his arms above his head and replied, "Good morning, Scooby, just give me a few minutes to get ready and we can go soon." I was somewhat excited to show him the new trail I discovered and tried to block out the awful experience from the previous night. We started jogging slowly as I took the lead. "Raggie, this is the trail I discovered. I usually run a 7-mile out and back route, but we can turn around at any point. Just let me know," I said as I looked back and he nodded.

He was always complaining about his knees and I did not want to get into any arguments, but I remembered that Brian appreciated the trails much more than road running and we ended up running the entire 7 miles in silence. After we showered, we took a ride around Asheville to start looking for a new home.

There was a new community being developed nearby in the Biltmore area that featured the popular YMCA and a strip mall with stores such as REI, Starbucks, P.F. Chang's, a bookstore and other smaller local stores. We parked and started walking around the beautiful neighborhood and saw a few open house events. We walked into one right on Heathbrook Circle. The house was a single-family home and had a finished basement, a cute backyard and was in great condition. The price was right below $200k and the annual taxes under $2k.

Brian asked me what I thought and I did love the house and neighborhood and told him so even though I felt so insecure about our relationship. Brian talked to the real-estate agent and would place a bid and the paperwork got started almost immediately.

After the house tour, we kept walking around the neighborhood and went to the YMCA to sign up for a membership. The Asheville YMCA was awesome and had multiple floors and special amenities such as an Olympic sized swimming pool, a jacuzzi, a child care center, spinning classes, aerobics room and much more. I inquired about becoming a personal trainer for them in order for my membership to be free and they directed me to an online form to submit my resume. It had been a nice morning and afternoon thus far. We decided to have brunch at the nearby Earth Fare which was their version of Whole Foods where they are dedicated to health-conscious foods, organic produce and grass-fed beef.

Upon moving to Asheville, I had decided to follow a more vegetarian and organic diet. We sat, ate and we were updating each other on everything while we were apart. "Scoob, now that we are going to purchase this new house, we are going to have to be more conscious of how we spend money. I know you will be going to school, but perhaps you can make some extra money working part time at a supermarket like this one," he said. I was flabbergasted not because I thought working at a supermarket was beneath me, but because my own husband was asking me to.

"Brian, I am going to apply to become a part-time personal trainer for the YMCA and while you were away, I was looking for a job as well and have sent in my resume to the Buncombe Board of Education for a part-time Spanish Interpreter position. The pay rate starts at $10/per hour. Apparently, that is the standard around here. This is not my fault and I am doing everything I can to contribute. I don't lay around doing nothing all day! I maintain our home by cleaning, cooking, doing laundry and picking up after you. I am sorry that I do not have parents like Jessica that can give you money and purchase us a house," I shot back angrily.

Brian's face got red and he grabbed my wrist as he realized that he had said something boneheaded. "I am sorry Scoob. I appreciate all that you are doing. I just thought working in a place like this in your spare time would be nice for you while also making some extra cash, that's all," he said. I looked down moving my egg whites from side to side on my plate with my fork trying to make sense of how Brian had gone from being a detailed, generous and thoughtful boyfriend to a stingy inconsiderate and unsupportive husband. Back in New York, Brian used to motivate me to be more. When I didn't think I could become a personal and group trainer, he believed I could and pushed me to get certified and teach classes. He was there for my first Triathlon and Adventure Race and I was there for him. We always developed goals together.

Judging by his actions and attitude, those days were finished over. I had gone from being an independent and a knowledgeable and respected Event Manager for a prestigious company to being completely alone, unemployed without a driver's license and having my husband ask me to work at a supermarket. I made the choice of moving here and now it was up to me to somehow make the best of this situation. If you really want to see what you are made of, try getting stripped from everything and everyone you know.

That evening after the movies, I reminded Brian about the driving lessons, so we went to a nearby parking lot. At the time, Asheville had so many open spaces that parallel parking was not a requirement on the driving exam because you could literally pull into any space. "Okay Scoob, you are going to get into the driver's side and adjust the seat to your comfort. Not too close or too far. Make sure your feet can reach the pedals and that your hands feel comfortable on the steering wheel," he said firmly while he sat on the passenger side. I had a big grin on my face while I followed his instructions.

As soon as I felt ready, I turned on the car and pressed on the gas a little too hard sending Brian into a panic mode! "Hey relax! Don't press on the gas that hard!" he yelled. I couldn't help but laugh at his reaction and I knew he didn't like me to laugh, but it was my natural reaction. I drove around in circles and practiced making left and right hand turns as well as 3-point turns for the next hour. That would be the first and last driving lesson Brian provided me with. He just did not have the patience, but knowing that, he agreed to me taking the car in the early mornings to practice by myself in the nearby parking lots after I obtained my driving permit.

That Monday morning, he drove me to test for my driving permit and I was able to ace it with no issues, so for the next couple of weeks before school started, I got up at 4 a.m. and drove myself to the parking lot to practice for an hour before my run and before Brian drove to work. I knew it was risky and Brian thought I was nuts, but I also scheduled to test for license 2 weeks later.

I was totally relying on the heavens to have my back on the morning of the driving exam. Brian dropped me off at the Asheville DMV and asked me to take a taxi back home which was fine by me. I was nervous enough and did not want the added pressure of him waiting impatiently to get back to his office. After a 20-minute wait, an older female driving Inspector came out. "Good morning young lady. Do you feel ready to take your driving examination now?" she asked. I looked at her and smiled nervously and replied, "Good morning, Inspector. This will be as ready as I could be. I start massage school next week and need this license to get there and also drive myself to church and other places because my husband won't."

I knew she was not expecting all that to come out of my mouth, but it was all bottled up inside and I had to let it out. "All right then. Get in the driver's side and wait for me before you start preparing and when I tell you to start the car, then we can take off," instructed the Inspector. I opened the door, sat down and adjusted the seat, wheel and mirrors before she asked me to start the car. "We are going to head down that residential street and at the stop light make a right and at the corner make a left, "she said. I turned on my signals at each turn and then she instructed me to do a 3-point turn which I made in 4. "I apologize Inspector. Can I please try again?" I asked and looked at her with tears inevitably filling my eyes.

Her bright blue eyes stared back at me and she gave me one nod of the head. I tried again and this time I got it perfectly at least that was what I thought until she said, "That concludes this exam. We can head back now." She did not look at me and through the corner of my eye, I saw she was marking up the official form. I felt nauseous, but relieved it was over and I would just need to keep practicing and schedule another exam as soon as I was allowed, but then as I turned off the car, the Inspector handed me the score card and said, "Congratulations on your license. Please be careful and make sure to keep practicing before you get on the highway."

"Thank you, God," I whispered quickly before I opened my eyes and replied, "Thanks so much Inspector! I will." I was about 6 miles away from the apartment and decided to walk back home instead of calling and waiting for a cab. Having this license was going to allow me to do so much. I called Brian and told him the good news and I know he was also relieved that he was not going to have to drive me everywhere. He said that his brother was looking to get rid of his old car, so he was going to take it off his hands and get it ready for me just in time for when I started school in a week.

As I walked home, I thought about all the things driving was going to allow me to finally do. My plan was to keep practicing and better my driving skills using the side roads for a month or so before I ventured into the highways to go to the IDMJI Church. In my research, the drive to IDMJI Church in Charlotte was 2 hours 20 min on the highway versus 3 hours and 50 minutes on the side roads.

On Thursday evening, Dan Brannen arrived to our apartment. It was awesome to see a familiar New Yorker even if he lived in New Jersey! I knew he was tired from traveling, so we chatted for a bit and briefly discussed the schedule for our hike the next morning. We were all up by 5 a.m. and out the door by 6 a.m. and on the Mount Mitchell trail by 7 a.m. The drive there was scenic and about an hour. I didn't realize that we were so close to the border of Tennessee. The trail started inside the Black Mountain Campground. Dan was excellent in educating us about the route. We would be following the blue trail markers which had blue blazes on the trees.

The trail started along a stream and we quickly started to ascend on trails that had significant roots and rocks. I experienced feelings I had never felt before. I didn't need anyone to be chit chatting nor did I feel the need to speak. I was focused on every step, every breath while I felt the skies, trees and mountain's embrace. Around the 2nd hour of the relentless ascent, there was a section where I was literally on my hands and knees grabbing on to trees sweating and trying not to slip down before we took a much-needed water and snack break. "So, how do you like the hike so far?" asked Dan. I burst out laughing uncontrollably and Brian followed and then Dan!

Brian knew that I once thought hiking was for grandparents. "I LOVE THIS! I never thought hiking could be like this Dan!" I replied with my mouth still chomping away at a Clif Bar. We got back on our feet after a brief 5-minute break and the brutal climb started up again. The higher we climbed the cooler the air got. After about another hour as we approached the summit, we reached another beautiful challenging section where the mountain became alpine, mossy and mystical and it certainly filled all my insides with indescribable feelings of joy.

With my legs feeling like jelly and my heart about to burst from emotion, we walked over to a big red sign that read, "Mount Mitchell, Highest Peak East of Mississippi River, Elevation 6684 Ft." I took in the 360 degrees views and closed my eyes and said a prayer while I felt the skies blow a warm breeze on my face. "This is what it feels like to be happy," I thought to myself as I wiped a tear away and would remember this first hike forever. The descent took nearly as long as the ascent, so we were all wiped out by the time we finished 7 hours later.

Arriving back in Asheville that evening, we took Dan to one of Asheville's best vegan restaurants called, "Laughing Seed Café" located in the heart of Downtown Asheville. We had a great time talking about the hike and old times before getting back to the apartment to shower, sleep and get back up to work the Cancer Walk/Run event the next early morning. We drove to South Carolina which was also about an hour drive away. Brian and I started moving barricades, helping set up the pre and post finish refreshment areas and setting up signage. Every event had similar elements. You just always need the right team to execute the logistics as best as possible.

As with any event, this Cancer Walk/Run had its challenges, but we made it work and it seemed to have gone fairly well. Before we departed, Dan mentioned that the New York Road Runners were no longer handling the JPMorgan Chase Corporate Challenge Event and that one of his associates and him were running the event for the bank now. He added that if I was available to work and help out in some of the logistics as I had done for the past few years, he would hire me. I didn't hesitate to jump at the offer and mentioned that I would be traveling to New York every few months or so and can be there to work the event in the summer, so we agreed to stay in touch.

It was a very fulfilling weekend and I was feeling melancholic on the drive back home. I hiked and reached a significant summit for the first time and worked a 12-hour day, so I also felt accomplished. Brian took the opportunity to point out that the holidays were quickly approaching in less than a month and that his father had invited all of us to his new home in Florida to spend a weekend with his wife, newborn son and also meet his in-laws. I tried not to visibly cringe, but something in my face must've given my feelings away. "It is just one weekend Scoob! I haven't seen my dad in over 6 months. This is not easy for anyone!" said Brian in a borderline high tone.

He would not go to church with me, meanwhile, he wanted me to go all the way to Florida and put on a fake smile to meet his new baby brother and his father's new in-laws. "Yeah, okay Raggie. I am glad you realize that this is not easy, but I will try and put on a good face for Thanksgiving weekend. Right now, I would like to focus and get ready for school on Monday. I will drive myself, so you don't have to worry," I said with heaviness in my chest.

The next day, I went for a long run by myself as I knew Brian would want to take the day to rest. His new thing was to binge on the Netflix mail service that allowed you to rent series and movies. He loved to watch the entirety of a 12-episode series in one sitting, which would take up an entire day. He was currently watching the 1st season of "Damages" with the actress Glen Close. I joked around and called him a bum, but he didn't care. He always shot back saying that he deserves a "bum" day after working hard all week.

I drove myself to the Asheville School of Masasge & Yoga that Monday morning promptly as 8 a.m. while the rest of my classmates strolled in after 8 a.m. One of the things that stayed with me from the Anthony Robbins seminars I attended in the past and the books I read was that being late is inconsiderate, so I did everything I possibly could to not be late, especially on my 1st day of classes. When the class of 12 women and 1 guy: Brandi, Emily, Gina, Heidi, Jamie, Jody, Kayce, Kate, Lee, Lisa, Lyndia, Mark and myself was complete, the school founder and director, Shala guided us through a series of gentle yoga exercises and finished with a meditation before we each introduced ourselves and went over the 8-month intense certification course.

Most of the women were from nearby areas and they quickly started to form their own cliques during the breaks throughout the 8-hour day. I felt as if I was reliving my elementary and high school years all over again. It was challenging to make friends and fit in. The women were never mean though, they just did not go out of their way to be friendly nor made any effort to get to know me. I hoped this would change. For now, I was sad and puzzled after my first day of classes, but I was determined to get through this course so that I can have my certification and obtain the skills needed to get a better paying job in Asheville.

On my drive back home, I remembered one of our instructors that we were introduced to, Martina Barnes who was a practicing psychologist in Asheville and she would be our instructor for Ethics and Psychology. I had not spoken to any counselor since Father Joe and I had not been to church in a few months, so I felt so much was bottled up inside. She had shared her email during the introduction, so I thought about writing her soon.

I was so drained when I got home and I realized it was mostly emotional. I straightened up the house cooked some rice that would go along with the roasted chicken I picked up from Earth Fare and I had it ready on the table as I waited for Brian to come home, but he called saying that he had to finish packing an urgent order for a client and he wouldn't be hone until much later. I didn't even bother to eat and put away the food and turned on my computer instead and was comforted when I received an email from petfinder.com alerting me that there was a 6-week-old male Jack Russell/Chihuahua mix puppy in need of adoption.

Someone left him, his mom and brothers on a side of a road in Lexington, North Carolina which was about a 6-hour drive from Asheville. His mom and brothers were adopted already and only "Brownie" was available. I saw his picture and fell in love immediately. This is the dog I have been waiting for my entire life! I emailed them and asked when I could pick him up and they responded right away and asked me to pick him up as soon as possible. I would plan to go that weekend on Saturday.

I couldn't stop thinking about "Brownie" who I would rename "Jack" as that name reminded me of some of the strong men I admired. Jack was the name of one of a great mentor to me named Jack Walston, a tough Navy Seal who taught me so much amount mental fortitude and toughness, Jack Dawson from the movie "Titanic" and Jack Bauer a Counterterrorism agent from the "24" television series played by Keifer Sutherland.

I saved his picture and forwarded the petfinder.com email along with a note to Brian that read: "Raggie, I understand that you have to work long hours and travel much more now. We will be moving into a bigger house soon and I think it is the perfect time for me to become a dog mom. Please see the attached picture of Jack who I would like to pick up this Saturday in Lexington, NC. I can drive myself if you want. We can talk about it when you have time this week. Love, Scooby"

I felt my lower back throbbing as I laid in bed drowsy seeing the image of Jack before I passed out. Throughout the remainder of the week, I struggled to wake up early and go for my run before classes and decided to run every other day instead of every day until I adjusted. One of the things I learned to really appreciate at the Asheville School of Massage & Yoga was starting out our day with stretching and meditation. It was part of our required self-care practice which we would also do throughout the day during breaks.

We learned about the different modalities of massage and we also started learning anatomy with one of the astoundingly knowledgeable instructors, Marion Stone whom also was a practicing Massage Therapist and former registered nurse. Anatomy was by far my favorite subject because it was challenging and I was amazed of the complex but wonderful ways our bodies' function. We would be tested every Friday which kept everyone on their toes and we also needed to practice our massage techniques at home and then perform our techniques on our instructors.

One day after school, I asked Brian if I could use him to practice my massage skills and his face lit up. Massage was something he loved getting whenever possible. His face lit up and he happily volunteered to be used for any and every practice session I needed. The constant bending over did not do any favors for my lower back which seemed to get progressively worse each day, so I scheduled an appointment to see an orthopedic specialist the following week.

The massage session that Friday evening softened Brian up and he offered to drive me to Lexington the next day to pick up Jack. We were on the road by 6 a.m. and arrived at noon. When we opened the door, 2 little light browned runts sprinted to us jumping up and down. They were both insanely cute! I picked them both up and they started licking my face and wagging their tails non-stop. "Raggie, can we adopt both? They are brothers and should stay together. Pleeeease?" I said overwhelmed with tears. Brian never had a dog, but I could see his heart melting with these precious little ones.

He observed my interaction with the tiny puppies. I put the puppies on his lap and they were also loving on him before he replied, "I would hate to separate them too Scoob. I will offer to pay for both dogs and take them home right away if the foster parent agrees." The vaccination/ adoption fee was $250 but Brian offered to write out a $500 check for both dogs on the spot. It was Jack and his brother Peanut, but the foster parent informed us that she had promised Peanut to a lady who was on her way driving in 13 hours from New Jersey. "The only thing I can offer you is to take either dog, but not both," she said.

I was heartbroken but I went to the other end of the room and extended my arms and closed my eyes. Whichever puppy ran to me first would be the one I took home. When I opened my eyes, Jack was wagging his tail and jumped into my arms. Ever since I saw his picture, I knew we were meant to be together. We were inseparable. On the ride home, we stopped at a pet store and purchased his food, leash and some toys.

Brian had made it clear that Jack would need to sleep in his own bed. Jack was so tiny at barely 3 pounds, but then again, he was only 6-weeks old. He loved hanging out around my neck to stay warm. We got home in the late evening and headed straight to bed. I put little Jack in his bed and a few seconds later, he started scratching my bed and crying. Brian put him outside our bedroom door and then we discovered how loud he could howl. About an hour later, Jack was sleeping in our bed underneath my armpit and has never slept in his own bed at night in the past 14 years since I adopted him.

While Brian indulged in his television series the next day on Sunday, I spent the day studying with Jack, training and walking him. I was fascinated by his preciousness and innocence. I gave him 100% of my love and affection and it was reciprocated for the first time in my life. It felt so good to tell Jack "I love you" throughout the day. I knew by the look in his big brown eyes that the feeling was mutual. I didn't need nor use a leash when we walked. Jack followed me and listened to my instructions. Training him felt effortless. I put everything I learned from Cesar Millan's books to use and it was working like a charm.

It was difficult to leave Jack when I went to massage school during the week, but I would come home for lunch to check up on him and rushed home after school. Jack became my study buddy, my confidant and my best friend. We moved into the new house on Heathbrook Circle in the Biltmore Community a few weeks later. It was the first time for me living in a house and I felt out of place. It was nothing extravagant, but nonetheless, I didn't feel quite at home. What did make me happy was that the house had a cute backyard that had a pet door that allowed Jack to go out into the yard as he pleased. One time I came home early from school to find Jack sunbathing in the yard and that image made me smile day after day.

Soon after we moved in, we went to visit his father in Florida and spent the Christmas holiday and New Year's in Miami. His cousin who owned a luxurious penthouse that featured fluffy rugs on the walls of his in-home theatre invited everyone to spend New Year's Eve at Miami's Prime 112 Restaurant.

It was one of the worst and loneliest New Year's I had ever spent in my life. There were notable people in this celebration like the singer Michael Bolton, models and people with a lot of money, but ultimately, they were all strangers to me that I had absolutely nothing in common with. At the stroke of midnight, I gave Brian a hug, but I had never felt so distant from him.

Although the celebration into the new year was uninspiring, I took the time to write down my goals on a piece of napkin while everyone got drunk. My New Year's goals included seeing a counselor again, driving on the highway so I can finally go to church, find a job, find a college to transfer to upon my completion of massage school and start my courses next fall, visit my sister in New York and start boxing again. As soon as we got back to Asheville that weekend, I got started on my goals and wrote an email to Martina Barnes, my Psychology teacher at the massage school.

I wrote to Martina telling her how sad I felt lately with my marriage situation, about the feelings of uncertainty of what I was supposed to do or be and dealing with past trauma. I expressed my interest in having a session with her if it didn't pose any conflicts. I also asked how much each session would be as that would also be a big deciding factor.

Within a few minutes of sending the email, I received a call from her! "Hi Martina! Happy New Year! It is really good to hear from you," I said in one breath. "Hello Patricia. Happy New Year to you too. Thank you for your email. I have some openings in my schedule this week on Monday or Friday at noon if you'd like to come in for a session. If you feel we are a good fit after that, perhaps we can arrange something. I know you are a personal trainer and I have been looking for one to start exercising again, so perhaps we can barter a training session a week for a counseling session. How does that sound?" she replied. I was elated by her reply and agreed to see her the next afternoon. What made me most happy was the fact that I did not have to ask Brian for any money and I could finally start relying on myself again.

Although I was off from school for the week, I had a busy week ahead and had something scheduled on every day of the week from doctor appointments, job interviews, college tours and looking at gyms. The next morning at 5 a.m., I took Jack on his first run/walk session. We jogged 1 mile and walked 2 miles for a total of 3 miles! He was now almost 3 months old and he did so well! I smiled the entire time from looking at his little legs run. It was inevitable that he would soon become my running partner. I was so excited to tell Brian, but when we got back to the house, he had already left to the gym.

I quickly showered and got ready to drive myself to see the orthopedic specialist about the constant pain in my lower back at Asheville Orthopedic Associates. I checked in with the nurses upon arrival and filled out the insurance forms and was taken in to get x-rays before I was put into a separate room to see the doctor. There was a loud knock on the door as the doctor came in looking at my x-rays. "Hello, my name is Doctor Smith. Good morning, Patricia. Can you tell me anything about any injuries you've had to your lower back?" asked the doctor as he shook my hand.

I gave him a blank stare as I could not remember specifically injuring my back. "Nice to meet you doctor. I am sorry but I cannot really remember any specific events where I injured my back. I started massage school a few months ago and have been sitting for long periods and bending over. That's about it. Do you see anything in the x-rays?" He scratched his head and looked at the x-rays again and said, "Well young lady, the reason for your lower back pain is that your L5 (lumber spine disc 5) has slipped from your S1 (sacral spine disc 1). In addition, you have an old fracture on your tailbone that never healed properly which contributed to that slipped disc. I would highly recommend surgery as soon as possible."

Feelings of déjà vu resurfaced to when the doctor told me that I fractured my wrist and needed to be put in a cast, but this was much worse. I also remembered that my father had beaten me up so badly a few times where I could barely walk or lie on my back for weeks. It was probably one of those beatings that fractured my tailbone. I didn't cry hysterically as I once did. I did my best to not react as dramatic as I had in the past, but tears streamed down my face as I said, "Doctor, I am a competitive athlete and have goals of turning professional as a boxer as well as long distance running goals. Please think of me as your daughter and advise me on any other treatment besides surgery. The old fracture was probably one of the many beatings my father gave me when I was a kid."

The doctor's face was bright red as that was probably not something he heard often. He paced back and forth and then said, "This is not by any means the solution, but the only thing that I can suggest is aggressive physical therapy. We can refer you to a couple of places and if after 12 weeks there is no improvement, then we can schedule you for surgery." The option the doctor offered meant hope- anything, but surgery. I went to the front desk and got the referral and decided to go there immediately since I still had a couple of hours before my session with Martina. I drove a few minutes to Asheville Physical Therapy and met the kindest and best physical therapist, Brian K. Lawler, MS., founder and owner of Asheville Physical Therapy.

Brian Lawler had recently opened up his own business. He patiently listened to my story and my goals of becoming a professional boxer, but what really changed his demeanor was when I said, "I am willing to do the work. I have faith you are God sent and that this physical therapy will save my back from surgery." His big blue eyes opened widely as he said, "I will help you as much as I can, but as Dr. Smith told you, there are no guarantees with physical therapy. However, you have the right idea about faith and working hard. I am glad you are a believer. We can get started right now and I can start you off with a few exercises and then put you on the table for electrical stimulation and ice packs to help with the inflammation. I can schedule you for 2-3 times a week for now and you must do the exercises I give you."

We did a few rounds of back and core strengthening exercises as one of the focuses was to work on the opposing muscles to help support my lower back. It was an important principle that would be reinforced in massage school which is to work on opposing muscles when a specific area was injured. The tens electrical stimulation on my back was intense and as I laid on the table, I said a prayer.

Although the relationship with my husband, Brian and being alone in North Carolina was challenging, I was starting to see that being here also had its blessings. I was discovering the beauty of strength, courage, faith and healing from the inside out. I would have never found out about my back, about the exquisiteness of nature and I knew deep down that there would be many more lessons to come. I was scheduled to see

Brian Lawler again later in the week on Wednesday early morning before he opened up and moving forward so that I would not be late for school.

I hurried to make my appointment with Martina at her in-home office and arrived just in time. Martina greeted me with a warm hug and I immediately felt comforted as her male tabby cat, Sugar and her husky shepherd mix dog, Angel also greeted me. Martina was warm and empathetic and I felt at ease speaking with her. She was completely different than Father Joe. It was a refreshing change and although I cried a lot, it felt great to speak to someone again. We agreed to exchange services and I would start personal training her on Saturday or Sunday mornings. She was involved in a car accident that affected her back and neck a few years ago and wanted to get back in shape.

For the next 16 weeks, I concentrated on my classes, physical therapy, counseling, spending time with my dog, Jack and working a few interpreting assignments from the Buncombe Board of Education. I was barely making $100 a week there, but something was better than nothing and I liked that I was busy. It helped ease the pain from my deteriorating marriage. Soon enough, I gathered up the courage to drive on the highway and go to the IDMJ Church in Charlotte, North Carolina. The drive there in the day light was not as bad as I thought it would be and I remember the joy and relief I felt from finally arriving to such a special place.

The pastor, brothers and sisters were warm and welcoming. I sang, prayed and meditated in the teachings during the 90-minute service. I was overjoyed until I walked out at nearly 8 p.m. and it was already pitch dark outside. I had never driven in the night time and now I was faced with driving in the unknown and to make matters more interesting, there was fog developing.

Driving in the North Carolina mountains in the dark foggy night with no street lights and curvy roads had my stomach twisted in knots the entire time. "God, the only reason I am out here driving at this hour is because I needed to show my presence in your house. Please guide my eyes and hands and protect me from all danger," I said in a desperate whisper as I clenched the steering wheel. I made it back home by 10 p.m. and debated whether to tell Brian, but he was already snoring in bed when I arrived. Driving at night was frightening, but I made it my priority to drive to church every other week for now.

With every week that passed, my body, mind and spirit got stronger. Brian Lawler challenged me with newer and harder exercises during our physical therapy sessions and at the end of the 16 weeks, I went back to Asheville Orthopedic Associates for a follow-up. Dr. Smith walked out with the updated x-rays rubbing his chin as he did the first time we met. He said, "Well, well young lady.... It seems you have been working hard. I am not quite sure how you did it, but it seems that your L5 and S1 are stable and not slipped anymore." I closed my eyes for a few seconds and breathed deeply and said in a soft whisper to myself, "Thank you, God." I knew from the initial diagnosis that surgery was not the option for me and with hard work, faith and perseverance, I could get healed.

I opened my eyes and replied to the doctor, "Thank you so much Dr. Smith for referring me to Brian Lawler at Asheville Physical Therapy. He has been essential in helping me strengthen my core muscles. I worked hard on my own as well and believed that healing was possible without the surgery." The doctor added that I was a true testimony on the positive outcomes of physical therapy and advised that I continue to do the physical therapy exercises on my own for as long as possible for maintenance and selfcare.

I graduated from the Asheville School of Massage Therapy & Yoga and obtained my NCBTMB (National Certification Board for Therapeutic Massage & Bodywork). I had the summer off and would start my college elective courses in the fall at Asheville-Buncombe Technical Community College (AB Tech) before I transferred to the University of North Carolina-Asheville (UNCA) in the winter. I loved all the valuable lessons and experience I learned from massage school, but I realized it was not the path I wanted to take. Staying grounded and providing people a comforting massage was not possible for me. This was not the correct career path for me.

CHAPTER 10

Chapter Ten - Round 10

My Why

"You have to accept whatever comes and the only important thing is that you meet it with courage and with the best that you have to give." Eleanor Roosevelt

After graduating from massage school and healing my back, I was focused on getting back to boxing. I wanted to feel a sense of purpose again. I wanted my life to have meaning. I wanted to challenge myself and see how far I could go in the sport and that would mean I would have to turn professional. I had no idea how the business worked, but I would at least start by getting back into boxing shape and enter the North Carolina Gloves which upon research would be in a couple of months.

After my morning run, I drove to the Mixed Martial arts center on Hendersonville Road. This gym was a located inside a steel aluminum warehouse like many businesses in North Carolina. I met the two managers named Shayne and Dave. "Hello, my name is Patricia and I am looking for a place to train. I am entering the North Carolina Gloves in September and have to get ready," I said. Shayne was over 6 feet tall, lean and muscular and smirked as he listened to me and Dave was not as big, but his blue eyes were fixated momentarily on sizing me up. "That's great Patricia. We are a new gym and we don't have too many fighters just yet, but why don't you come back this evening and workout with the class and speak to the owner. I can also talk to my wife. She has some good moves and perhaps you can spar together."

I wasn't keen on coming back in the evening as my energy level tends to drop significantly by then, but I would make an exception and hoped it would be worth it. I went back home and walked Jack around the neighborhood and bumped into a neighbor that apparently lived down the block from me. "Hi there! I always see you in the neighborhood and had meant to introduce myself. My name is Candace and this is my dog Harmon short for Harmony. Forgive me for being so forward, but would you be interested in a small job walking my dog? I am looking for someone to watch and walk Harmon for the next 3 weeks while I am away visiting family," she said. Candace was a sweet lady in her late 60's and did indeed live a block away in a beautiful well-kept house with her dog, Harmon. I was also off from my interpreting job with the Buncombe Board of Ed for the summer, so I could use any extra income.

"Hi Candace, it's very good to meet you. This is my dog, Jack and I am free this entire summer because I am a part-time interpreter for the Buncombe Board of Ed, so I would love to take care of Harmon." Candace was very happy and invited me for tea back at her place to show me around. Harmon and I got along really well and Jack immediately liked Candace as well, so this was a good sign on both ends even though I was confident I would get the job. There was no doubt that I had a special connection to animals. I took an immediate liking to her and answered all her questions. She offered to spread the word around the nearby neighbors about my dog walking availability for the summer and not long after, I had 4 additional furry clients on my morning and afternoon walks.

I went back to the Mixed-Martial Arts gym in the evening. There were 6 guys and 1 woman named Jennifer who was David's wife. I wrapped my hands and joined the class who were shadow boxing in place before we started hitting the heavy bags and took turns hitting the pads. After 45 minutes, they put headguards on Jennifer and I so we can move around for 3 rounds. I was taught that whenever 2 people go inside the ring, your internal guard must go up.

The bell rang and I started the round with a quick one-two (jab-right hand) that caught Jennifer as she did a 360-spin. David had built her up to be this incredible athlete with good moves, so I was surprised and disappointed as I was looking forward to a regular sparring partner in Asheville. We could not even finish one complete round as she blinked at every move I made. It became apparent that she only stepped into the ring because of David and had no real boxing experience.

However, she was a very kind woman and dedicated mother to a teenage son who would later on divorce David and open up her own Chiropractic and Wellness center in Asheville called Crystalign Chiropractic.

Before I drove back home, the owner came outside and handed me the keys to the gym. He said I was welcomed to use the gym in the early mornings to train and get myself ready for my upcoming bouts. I was very grateful and was going to do the best with what I had. I would make it my business to train here a few times a week and would have to keep searching for sparring partners.

The next morning, I started searching and calling boxing gyms in the surrounding areas. I called a place in Charlotte named Ultimate Boxing Gym and the guy who answered the phone invited me to come in on Friday afternoon to spar with one of their female fighters who was also getting ready for the North Carolina Gloves as well. I agreed right away and decided to keep calling around just to have a back-up. In boxing, you always needed a plan b as the chances of things falling through was always high. I called a place named White Rock Boxing in South Carolina. An older guy answered the phone enthusiastically and invited me to spar sometime next month. I agreed and was happy to have made 2 new contacts. I would go to Charlotte on my own, but would invite both Brians- my Brian and Brian Lawler to come with me to South Carolina whenever that was scheduled.

My days became busy again. I got my early morning training in and then I walked my furry friends in the mornings and afternoons and then before Brian got home, I would sometimes get in a 2nd workout. I would sometimes join him to watch whatever series he was into, but the lack of intimacy continued. Feeling and watching a relationship die is one of the most painful experiences ever and I trained even harder to numb the pain.

On Friday morning, I stretched and prayed instead of working out as I needed to be fresh for my sparring session later. I walked the dogs in the morning and afternoon and called Brian to tell him that since I was going to go the IDMJI Church in Charlotte after sparring. I had become a better driver and getting on the highway was no longer as intimidating as it once was. I arrived at Ultimate Gym and the owner; Doug shook my hand and showed me where the changing rooms were. When I went in to change, I met Janet. "Hi! You must be Janet. Good to meet you. I believe we are sparring today?" I asked. She had a very serious face and shook my hand and walked out. She was not friendly at all initially, but we were about to spar after all, so I understood the mindset. When I walked back out, Janet was shadow boxing in the ring all geared up and ready. So, I hurried and put in my mouthpiece and head gear, but needed Doug's help to get my gloves on.

The bell rung and we tapped gloves. I moved from side to side, forward and back and then threw 2 quick jabs that made contact with Janet's face. I could see her face turn red from anger even through the headguard. It was as though I had initiated war because she charged at me right after that. Boxing is an emotional trigger for many and I understood why. However, I used that to my advantage and the more Janet chased me, the more I could practice my defense. I went back to my empty corner and took a quick sip and I could see Janet and Doug arguing. Although, he was coaching her on what to do for the next round, their body language indicated that they were or had been a couple at some point which was common in Women's Boxing. Female fighters were usually involved with the Coach, Trainer, Manager, Promoter or someone from her team.

The bell rang for the 2nd round and I initiated contact with a 3-punch combination which Janet answered right back. She was very fit, lean and strong at 132lbs, but as a mixed martial artist, she telegraphed her punches. I felt her punches, but they didn't hurt. She had a better round and we sparred for 6 rounds in total. I was shocked when she gave me a hug at the end of the 6th round just because I thought she hated me. "You are really good Patricia! Thank you for the work today. I hope you can come back soon before the tournament," she said. As I was leaving, Doug invited me to a boxing show he was putting on at the end of the month and said he had another mixed martial arts female fighter in mind that was 125 lbs. that he could match me up with.

During the week, I opted to go to the MMA gym instead of my morning runs. I could not let having the keys of this gym go to waste and besides, I had to prepare for the boxing show in Charlotte and also be ready for the North Carolina Gloves. There was a small mirror full length mirror that I used to watch myself shadow box.

I always felt awkward looking at my reflection in the mirror when I was shadow boxing in front of Coach and others, but there was no one around except Jack, me, and my shadow, so I was able to watch my reflection, my moves, and my eyes carefully in the mirror. As I did that, I also remembered my sparring sessions, bouts and all the years of training.

I finished my 10 rounds of shadow boxing and moved on to the heavy bag. I bobbed, weaved, and ducked imaginary punches and countered with intense combinations one after the other. I moved around the bag moving side to side and practicing my footwork for another 10 rounds. I completed my workout with some good old sit-ups, push-ups, and pull-ups while I played the "Rocky" theme song in my head. By the end of my 90-minute workout, I was proudly drenched in sweat. I continued to do this morning routine every other day and the days in between, I supplemented with running on the trails and weight workouts at The YMCA and the exercises I learned from my physical therapy.

Upon the arrival of Fall, I started my classes at AB-Tech three times a week from 9 a.m.-12 p.m. and I managed to continue to keep walking the dogs in my community in the afternoons. I really enjoyed spending time with dogs while making extra cash. They didn't judge and any time spent with these furry creatures was time well spent in my eyes. The time left over, I dedicated to the maintenance of the house, spending time with Jack and going to church.

The weekend before the Boxing Show, Brian told me that he had to drive out to Raleigh, North Carolina for a 5-day textile show, so I would be on my own for this show. I was depending on him to be my corner-man, but now, I had no one. I was disappointed, but it didn't matter. My mind was set, and I was going to go alone and be my own corner-man if needed. Brian was very apologetic, but it was my fault for relying on him at all. Thankfully, Martina loved Jack and agreed to watch him while I drove to Charlotte. Jack got along wonderfully with both her dog Angel and her cat, Sugar.

On the drive to Charlotte, I remembered when I was training in New York for the Western States Championships. I worked briefly with a performance coach named, Joe Garafolo. He was a former football player who got injured and became focused on working with elite athletes. Working with him gave me a great insight on how to develop speed and power through specific training of the fast twitch muscles like plyometrics, snatches, cleans, sprints and other exercises that required 100% intense output.

There was a noticeable increase in my speed and power. I owe a big part to winning the Western State Championships to working with him and I took all his teachings and applied them to my trainings whenever I needed. Joe would also take the time to give me advice on life. He once told me that the road and journey of a Champion was a very lonely one and I had to be willing to walk alone. It was not only in sports, but I felt that I walked alone in every aspect of my life. I was thankful to have my faith which I knew was the foundation of my strength and courage.

I arrived at Ultimate Gym at 5 p.m. and had about an hour to change and get warmed up as the show started at 6:30 p.m. I saw that the gym had been converted into looking like a boxing arena with over 100 chairs fanning out around the perimeter of the ring. Although Doug said this was only a "show" where there is no winner declared, I knew that it wasn't. When 2 athletes put on boxing gloves, whether it is in their minds, their coaches' minds or the people watching, there is always a winner and a loser.

I changed into my favorite black and gold trunks, I put on my yellow Golden Gloves tank top, tied on my blue and red boxing boots from the Nationals and felt the fire burn within. I looked into the mirror and whispered, "Be Relentless tonight." As I started wrapping my hands, I realized I had no beta on my opponent, no one to give me any pointers and no one to hold the pads for me to help get me warmed up.

I went back out, and the gym was already 90% filled with people sitting, standing, and drinking. Thankfully, Doug is a hard to miss guy and I found him amongst the crowd quickly and told him I didn't have anyone to work my corner and he assured me when it was my turn to box, he would have someone ready in my corner. He also pointed out the girl I was scheduled to box. It was a girl named Tracey who was an experienced mixed martial arts fighter transitioning into boxing. She was my height and 125 pounds.

I was the 3rd bout, so I started jumping rope for 3 rounds in the back of the gym and then shadow boxing. About a half hour later, I heard the announcer call my name and I shuffled down in between the crowds and entered the ring for the first time in over 3 years. I saw a random guy in my corner and I went over and high fived him with my gloves. The announcer called us into the middle of the ring, we tapped gloves and then the bell rang. I charged across the ring and threw a hard jab that snapped Tracey's head back and the crowd went crazy.

I remembered what Coach used to say to me, "When the bell rings, make sure you establish who's the boss right away." Tracey was tough though and kept pressing forward no matter what I threw at her. As soon as I heard that she was an experienced mixed martial arts fighter, I knew she would be tough. My first discipline was martial arts, and it was what helped me develop that "no quit" mentality and heart which stayed with me forever. Tracey telegraphed her punches, so I was able to beat her to the punch and get out of the way. My defense didn't allow her to score much. At the end of the 3 rounds, we both had our hands raised, but the crowd, the corner and we knew who had won this bout.

This "show" did not get recorded in our boxing passbooks, but it was a great tune-up before the North Carolina Gloves. I agreed to drive in whenever possible to spar with Janet and/or Tracey to help Janet get ready as well. I hoped that whatever was going on between her and Doug would not interfere with her training. Right now, I had to take care of me and hurried out as it was past 8 p.m. and dark outside.

I picked up Jack before I got home and got a call from Brian asking about the show. When we hung up the phone, tears streamed down my cheeks because I was touched that Brian at least cared to call to see how everything had gone. As much as I wanted to let go of the hurt, I felt that somehow it was too late. We disagreed on almost everything, he refused to go to church with me and thought I should work in a supermarket and a huge wedge between us was also not being intimate for a very long time. I felt that his love for me had developed into something you would feel for your sister.

I talked to Martina about this during our sessions and she suggested that I try my hardest and "just do it". But I couldn't force myself. "If my heart and soul are not there, I just cannot force myself," I would say. Although Brian cared, I felt that his patience was running out. He was never violent or demeaning when we argued and he never ever raised a hand to hurt me physically in any way. I just felt that the lack of intimacy and understanding had reached a point of no return. All I could do in the meantime was keep praying for a solution and keep moving forward with school and boxing.

I decided to call White Rock Boxing and follow-up on the sparring invitation. The older man on the other end of the line again with the deep southern accent was the manager of the gym named, Billy Stanick said when he heard my voice, "Well hello again! I am glad you called! Angel and her Coach, Dominic would be glad to have you in this Sunday at their usual training time of 10 a.m. We look forward to having you!"

Angel fought in the 132-pound women's division. I was used to sparring with heavier women and did not worry much as speed equals power and I had some of that to help balance things out. I invited both Brians to be my corner men and on that Sunday morning we all met at the Ingles Supermarket in Asheville and started driving from there. We were due in Chapin, South Carolina at 10 a.m. which was about a 90-minute drive from Asheville. As we got closer to the gym, there was a few houses that we passed that had a flag I had never seen before hanging in the front porches.

"Raggie, that is a funny looking flag. What country is it?" I asked. Brian looked at me confused and amused at the same time. "Are you joking with me Scoob? You've never seen a confederate flag before? I am glad you are not here by yourself. I don't like you coming to these places on your own," he replied. I was relieved that I was not alone today too. We arrived at White Rock Boxing at 9:45 a.m. and an older fair skinned colored man with white hair in his 60's greeted me loudly, "You must be Patricia Alcivar, USA National Champion and NYC Golden Gloves Champion... Welcome to White Rock Boxing!"

I was startled by the loud and forward welcome. He came over to shake my hand and I replied, "Very good to meet you sir. Thank you for inviting me to spar here. This is my husband Brian and my strength coach Brian Lawler who will work my corner today.

We have a long drive back, so I am going to get changed and warmed up," I said. While I warmed up, Angel and her Coach, Dominic walked in. Although she boxed in the 132-pound division, she must have been easily walking around at 150 pounds. She looked round and was a few inches shorter than me. I could see her coach sizing me up and looking at my every move while I shadow boxed in front of the mirror. That is what coaches do though and I was envisioning my moves on this chick.

Boxers that are shorter and heavier like Angel will try to use their power but get tired easier, so I already knew I was going to have to use my footwork, speed and conditioning. I saw Angel getting in the ring and getting her headguard and gloves put on, so I did the same. I instructed both Brian's about taking out my mouthpiece and giving me water and any words of advice during the one-minute breaks after each round. The plan was to spar at least 6 rounds. I was initially intimidated by the environment, but I said a prayer before the bell rang and then that magical switch went on just in time.

I met Angel in the center of the ring and landed 2 quick hard jabs to her nose. She shook her head and threw 2 solid body punches to my obliques. If I had not been in shape, they would have caused me to take a knee. I did the mistake and stood there exchanging heavy punches with Angel. When the bell rang to end the first round, everyone in the gym was watching. My nose was already bloodied and I could see the look of concern from both Brians. "You gotta move Scoob! This girl is a lot heavier than you. Do what you do best," said Brian. I nodded while I got a sip of water. I knew he was right, but I had let my pride get in the way. I could see her breathing hard, so I was going to take advantage of that now.

The bell rang for the 2nd round and I still met her in the center of the ring, but now was moving quickly after each punch I threw. "Stick and move," I kept saying to myself. She chased me and was missing big time. I don't think she connected with any punches in the 2nd round. We could hear her coach yelling at her during the break. "Nice job Scoob! This was a better round for you. Keep moving and do not let her connect. She is breathing heavy and is tired!" said Brian during the break.

The bell rang for the 3rd round and my plan was to continue to use my defense but not moving as much. It was risky but I started throwing hard combinations and using my hands to take the weight off her punches as well as ducking and weaving. I was able to get the better of the round again while she went back to her corner and kept getting yelled by her coach. We ended up sparring 10 rounds! That was a record for me! After the 6th round, Dominic kept saying "One more!"

Billie Stanick came up to me before we left and said, "You are going to be World Champion. You are welcomed to come back anytime." This was a great sparring session and I was very thankful. It was exactly what I needed before the North Carolina Gloves tournament which was the following weekend in Wilmington, North Carolina- a 5-hour plus drive from Asheville. On the drive back to Asheville, both Brian's were impressed and continued to give me advice on what they thought I could have done better.

For the moment, it looked like things between Brian and I could have a chance. I asked him to work my corner at next weekend's tournament and he offered to drive me as well, so I saw it as a sparkle of hope. Gratitude for me is where it all starts in my heart, so I hoped that somehow it could rekindle those special feelings. I needed his support more than ever. I had felt so alone since we moved here and I've had to rely on prayers and my faith. I was trying so hard to be a wife, but did not want to give up on my dreams either.

We started the drive at 5 a.m. the Saturday morning of the North Carolina Gloves. This tournament was not as big nor prestigious as the New York City Golden Gloves and the tournament for the women's division would just be on that Saturday afternoon. There was also no guarantee that there would be anyone in my division either. Brian was listening to stand-up comics on the satellite radio while I slept most of the way. Once we arrived, I was so glad to see Janet!

"Hey Janet! I am so glad to see you here!" I said with excitement. I didn't see Doug there and was afraid to ask. While we waited in line, she hesitantly told me that they had dated, but it didn't work out and she was trying to do the boxing on her own. She did not come with a coach and was relying on the event to assign her a random coach to work her corner.

We finally came to the front of the line and Janet would get matched up with the only other female in her weight division. There were no women at 119 besides myself, but there was one other female boxer at 139 pounds that also really wanted to fight.

The USA Boxing Official told me and the 139-pound female boxer that they could have us box each other, but it would not get recorded in our boxing passbooks as an official bout. The 139-pound woman was taller and looked so much bigger than me, but I took a deep breath and told the Official that I would box her. I reasoned with the fact that in training, I always spar with heavier boxers and Coach always told me that I had a good chin which was a term used when a fighter could take a hard punch and still keep coming forward. The truth was though, I had taken much more pain in by my parents and in life and a punch did not sting nearly as much. I also didn't have Brian drive for over 5 hours for nothing and I needed the exposure. I was going to show myself and the people in attendance that I could fight a heavier boxer and win.

Janet was the 1st bout and was extremely nervous. I held the pads for her and helped her warm up. I could see that her nerves were getting the best of her. "Let it all go when the bell rings," I said right before her name got called. She was assigned a random coach to work her corner and then the bell rang. "You first Janet! Jab! Jab!" I yelled. She was bouncing around the ring and was not able to connect at all in the first round. I wished I could be in her corner and hoped the random coach was giving her good advice. The bell rang for the 2nd round and Janet came out and threw 2 nice jabs that finally landed. She was moving better, but her opponent answered right back and they exchanged punches in the center of the ring before the bell rang again. "Janet has to win the 3rd round big if she wants to win the bout," I said to Brian.

The final bell rang and Janet came out swinging. She knew she had to take this round as well, but her opponent was now the one bouncing around the ring not letting Janet connect. No one landed anything significant and then the bell rang to end the bout. Her opponent won the 1st round and round 2 and 3 were even with a slight edge for Janet, but her opponent was a local Wilmington girl. In boxing, you cannot rely on the judges to be fair. You had to decisively win each round to ensure a win and not allow judges to be blinded by any politics that could cloud their judgement.

The referee brought the ladies to the center of the ring while the winner was announced, "The winner of the North Carolina Gloves in the 125-pound Women's Division is.... From Wilmington, North Carolina....". The decision could have gone either way and somehow, I felt Janet's pain. "Scoob, you have to get warmed up NOW! Your bout is right after this one," said Brian. I jumped rope for 3 minutes and shadow boxed for another 5 minutes and then my name was called. My opponent was also a local fighter, so I knew what the deal was here. We came to the center of the ring and tapped gloves and I noticed how much taller she was than me and I thought to myself, "I gotta pound that mid-section".

The bell for the 1st round rang and I rushed over to her and threw a hard jab to her nose and came right down to her body with a right and left hook that landed solid in her obliques and solo plexus. I heard her gasp and her eyes were opened widely. I ducked and weaved out of the way of her punches immediately after. I was surprised at how silent the crowd was after such a beautiful combination, but then I realized, this was not my hometown. The bell rang to end the 1st round and Brian did not take out the stool for me to sit down during the break. "You look great Scoob. Keep doing exactly that for 2 more rounds. Remember, this is your show. Show everyone what you have," said Brian before the 2nd bell rang.

My opponent rushed at me this time, but I did not let her connect with anything solid. I wanted to practice and display my footwork and defense this round. One of my all-time favorite fighters inside and outside of the ring was Sugar Ray Leaonard. I had watched countless hours of videos of his fights. My favorite was when he fought Roberto Duran where he made him miss almost every punch in the final round before the fight was stopped. I remembered that as my opponent kept throwing bombs at me and kept missing. The 3 rounds were up and although the referee raised both of our hands, the people in attendance knew exactly who won.

I was pleased to have boxed in front of a crowd and out box a woman almost 15 pounds heavier than me. As I made my way out of the ring, people reached out to congratulate me. One petite lady in particular with a southern accent came over and shook my hand and said, "Congratulations Lady! You looked awesome! Too bad it didn't count, but you impressed a lot of folks. Where do you train out of and where is your coach?" she asked while she grabbed my arm and pulled me aside and out of the crowd. "Oh! Thanks so much! I don't really have a gym that I represent at the moment. I go everywhere to train and spar. I am really from NYC and moved to Asheville because of my husband's job a few years ago. I am just trying to get a few fights in, but really would like to turn pro soon," I replied.

In our brief exchange, I found out that this woman named Terri was a former Professional Female Boxer who had won a World Title a few years prior but had recently retired and was a coach in Decatur, Georgia. She mentioned that she had a few female boxers and she would be happy to help me turn pro. She gave me her contact information and I agreed to drive to Decatur the following weekend for some sparring with a professional female boxer she trained named, Jackie who was currently 2-2 (2 wins, 2 losses).

Brian came over and said, "Scoob! I have been looking for you! Are you okay? We should start driving back." I introduced him to Terri who was fast talking, witty and quickly disappeared into the crowd again. I was naïve, much younger and thought the best of Terri not yet realizing that I should have had my guard way up when it came to dealing with anyone in boxing even much more when it came to Professional Boxing. I made my final rounds of pictures and we started driving back to

Asheville. I was excited and told Brian all about Terri and that I would be driving to Decatur the following weekend.

"Scoob! How much more do you want to do in boxing? I thought you were phasing out of this?" said Brian. My hopes of any sparkles and rekindling anything went out the window. I was never able to hide disappointment and my face clearly showed that and much more as I turned and looked at him with tears coming down my cheeks. "Raggie, you met me while I was still boxing and yanked me out of the city where I was shining. I told you that I was not done with boxing and wanted to turn pro. I never leave anything unfinished. You said you would support me until the end. Have you changed your mind?" I could see him clenching his teeth and he chose to remain quiet for the remainder of the drive home.

I learned throughout my life that no reply is indeed a reply. Silence is painful and a form of mental abuse. When we got home, Jack came running out and jumped all over me. He loved Brian, but it was clear who the apple of his eye was. He finally calmed down when I picked him up. I laid down with Jack on the couch and cried. I remembered Father Joe telling me that crying did not make me weak and it was a healthy way to deal with painful emotions. He said that not crying and bottling up the pain and anxiety in the end would be worse for my mental and physical health. Judging by how much and how often I cried, I knew I had a lot of pain inside.

A few days after the tournament, there was a small article in the local newspaper highlighting the tournament and my bout. At the same time, I received a call from a guy named Dan from a Media Company. He was looking to film me for one of his projects. I explained that I was looking to turn pro very soon which sparked his interest even more. He mentioned that he was willing to cover my expenses in the process as long as he could film my professional debut. I was way too excited, but maintained my composure and said I would stay in touch and update him when I had the date and fight lined up. I needed to get to Georgia and speak with Terri and would make those arrangements soon. For now, I also needed to start my classes at UNCA.

I had finished the fall semester of college electives at AB-Tech with above average grades and transferred to UNCA (University of North Carolina- Asheville Campus) as planned and had started the winter semester there. The UNCA campus was beautiful and I was intimidated by the size of this University and of the students attending and felt out of place. My goal was to finish my degree in Health and Wellness and I had to do my absolute best. At the end of my anatomy class, I was hurrying down the halls to get home to walk Jack and then a flyer on the announcement board for a sports psychologist caught my attention. It read: "Get to the next level in sports and in life with Bob Swoap, Sport Psychologist, and Professor of Psychology".

I loved my therapy sessions with Martina, but having a session with a specialized Sports Psychologist could only help especially with my intentions of turning professional in boxing, I felt that I should at least inquire. I took a picture of the flyer and made up my mind to call when I got home. On the way home, I stopped at Earth Fare and decided to sit down and have lunch by myself. I sipped my chai tea latte with oat milk and ate my scrambled eggs and thought of my eldest sister. She would go into sweats of the mere thought of going anywhere by herself and here I am doing everything by myself and I was okay with it. I always wondered why all my sisters and I were so drastically different.

I arrived home and quietly tried to sneak up on Jack. I realized as I saw a tail up in the air through the kitchen window that Jack was in the backyard. I watched him digging holes in the backyard with such joy. After he got tired, he found a perfect sunny spot to enjoy the warmth of the sun. Watching him do his dog things and be so carefree was soothing to me and I found myself smiling the entire time. He was precious and I felt fortunate that we found each other. I walked out to the backyard and Jack's ears stood straight up and then he ran over to me with his wagging tail. I rubbed his belly for a bit and fed him the sausage patty I saved for him from Earth Fare.

It was time for me to make that phone call, so I dialed Bob Swoap, "Hello, this is Bob," he answered the phone. "Hi Bob, my name is Patricia and I am a student at UNCA and I saw the flyer for your sports psychology services and would like to have a session with you. I am an accomplished female amateur boxer looking to turn professional soon and I think your services might help me," I said. We spoke for a few minutes and he asked me a few questions about my background. It was not as hard as it used to be to say that I was abused by my father and come from a dysfunctional family. I agreed to see him for a lunch time session the next day.

I sat in the kitchen table to do my homework and was distracted by Jack's big brown eyes staring at me. I picked him up and he laid on my lap while I continued with my studies. I took a few minutes to acknowledge how beautiful it was to feel such a precious furry soul on my lap. It was something I longed to feel my entire childhood and despite the current disarray that my marriage was in, I was grateful to have Jack. We hiked, exercised, drove, ate and did so much together. We were inseparable.

After a couple of hours, I felt the urge to go out on a run before it turned dark and before Brian got home, so out we went in the back trails of the Biltmore Community. Jack had become a good little runner and he ran steadily by my side for a solid hour except when he saw the rabbits hanging out and tried to sprint ahead. "Good Boy, Jack!" I said as we kicked it in to finish our run. Jack looking up at me with his smiling face sealed it for me. Happiness requires being grateful and I was indeed thankful for these moments. I didn't need anything else for tonight. I took a shower, left a note for Brian with his dinner for whenever he got home and went to sleep with Jack by my side.

Jack was not only my best friend and daily companion; he was also the protector of my sleep. He usually snuggled underneath my neck or pressed up against my stomach and was keen on detecting when I was going to have a paralyzing dream. If and when he sensed one of those awful nightmares, he would bark at the dark or start scratching at the bed to wake me up. Tonight though, we both were sound asleep throughout the entire night.

A dull pain in my stomach woke me up and it was my menstrual cycle. It crossed my mind to cancel my session with Bob Swoap, but I had learned to recognize the moments when I had to stand up to my own self. The mind and body seek comfort and anytime I had to talk about my past and/or tried to better myself, I felt like another part of me was comfortable where I was. I fought the urge to stay in bed and woke up before dawn. I went downstairs and remembered the yoga exercises we did every day before started classes. I did a few rounds of the Sun Salutation sequence from massage school and then ended with a prayer before taking Jack out on his walk.

After my morning classes, I walked right into Bob Swoap's office. He was a tall slim, fair skinned about mid 30's man with dark blonde hair. He extended his hand to introduce himself and I did the same. "I know you mentioned briefly some of your background, but let's start over and tell me where you grew up and about your family and how you ended up here in Asheville," said Bob Swoap. As I started telling him about the abuse and beatings I endured at the hands of my father, about how I called the police on him that night when I was 10 years old, how I survived living on my own at 15 years old in New York City after refusing to take any more verbal and mental abuse from my mother, I saw a beautiful picture of him and his family on his desk. He was married and had 3 great looking children. They looked so happy like any family should, but I had that unsettling feeling that he would just not understand.

Bob was compassionate and kind and then asked me about my athletics. I told him how I ran my first marathon at the age of 16, how I won the World Kyokushin Full Contact Martial Arts Tournament shortly after, about winning the first USA Women's National Boxing Championships and about my current goals of turning professional. I also confided in him the difficulties in my marriage and my fears. Hearing myself voice my feelings out loud and talking about my painful past was empowering.

I did not realize at the moment that speaking about them is just one small step. Forgiving and letting go are other important steps that require a different level of spiritual and mental maturity and faith. I understood that many of the past and present events still caused me significant sadness. However, I wanted to address the reason I was seeking Bob's help and that was to move forward in my life and athletics. I did not want my past, my fears and my current situation to hold me back.

"When it comes to boxing, what are you afraid of Patricia?" asked Bob. It didn't take me long to reply, "I get very afraid of losing. I don't want to lose my titles. I do not want to be known as a loser. I don't want to end up being a nothing as my mom used to tell me growing up." Bob had a very calm demeanor about him, but when he heard my answer, he straightened up his back and his tone changed. He said something that changed my life forever, "Patricia, you will forever be a Champion. You won the New York City Golden Gloves, You won the USA National Champions and all the other Championships. No one can ever take that away from you. You are **not** the defending Champion. You are the Champion. For the rest of your life. Period."

Bob gave me pointers on practicing detailed visualization as we were nearing the end of our session which he wanted me to do before my next sparring session this coming weekend in Decatur, Georgia. He wanted me to visualize from the drive to Georgia to me entering the gym, the warm up and then how I wanted to perform in that sparring session. I was grateful for this session with Bob and would put the lessons learned into practice right away. I walked away feeling better about everything. My situation at home was heartbreaking, but I knew I had to keep moving forward and keep praying that somehow things would fall into their place.

The best part of my day was always coming home and seeing Jack's smiling face and wagging tale. I planned to leave him at Martina's house after our session tomorrow so that I could drive to Georgia on Saturday. Brian would be away again this weekend at some textile show, so I needed to continue to be strong and do things on my own. I ate my dinner while I held Jack in my arms and fed him tiny pieces of my chicken burger. I had started to reintroduce beef and chicken back into my diet after learning that my blood type was O positive. According to Dr. Peter D'adamo's book, "Eat Right 4 Your Blood Type," people with my blood type which is the oldest blood type in existence needed beef in their nutrition to survive. Furthermore, he advised on avoiding shellfish, dairy, wheat and gluten among other foods.

I had started to follow Dr. D'adamo's guidelines a few months ago when I was desperately trying to find a solution for the strange fatigue, heart palpitations and weight gain I was experiencing. After a few weeks, I saw and felt a notable difference in my body composition and energy. It all made sense as I am allergic to almost everything on the list of foods to avoid for people with blood type 0, so eliminating them and sticking to the highly beneficial food list which included beef, bananas and vegetables was an important daily mission. I saw Brian's packed bags ready as he was leaving for his flight very early in the morning. I wanted to wait for him, but I was exhausted and took Jack to bed and left a note for him with his dinner wishing him a safe flight.

As I snuggled in bed with Jack, I wondered what Brian was feeling. He knew how he pushed me away each time he sided with his father and brother. He saw the pain in my face each time he rejected my invites to accompany me to church. He didn't support my goals of becoming a professional boxer or continuing my studies. Instead, he preferred for me to work at the Earth Fare Supermarket as a cashier and be a good housewife. He had told me how special I was and how I was destined for great things when we were dating. I owed it to myself, to that little girl who forever lived inside me to keep fighting to make her feel special even if no one else did. Tears rolled down my face as I saw an image of myself when I was 6 years old holding my teddy bear. My heart knew what it was fighting for and "My Why" started to finally become clear that night.

When I woke up, Brian was already gone. I was going to take the day to rest from training so I could be somewhat fresh when I sparred in Georgia tomorrow, but I couldn't. Running was an essential part of my well-being, so I took Jack and off we went jogging in the woods for a good 10k. We were both smiling afterwards. Later in the afternoon, I had my session with Martina and left Jack at her place. Jack loved her and her dog, Angel, so he was in good company. The only negative part about leaving Jack was that now I would be completely alone tonight in the house. I forced myself to drive away quickly before I changed my mind.

I had spent so much time doing things alone for as long as I could remember. Growing up, my sisters played amongst themselves and kept me at bay, so I played by myself. Throughout my school years, I mostly kept to myself because the kids also kept their distance from me. I discovered running at the age of 14 and fell in love with being alone with my thoughts. I couldn't help feeling strange in being so comfortable with the fact. The only time I did care about being alone was at night.

I could see the sun setting from the kitchen window. I packed my bag with my boxing gear and clothes and also took a pillow and comforter and brought everything downstairs to the couch. I had a large baked potato for dinner while I watched "I Love Lucy" videos. I missed having Jack by my side tonight and as I closed my eyes, I visualized a smooth drive to Georgia in the early morning and getting to the boxing gym in Decatur and seeing Terri and the female professional boxer I was going to spar with. I visualized being focused and strong during my warm up and then getting in the ring full of energy and power throwing every punch with exact precision and force for the duration of the sparring session.

The GPS estimated the drive to be 3 hours to Decatur, Georgia and we had scheduled the sparring session at 10 a.m., so I started my drive to Georgia at 6 a.m. to allow myself time to make the necessary stops for gas and coffee. Driving for extended periods of time had become the norm for me and it did not bother me which made me wonder why Brian disliked the long drives so much. I was not a fan of getting stuck in traffic, but my reaction was never rage.

I arrived at the Decatur Boxing gym at 9:30 a.m. and could see that the gym had not opened, so I waited inside my car and locked the doors and windows. I always missed the earlier openings and the faster pace of New York City. At 10:20 a.m., I heard a loud engine pulling in and saw that it was Terri driving in a small red BMW with a woman that I assumed was the pro boxer. They got out and hurried over to open up the gym. "God, please protect me and help me have the courage and strength to box well this morning and get back home safely today, Amen," I said mentally and then walked out. When I went inside, Terri came over right away and said, "Hey Girl! Glad you made it! This is Jackie, she is a pro and she will be sparring with you today. Jump a few rounds of rope, shadow box and get geared up. We can get started in about 20 minutes and we can see what you got."

I was not a big talker in general and worst before a sparring session, so I just nodded my head and jumped rope for 3 rounds on the other end of the gym in a small corner. I could see that Jackie was at least 140 pounds and about 5'6", so I would have my hands full this morning and had to stick and move. I could see Jackie shadow boxing in the ring and her punches were quick and short and her movements were somewhat stiff and her footwork was not fluid.

I wrapped my hands and put on my head gear and Terri came to check what size gloves I would be sparring with which were 14 oz. They claimed to only have 12 oz gloves and I could tell by the look on both their faces that they knew it was not right. Jackie outweighed me by at least 20 pounds, but it would not be the first or the last time unethical things like this would occur in boxing. I was on my own here and needed the boxing and guidance to turn pro, so I just shrugged my shoulders and got in the ring after Terri tied my gloves.

The bell rang for Round 1 and I met Jackie in the center of the ring, tapped gloves and jabbed her right in the nose. She did not like that at all and responded with a hard over hand right that had bad intentions all over it. Luckily, I sensed her vibe even before we got in the ring. When you come into a boxer's turf, you have to earn their respect. However, her pro record at the time was 1 win 2 losses. Terri mentioned that Jackie let her nerves get the best of her. Jackie was strong, but there was something indeed lacking. I was faster and had better foot work and most important of all, I ironically had confidence.

We were able to get 5 good rounds of sparring before she caught me coming in with my hands down and wacked me pretty good right on the nose. My nose was not broken, but I was bleeding a lot and we called it a day. She was bigger and was wearing smaller gloves than me, but some fighters need to do whatever it takes to boost their self-confidence. I shook it off and decided to talk seriously to Terri. "Hey Terri, I want to turn pro as soon as possible. A Media Company called me the other day and wants to film my pro debut and said they would cover my expenses in exchange," I said. That got Terri's attention immediately.

"That's awesome Patty! Well, if you give me their number, I can speak with them and tell them all the costs involved. You are a very decorated fighter, so no one is going to want to fight you without some incentive. We are going to have to pay for your opponent and that is gonna cost, but if they want to film you, they are gonna have to pay. Let me take care of all of that. You just need to worry about training. I will coach you and manage you until we find a big manager for you that can pay for everything," she said with sparkling eyes.

I was confused and did not understand why we needed to pay someone to fight me. I was going to be a Professional Fighter and thought I would be the one to be paid to fight. She explained to me that in the beginning of upcoming fighter's careers, their management paid for their opponents in order to build their professional experience and records. Once the fighter had a few wins, that would attract promoters, managers, backers and sponsors which would eventually lead to fighting for a title.

So basically, you had to invest in your own boxing career in the beginning and once you obtained appropriate management, the promoters would pay you to appear on their show. However, paying for your opponent did not guarantee a win. All of Jackie's opponents were paid for thus far and she had 2 losses already on her record. Terri explained that just because you pay for someone to fight you, that does **NOT** mean they are not going to fight. It does **NOT** mean you are guaranteed a win. You have to fight as if your life depended on it because they are going to do everything possible to win.

This information blew me away and I was very nervous. Once again, I ignored the red flags and I would let Terri handle my Professional Boxing debut. I gave her the Media Company's owner's contact info and agreed to come to Decatur once a week for sparring and training and do the rest of the training on my own in Asheville. We finished up the training for today and I drove back home thinking about everything. I wasn't sure how to tell Brian. I feared he wouldn't understand nor support it either, so I would just keep it to myself for now. My focus had to be on training and being ready for my Professional Boxing debut.

For the next few weeks, I concentrated on my nutrition and training. I cut out all junk food from my diet. Although I always stayed within 10 pounds of my 119 lbs. fighting division, losing any weight was extremely challenging for me as I was already active and had a petite frame with low body fat. My weakness for as long as I could remember was sweets. I still occasionally indulged in the bag of sour patch kids when I went to the movies or added the extra tablespoon of sugar in my morning coffee.

I had flashbacks of Coach yelling at me for being over the weight limit a few days before my bout and how I promised it would never happen again. These flashbacks were enough to make me stick to a strict sugar free low-calorie diet immediately.

I kicked my own behind on a daily basis. My mornings began at 5 a.m. with a speed workout at the track. Jack would bark his head off and chase me for the first few laps and then got tired and then would just stand guard lap after lap. Immediately after my sprinting fest, I drove to the MMA gym to shadow box and hit the heavy bag for 20 rounds straight and I would finish with 10 rounds of calisthenics or a weight workout at the Biltmore Community gym and still manage to be in school by 9 a.m. for my first class.

One evening while I was doing my homework, Terri called and said, "We got the fight for you! You are fighting on Friday, October 9th at the National Guard Armory in Columbia, Tennessee against another woman also making her pro debut named Jennifer Batchelder." I felt my adrenaline rise as if I had just finished one of my sprints at the track. This was 2 weeks away and I had trained hard for the past 4 weeks, so I felt ready as I could be. "Awesome Terri! I am ready. I am 122 lbs. right now, so I will be on point with my weight on the 9th," I replied. I was scared, but I had to take this leap. I was due to go to Decatur this weekend for a final sparring session and we would talk about the final schedule and plan.

Now, I had no choice now and I had to tell Brian, so I waited at the dining table with Jack until he got home from work. While I waited, I sent Bob Swoap an email requesting a session as soon as possible. Moments later, Brian came home and kissed me on the forehead and said, "Hey Scoob, everything okay?" I tried to swallow my saliva, but my mouth was completely dry. I replied, "Raggie, my boxing pro debut is all set to happen in 2 weeks on Friday, October 9th in Columbia, Tennessee. A Media Company is going to film it and absorb all the related costs and the promoter of the fight card is going to pay for my hotel, food and anything else I need. I would like you to be there if you can."

"Congrats Scoob. This is what you wanted, so you good for you. I will do my best to be there in the evening, but cannot take off from work the day before or the morning of. I am dead tired and going to hit the shower and relax a bit," he said before he walked away. His tone and words sent chills down my spine because I knew the end was inevitably near. I held Jack extra tight that night while I cried myself to sleep.

I was thankful to wake up and see an email from Bob who agreed to see me today after my final class at lunch time. I had an uncomfortable feeling in my stomach and I knew it was much more than just nerves from this pro debut. When I had to choose between staying in NYC or moving to Asheville to save my marriage, I chose Asheville. I could not give up on my goals now when no one gave up anything for me.

My biggest issue was feeling worthy enough to choose myself and be okay with it. This was the main thing I would talk to Bob about today. I made myself go out for a lite 5k run with Jack to help clear my mind for school.

As I was trying to concentrate on my morning classes, I was having the same uncomfortable feelings in the pit of my stomach I once had before I came home in New York to find that my Golden Gloves were stolen. I was just not sure what to think or do. After my final class, I ran to Bob's office and sat down and cried. "Hey Patty, are you okay? Tell me what is going on," he said calmly. I took a few deep breaths and calmed myself down before answering, "I am sorry Bob, I am just overwhelmed. I found out yesterday that my pro debut boxing fight is all set for 2 weeks from now on Friday, October 9th in Tennessee and I told my husband and his reply was not what I expected. I fear the end is very near if I go through with this fight."

Bob nodded his head and instructed me to close my eyes and to visualize what I wanted to happen in 2 weeks. I followed his directions and controlled my breathing while I closed my eyes and visualized arriving at the National Guard Armory and boxing for the first time as a professional with confidence and style and having my hands raised in victory at the end of the bout to a cheering crowd. I opened my eyes and Bob asked, "Why do you want to fight Patricia?"

Years ago, when I practiced Martial Arts and then transitioned to Boxing, I would not have known how to answer that question, but the answer became clearer each day now. "No one ever gave me a fighting chance. Not my father, not my mother, not my family or friends. No one ever fought for me. I owe it to myself and that little girl no one valued to make the best of what God has given me. I fight and will die for her and her honor." It was the first time I was able to voice "My Why" and now it would become the reason behind everything I did. It would clearly be my inspiration, my motivation to keep moving forward in spite of the obstacles- Little Patty. This session would be one of the most significant talks of my life.

The next day, I drove to Decatur and I had my final sparring and training session with Terri. "You are definitely ready to make your pro debut Patty! You go out there and do what you do here and you are going to knock that girl out. Just remember that Jennifer is thinking she is going to win, so you show her who's the boss," said Terri while I stretched and we talked about the schedule for the final days leading up to the fight. I would be riding down to Tennessee with the Media Company on Thursday, the day before the fight for the weigh-ins which would be held at the Armory in public and meet Terri there by noon.

The next few days I restricted my food intake even more and I made sure I went to the sauna at the YMCA in the evenings and kept my runs at no more than 3 miles at a time followed by 30 minutes of intense shadow boxing. By Wednesday evening, I was at exactly 119 lbs. On Thursday, October 8th at 7 a.m., the Media Company knocked on my door, "Hey Patty Boom Boom! Are you ready?" asked the founder, Dan with a huge smile. Brian had already left to either the gym or the office and I had left Jack at Martina's place last night, so I looked down momentarily and got my packed bag and replied, "I am ready! Let's go!"

There were 2 camera crew guys also in the van with us and talking with all of them made the 5-hour drive go by quickly. When we arrived at the National Armory Guard, I was surprised to see Terri shadow boxing in front of one of the mirrors at the Armory. She had been retired for over 5 years, so it was strange, but as soon as she realized I had arrived she and her assistant/friend came over to greet us.

"Hey Girl! How are you feeling? I just saw your opponent. She means business and she was already talking trash about how she is going to knock YOU out," said Terri. I was not sure why she would say something like this to me, but I knew what and why I was fighting for and I was not going to let anyone dishonor that. "Hey Terri! I am so hungry and thirsty! I am right on weight, so I want to get this weigh-in over with so I can eat!"

It was past 1 p.m. and the promoter came over to tell us that we would get started momentarily. The local newspapers, news and photographers were all gathered in the main media room while they started calling out the first few preliminary bouts. I was stunned to find out that my bout was the co-main event! I felt my hands trembling as I started to remove my socks, shorts and top to get on the scale in front of the people in attendance. "Patty Boom Boom, 119!" said the announcer. Jennifer was up next and she weighed in at 116.0 lbs. which meant she was ready as well! It reminded me of the time when I fought in the USA Nationals and weighed in under the weight limit each and every time.

During the face off pictures, I was able to look into Jennifer's eyes. She was just as nervous as I was, but there was something missing. Although I was nervous, I had faith and I had "my why" and somehow, I knew that was going to make the difference tomorrow night. She didn't shake my hand and just gave me a dirty look as we turned around and went our separate ways and the photographers finished snapping their final pictures of us. I saw Terri talking to the reporters and I managed to hear her saying that she was a world champion. It started to become clear that she wanted to be the center of attention and promote herself which was not cool at all especially during my pro debut.

We went to the local diner and I started rehydrating immediately and ordered 3 scrambled eggs over rice. Terri and everyone were surprised at my order, but I told them how this reminded me of amateur competition days at the USA Nationals and every major boxing tournament. It was my go-to food that I knew my digestive system could handle and provided the right amount of energy and nutrition. Terri like many female professional boxers, did not have an amateur background. I paid my dues with almost 6 years fighting as an amateur and had close to 50 fights winning almost every major award in the sport. And as Bob

Swope taught me, those awards and merits would be forever mine and spoke volumes on their own.

After dinner, we drove to the Days Inn, the hotel the promoter paid for us to stay in. It was not the best and looked run down and had an odd smell, but I was dead tired and needed to rest. I said my prayers and was thankful to fall asleep right away with no issues at all even though I did not have my little Jack. The sound of my cell phone ringing woke me up at 8 a.m. I could not believe I had over 8 hours of uninterrupted sleep. I was so glad it was my sister calling to wish me luck. Soon after she called, Brian called to let me know he would be driving down and be there early in the evening for my fight. Soon after my shower, Terri came knocking at my door to pick me up for breakfast.

While we ate our breakfast at the nearby Denny's Diner, we briefly went over the key things for tonight which was mainly to not lose no matter what. I really had no clue on what Jennifer was bringing to the table. She was slightly taller than me and was right-handed and wanted to win. I would adjust to whatever she presented in the first few seconds of the first round. All I knew was that it was my night to shine and once that bell rung, Patty Boom Boom would be fully present.

I went back to the ugly hotel and forced myself to take a good hour nap. I packed my bag with my gear, my new trunks and new robe that featured my favorite colors and I took a shower. I made sure I had enough time to pray and visualize and then Terri knocked on my door by 5 p.m. The Armory was a good 30 minutes from the hotel, so we had to rush as I had to get the mandatory pre-fight physical. The bouts started at 8 p.m. and it was a small card of 6 bouts in total and my fight was the 5th bout and co-main feature.

The Media Company greeted me as I arrived at the Armory and kept the camera in my face as I got checked in by the doctor and throughout the night. At 7:30 p.m., Terri started wrapping my hands for the first time as a professional boxer. The wrapping was very different than my amateur boxing days. This felt much more solid as if my hands were in a cast. The promoter had also given Terri the small black 8 oz gloves I was supposed to wear. As Terri cut off the ends off the glove's laces and I prepared to stick my hand in those tiny gloves, I felt my inner body temperature rise. No head gear, cast-like wraps and smaller boxing gloves.... This was serious business tonight!

The fourth bout was already in the ring and I had started to shadow box and Terri came rushing in so I could get in a few rounds of pads. After I broke a light sweat, she put on my robe and we were instructed to start making our way into the ring. My heart was racing and I then I remembered what Coach's brother once said to me before my first ever amateur boxing bout, "Turn on that switch as soon as that bell rings. Take all your love, your fears and all your emotions and let it unleash on whoever is in front of you. Don't let anyone take away what belongs to you!" I heard my ring song start to play out loud which was "En Barranquilla me quedó," by Joe Arroyo. It was a traditional Colombian song that reminded me of my mom. I started trotting down the hallway and down to the ring with Terri and the camera crew following behind me.

Jennifer was already in the ring with her coach. She was wearing black trunks, a black sports bra and black boxing shoes. I was wearing white and blue boxing trunks, a white sports bra and my red, white and blue boxing boots that were given to me at the USA Nationals. The crowd in attendance were cheering loudly for both of us as Women's Professional Boxing was and still is a novelty everywhere. We came to the center of the ring and the referee gave us final instructions before we went back to our corners and then the bell rang for my first professional boxing fight.

Something deep inside me was triggered when that bell rang. I ran out of my corner and did not allow Jennifer to breathe. Just as in my first ever fight in the amateurs against Barbosa, I started at a furious pace. Jennifer threw one hard overhand right hand, but I brushed it off and threw 10 unanswered hard punches that sent her to the canvas. The referee started his count: ONE, TWO, THREE, FOUR... Jennifer got up at the count of five. I saw the fear in her eyes and ran back across the ring with another barrage of punches that knocked her down for the second time. The referee did not finish the count this time and stopped the fight. I won by KO in the 1st round of my 1st Professional Boxing Fight. I went over to make sure Jennifer was okay and shook her hand and her Coach's before I celebrated in my corner with Terri.

CHAPTER 11

Chapter Eleven - Round 11

The Mourning

"We do not have to become heroes overnight. Just a step at a time, meeting each thing that comes up, seeing it as not as dreadful as it appears, discovering that we have the strength to stare it down." Eleanor Roosevelt

After I came down from the ring, I saw Brian and he gave me a hug. "Congratulations, Patricia!" he said. It was the first time in a while that he had called me by my name, but despite the awkwardness, I was glad that he made it to see my professional boxing debut and I had hoped that perhaps seeing me fight would inspire and motivate him to support my dreams of going further. He knew that this was just the beginning for me as I never did anything half way.

The Media Company continued to follow and record. I posed for pictures for so many people that asked for one before we left the Armory. It was a great night for me, but that strange sinking feeling in my stomach had returned big time when I went back to the hotel with Brian. Even though the fight had lasted one round, my body felt as if it had gone 12 rounds with Mike Tyson. I felt completely run down, sore and just off. I took a shower and passed out.

At 8 a.m., Brian woke me up and said, "Hey Scoob, I didn't want to wake you up, but I would like to start driving back soon. It is a long drive and I don't want to get caught in heavy traffic." I was disoriented and did not feel good at all. I felt feverish and also had rashes on my neck, back, arms and stomach and could not stop scratching myself.

"Good morning, Raggie. I also want to get out of here. I don't know why I have a fever, but I am going to take a quick shower and we can leave asap," I replied. As I let the cold water cool my body down, I tried to think of what I could have possibly eaten that prompted this allergic reaction, but nothing came to mind.

When we got in the car, I saw that Terri's car was not there. She had an even longer drive back, so it was smart of her to get out early. I felt so tired and dosed off for about an hour when my cell phone rang and it was Terri. "Hey Girl! How's the Champ feeling?" asked Terri. I wished I was not feeling as horrible as I did, but I replied, "Hey Terri, thank you, but I am feeling horrible. I've had a fever since I woke up and my body hurts and I have rashes all over! I don't understand what I am re-acting to." One of the things I did appreciate about Terri was that she knew a little about everything and it did not take her long to know what was wrong with me. "You need to go to the next hospital or urgent care Patty. It sounds like you are having an allergic reaction to bed bugs from that dirty hotel!" she said.

My eyes teared up as soon as I realized that I was afraid to tell Brian. The person who I had once confided in and I wasn't afraid to say any-thing to, I now hesitated, but I didn't have a choice. "Raggie, we need to stop at a hospital or urgent care as soon as possible. Terri thinks that I am having a bad reaction to bed bug bites," I said. Brian just nodded his head and did not say much. We pulled into a hospital half hour later. A nurse took down my information and I showed her the rashes and told her my symptoms.

Soon after, the doctor came out and confirmed Terri's feeling. "Sorry to inform you young lady, but you are having a severe allergic reaction to bed bug bites. I usually don't see cases as severe as yours, so I am going to prescribe Prednisone pills and Cortisone cream for the next couple of weeks. If or when the symptoms subside, you can switch to over-the-counter Benadryl pills," instructed the doctor.

My shining moment just the night before quickly was overshadowed by the agony of wanting to scratch my skin off, pain, discomfort and fever. Brian stopped at the nearest pharmacy and we picked up the prescription and extra boxes of the Benadryl. "Raggie, that's too many boxes of Benadryl. I don't think we need 4 boxes," I said, but then I noticed a similar rash on his arm. "I got bed bug bites too, but my symptoms are not as severe as yours, so I will just treat it with Benadryl and we can share the cream," replied Brian. Dealing with the severe itchiness and symptoms for the next few weeks was extremely challenging I thought, but as life would teach me, it can always be much worse and soon enough it would be.

Terri called often throughout the weeks that I was dealing with this condition to check up on me and to plan my next fight. She kept saying that she was talking to some potential managers and promoters who were interested in me and how I had to be "extra nice" to them.

"Patty, you have good looks and talent and you have to use those God-given tools to your advantage. You are not friendly enough to these men. They are loaded and are looking to spend money but only if you make it worth their while," she would say. Although I was naïve, I was upset that she was using religion to persuade me and I was also able to get a sense of her implications and I responded, "Terri, I appreciate all the hard work you are doing with making all these phone calls but I am not sleeping with any dirty old men. I do not have money to pay for my next opponent, but I will NOT sell my body! There has to be another way."

I also received many messages through my social media outlets from intrigued boxing fans and supporters asking when my next fight would be. One of these new supporters, JS from Florida took a special interest. He claimed to be knowledgeable in the sport as he was a "boxing reporter". He offered to help me as much as he could and provided his contact information. He said he knew of boxing managers and promoters and could talk to them about me. JS and I agreed to stay in touch and I hoped to God that he could indeed help me.

After 6 weeks, I finally stopped taking the Prednisone which had affected me negatively in every way. I felt bloated, tired and just not myself. I had gained 10 pounds throughout this bed bugs illness and did not want to continue going down this dark hole.

On a casual weekday morning, Brian offered to drive me to Earth Fare to get breakfast after a gym workout. He knew how much I loved their scrambled eggs and latte. I ordered it to go and on the short ride back home, I noticed how nervous Brian was. He was grabbing the steering wheel extra tight and he was fidgeting. When we arrived in front of the house, he took a deep breath and said something I would never ever forget and it still pains me until this day, "Patricia, I have filed for a divorce. I don't want this to get ugly and I want us to part ways amicably. You can stay with the apartment in New York and I will stay with this house here in Asheville. You can take one of the cars- the Toyota Prius and take anything from the house that you may need back in NYC. The business is my family business and I would like that to be untouched."

To this date, it was the most pain I had ever felt. The feeling is indescribable and inevitably tears streamed down my face. Something deep inside of me forced me to compose myself. For my dignity's sake, I was not going to ask him to give us another chance. I realized that this was something he had planned and discussed with his father, brother and friends, so I replied, "You have broken my heart Brian and you broke the biggest promise you made to us and God. But I will not fight your decision or your wishes. I will leave your business alone as I know how sacred that is to you. I will make arrangements to move back to New York as soon as possible."

I got out of the car and ran into the house while he drove away to his office. When I opened the door, Jack instinctively was there waiting as if he knew. I looked into his big brown eyes and said, "It's just you and me bubba," even though it had always just been us two and I held him tight and fell to the kitchen floor and sobbed. As I laid on the floor, I saw images of myself as a little girl. I couldn't let her down and then I remembered raising my hands in the ring just a couple of months ago and each time I crossed a finish line of any particular race. I raised my hands not because I won, but because I defied the odds and did not give up.

I got myself off the floor and went straight into the bedroom and started packing my things into large duffle bags which would be the easy part. After a few hours, I started to make the dreaded and painful phone calls to the people that absolutely needed to know. I first called my sister whose first reaction was complete disbelief and then anger. "Don't be dumb Patricia! Take him to the cleaners! Take half of absolutely everything he has. You deserve it! We will be waiting for you with open arms. Let me know if you need anything at all," said my sister. Money was never my motive and I did not want to get into an ugly legal battle for his business and other finances. I had always been independent and I was going to return to New York City and make the best out of this painful situation on my own.

The mid-sized red Toyota Prius was packed with everything I owned and at 5 a.m. in early March of 2010, I started my long drive back to New York City. Before I left, I sent a text message to Terri letting her know briefly about the divorce and that I was driving back to NYC. I should not have been surprised at her cold reply, "Well it was nice knowing you and I guess I will never hear back from you. Good luck," was the last thing she ever said or wrote to me. I wrote farewell emails to Martina, Bob, Candace, Brian Lawler and the few acquaintances I had made in Asheville during the last 4 years. In my emails, I was shocked to see the divorce papers filed by Brian via Legal Zoom. A lavish wedding with 200 guests in one of New York City's premiere spots comes to an end via Legal Zoom. I was disgusted, but I signed the papers immediately and left.

I felt nauseous throughout the 14-hour drive back and had to pull over a handful of times to throw up. I kept remembering how much it took to leave everything behind to move to Asheville and now it is taking even more to return to New York City. One of the last things Martina said to me before I left was to be kind to myself as a divorce could be as or even more painful than mourning the loss of a loved one. I could attest to that fact for sure. The crying, the vomiting and the praying were all necessary and cleansing.

The best part of this drive back was having my wingman, Jack by my side. I took the final exit to Forest Hills and was faced with the reality of now having to find parking and even worse, parallel parking! I had flashbacks of being relieved of the driving test in Asheville where parallel parking was not required because it was just not ever necessary there. But here in NYC, it was mandatory!

It took me nearly an hour to find parking and about another half hour to parallel park while other drivers honked their horns shamelessly. I opened my apartment door at nearly 10 p.m. and fell asleep out of complete exhaustion on the faux leather couch that was left behind by the people that were subleasing the apartment while I was in Asheville. At 3:30 a.m., I felt a choking sensation and I could see myself struggling to speak from above. "Padre nuestro que estas en los cielos...." I started praying in Spanish before I let out the biggest sigh of relief when I could actually hear myself. The paralyzing dreams were back with a vengeance.

3:30 a.m. became my new wake up time until this present day. I prayed and started my day with a list of things I had to accomplish today. I had to clean the apartment, unpack, set-up my computer, sell my engagement and wedding rings as I did not have a job or money, update my resume and start applying for jobs and contact JS in Florida to help me set up my next boxing fight. By 10 a.m., my apartment was squeaky clean and everything was unpacked and my computer was set up. Although we were in the month of March, I sent an email to Dan Brannen and told him I was back in NYC for good and to count on me for the Corporate Challenge event in the summer and to please keep me in mind for any other work opportunities.

Dan was very empathetic and assured me I would be on the event's list of workers. I registered online with several recruiting companies and I applied to multiple jobs as an Executive Assistant, Event Manager, Health and Wellness Manager and as a Spanish Interpreter/Translator. I also saw an opportunity to go back to school on a government sponsored scholarship in the Emergency Medical Services field that required an application/essay process, so I did that right away.

By noon time, I took the subway to the Diamond District in midtown Manhattan and went to over a dozen jewelry stores and sold my rings to the best offered price. I was relieved to have enough money to pay the maintenance fee for the apartment for the next 2 months which was just as costly as a monthly rent and enough money for food and transportation. I was confident that I would have some sort of income soon because I was willing to work pretty much anywhere if needed.

When I got back home, I saw an email from JS saying that there was a promoter there in Florida who was working on putting on Hector "Macho" Camacho's next and potentially final fight and was looking for a co-main event feature fight and was interested in having me fight on it. I called JS right away, "Hey JS! I saw your email! That is amazing news! I would love to be on that card. Who will be my opponent, where and when will this fight take place?" JS paused and then stuttered as he replied, "Hey Champ! This is exciting news for sure!

The boxing card is in Kissimmee, Florida on May 14th, but we have to get the opponent. There is a tough girl from Mexico who just fought in New York City named Laura Gomez that is willing to fight you for $2,500."

There was a long moment of silence before I realized what Terri was saying was indeed the truth when it came to having to invest in your professional boxing career. According to her, a professional boxer's team usually had to pay for at least the first 5 fights of the upcoming boxer to build up a solid record in order to attract the attention of major sponsorship and be a top contender. I had no back-up, no manager, no promoter, no coach, but I had to figure it out somehow. I had no money except the money I just got for my rings which I needed to pay for my home fees, food and essentials and the only thing left to do was sell my car. "Okay, JS, please contact Laura's people and let her know that I will fight her for that amount. I will sell my car as soon as possible and use that money to pay her fee and the next couple of fights. I will do this on my own without having to sleep with any of those dirty managers," I said.

JS was not attractive at first sight from the pictures I saw of him when we became friends on social media. He was about 5'3, 150 lbs. with thinning hair in his early 40's. That was not my taste at all, but his willingness to help me, his support and passion for the sport definitely had my attention. He had a brief amateur boxing background; he worked as a doctor recruiter and was separated from the mother of his 10-yr old son. He was a huge boxing fan and he would watch fights and write about them for free and shared his point of view across various social media outlets. He was not well known and had no real connections, but I did not know that at the time. I did not know that he had stalked my social media pictures and background. He would not have offered to help me if it wasn't for my looks and the incentive to somehow get involved romantically.

I did not get a good vibe from him and once again ignored the red flags. I noticed that his stuttering became much more noticeable any time he was lying and that was often, but I needed to get another fight and needed his help. All he was doing was talking to promoters about me and I was putting out my own money, but I would soon realize once again that absolutely nothing is for free.

We would be in constant contact as I needed to sign the official contract and he was my liaison to the promoter, Eddie. The next task which gave me scary goosebumps was to contact Coach. I did not have money to pay to train in a boxing gym and worse for training. I had it in my mind to train myself if needed. In the brief time I trained with Terri which was only a handful of weekends before my professional boxing debut, she did not teach me anything new.

My foundation in amateur boxing, my great physical endurance, my mental toughness and my faith got me through my first professional boxing fight and it will continue to get me through for now until I can get a real professional boxing trainer I thought. "Hi Coach, its Patricia. I am back in NYC for good. Brian filed for a divorce right after my professional boxing debut. Things just did not work out between us, so I am going to focus on doing as much as I can as a pro and I need a place to train. A guy I know from Florida helped me get my next fight which is in 6 weeks," I said in one breath over the phone.

"Hey yo, Alcivar! Oh man, sorry to hear things didn't work out between you and Brian. You can train here. Don't worry about it. I can have one of our new trainers, Steve work with you and I can jump in whenever I can. If you need someone to work your corner in Florida, I can go. I just need my flight and hotel paid for. I gotta go train some people, but get back in here tomorrow!" said Coach before he hung up. I let out a loud and long sigh of relief.

That was not nearly as hard as I thought it would be, but I had that nagging feeling in the pit of my stomach which was never good. I had a habit of not looking into people's ulterior motives. I believed the best in people despite the red flags and uncomfortable vibes. I would pay dearly down the road for not listening.

My next big task was to sell my car, so I looked up its value on Kelly's Blue Book and then put ads out on Craig's list. Within a few minutes of putting the ad out, a guy with a foreign accent called me and said he was interested and wanted to see my car ASAP and if it matched the description I provided, he would pay me cash on the spot! Craig's list sellers are notorious for scammers to prey on, so I was skeptical, but I desperately needed to sell this car, so I agreed to meet the guy within the next couple of hours. I prayed and then got ready to meet this guy.

In the distance, I saw a lean man slightly taller than me rushing past everyone wearing black jeans, a slim fitted black t-shirt and dark sunglasses carrying a brown paper bag tightly. The only thing missing were leather gloves for when he murdered me, I thought. "Hallo Patricia. I am Andre. Is this the car? Here is cash that you hold while I test car," he said. I handed him the keys and held on to the brown paper bag nervously. It only took him 5 minutes and when he returned, he inspected the car from the inside out for another 5 minutes and then shook my hand and said, "The money is all there I assure you. I must go now. Thank you," he said before he sped away.

I ran home as quickly as possible and counted the money and it was all there. I now had enough money to pay for Laura Gomez, flights and perhaps the next 3 fights if needed. I ran back out to deposit the money in the bank and considered this first full day back in New York City a highly productive day. Tomorrow, I planned to get up early and be at the boxing gym by 6 a.m. As I laid on the couch with Jack, I visualized the checklist I had created in my mind. I still had to go to the IDMJI Church this week, I had to call my sister tomorrow and my mother and follow up on all job leads.

At 5 a.m., the subway platform was already busy with people waiting for the train. I was glad to get a seat on the E train as it was a solid hour train ride into Manhattan and I could get a much-needed nap before my boxing workout. I had flashbacks of my good ole sweaty boxing days as a young teenage amateur boxer as I approached the front of the boxing gym. "Hey Alcivar! Welcome back Kid!" said Coach as he high fived me. The gym smelled like sweat and was packed with the morning people getting in their workouts before work. It was good to hear the sounds of people jumping rope, hitting the speedbags and heavy bags while an Aerosmith song played in the background.

The bell rang to end the 3-minute round and during the one-minute break, Coach went around saying, "Do you know who this kid is? She was the 1st Female ever to win "Fighter of the year in boxing! She is the USA National Champ and now is a Pro!" I was never sure why he did that, but it always made me feel awkward as people's reaction ranged from admiration to not caring to envy.

It was my first day back to boxing since my pro debut fight and after the bed bugs illness, so I felt rusty, but I jumped rope for 5 rounds, shadow boxed for another 5 rounds and hit the heavy bags for 5 rounds. Then Coach introduced me to Steve who was a relative to an up-and-coming boxing promoter named Ronson. Ronson had a great amateur boxing career and was currently a pro boxer and boxing promoter.

I knew of him when I sparred at Gleason's gym in my amateur boxing days. He trained at Coach's gym occasionally and Coach mentioned to him that I was now a pro as well hoping he could put me on some of the boxing cards he was promoting. His nephew, Steve was in his early 20's and already had a kid of his own. He supposedly had a few amateur boxing fights and was a boxing trainer at different boxing gyms. He came over to shake my hand and held pads for me for a few rounds. I was not crazy about working with him. He seemed unsure of the pointers he was giving me, but I stayed quiet. I needed to train and was going to make the best out of this situation.

Before I left for the day, Coach called us over to see a video of Laura. She had recently fought Keisha Wells here in NYC on a Lou Di-Bella Boxing Card. Coach had gone to High School with Lou DiBella, who was currently one of New York City's biggest Boxing Promoters. Most of the boxing shows he promoted were televised. However, Coach mentioned that DiBella was already promoting Keisha who was in my weight division and besides, they had some sort of unresolved issues going back to their adolescence. Laura was tough and gave Keisha a good fight that went the distance.

When I got home, I saw that my email inbox was full. Among them was an acceptance for the Emergency Medical Services Program. The Scholarship Committee at LaGuardia Community College had reviewed my application and essay and I would need to go in person next week for an interview. If everything went well, I would take the 6-month intensive college program to officially become an EMT. The scholarship program would pay for my studies, books and uniform and I would start in late August. When I was going to school in North Carolina, my favorite class was Anatomy and I've always felt an inner peace when I helped anyone, so I thought this would be a great field to consider.

I also received an interview request from one of the Translation Companies who was impressed with my resume, so I called them right away. They interviewed me right over the phone. I was on the call with them for almost a solid hour.

Along with the required questions about my work history, they tested my Spanish verbal skills and I was thankful to have passed with no issues at all. I would later obtain certification as a Professional Spanish Interpreter/Translator as well. Desiree, who was one of their top coordinating managers explained that the work they were offering me was on a contractual basis and I would get paid $20/per hour to start with a minimum of 15 hours per week.

It was not a lot of money, but it would be rewarding work while I boxed and possibly went back to school. I could always find additional part-time or contractual work as a personal trainer as I was certified and loved doing that work as well. Desiree was sent from above as she got me set up in their system for payment immediately and asked me to send her my availability on a weekly basis and based on that, she would send me assignments. My first assignment as a Spanish Interpreter was the very next day in a hospital. I served as an interpreter for a doctor and elderly patient on an 8-hour shift for 3 consecutive days!

The end of the week was here and in my first week back to NYC, I had checked almost everything off my to do list and now it was time to call my mom. "Hello Mami, it's Patricia. How are you? I am back in New York for good. Things did not work in North Carolina, but I am okay," I said trying not to cry. My mom's reply and tone were melancholic, sad and uninspiring, "Well Patricia, you know how men are. I told you how they get bored and tired after they marry you. Just move on and something better will come along."

My mom had retired before I left to North Carolina and my sister had mentioned that she was falling into a depression since she did not have a plan for all the free time she now had. My mom was all alone in that apartment in Woodside, Queens and was desperately needing any sort of interaction. That neighborhood was also toxic at the time with gossipy neighbors and past acquaintances that all knew what had happened with my father. My sister had mentioned to me the idea of my mom moving in with me since I had a spare bedroom that she could take and she could also take care of Jack while I was at work, training or traveling.

The Forest Hills neighborhood was a healthier option overall for her. Although I was very hesitant, my mom wasn't. When my sister mentioned it to her after it was confirmed that I was moving back to NYC, she jumped at the idea, so they were waiting on me. My mom and sisters had severe co-dependency issues and would rather die than be alone.

I on the other hand, valued my alone peaceful time more than anything and was extremely reluctant and I felt remorseful that I was being made to feel guilty for even hesitating. The pressure fell on me as none of my sisters had the space or ability to move my mom in with them. They all had children and just had different lives. I have and will always love my mom despite everything that happened with my father and her lack of support and protection throughout my life. I had unresolved emotional issues that I did not know how to deal with. It was a deep resentment and sadness of not ever receiving love, affection, support and protection from my mom. I internalized it and hoped it would go away some day. I put my feelings aside and would welcome my mom to move in to my home a month later right before I went to Florida for my 2nd Professional Fight.

For the next 5 weeks before my fight in Florida, my busy life started to come together again in New York City which helped mask the pain of the divorce, the resentment I had with my mom and any other pain I was feeling. Each punch I received and gave helped take the pain away temporarily. I boxed in the early mornings, worked during the days and studied in the evenings. I had also started to teach bootcamp again for Navy Seal P.T. in Central Park at 5 a.m. a couple of mornings a week for one of my past mentors, Jack Walston.

Although my main training was done at the boxing gym, I always went the extra mile and did the running and strength training on my own. I had to do what my opponents were not doing. My legs were usually shaking with exhaustion at the end of the day. A week before the fight, I woke up and could hardly put pressure on my right foot. I did not remember injuring it, but I did remember a nagging discomfort after my runs and would just ignore it. I had to go see the doctor asap and would need to pay for it out of my pocket since I didn't have medical insurance.

My mom had a foot doctor in the old Woodside neighborhood we grew up in and I decided to just show up without calling. The podiatrist was an attractive older gentleman in his late 40's and I told him I was getting ready to fight my 2nd pro fight in Florida, but woke up limping. He was stunned and did an x-ray right away that revealed a stress fracture on my 4th metatarsal! "Doctor, I signed a contract to fight. Tickets have been sold and there is no way I could back out now. Please, is there anything you can do?" The podiatrist's clientele was mostly retired people seeking comfort from their bunions and hammertoes. I could tell that my situation was a first for him.

"Listen young lady, I will do as much as I can to help you, but you are taking a big risk here. I can inject something directly in that bone to relieve the pain and then customize your shoes to elevate your foot and relieve the pressure to that metatarsal, but you will eventually need to be in a cast or a boot," said the podiatrist. Another Godsent angel who refused to charge me. I decided not to tell anyone about my broken foot as it would only create unnecessary worry. The pain was manageable and I needed to avoid the pounding of the running while still keeping a close eye on my weight. I was physically ready, but now had to deal with this extra challenge.

Coach and another of his favorite boxers, Peter would be working my corner for this fight. They took their flights the morning of the fight while I took my flight 2 days prior so that I could be somewhat relaxed and not worry of any water retention weight due to the flight. JS picked me up at the Florida International Airport and insisted that I stay at his place in Delray Beach. On the ride to his apartment, he told me that Sports Connection, which was the Floridian version of ESPN and featured highlights and news on all major sporting events, wanted to do an exclusive interview and feature tomorrow before the weigh-ins, during and after my fight. I would have declined, but I needed to draw the attention to obtain that proper management I needed, so I agreed.

First things first, "Hey JS, do you have an accurate scale in your home? Flights make me retain water, so I need to find out if I put on any weight because I was exactly 119 last night," I said as he pulled into the parking space at his apartment complex. Thankfully, he did have a scale and I jumped on it immediately. It read 121 lbs.! The weigh-ins were tomorrow at noon, so I had less than 24 hours to lose 2 pounds which was more than enough. However, it meant I had to starve today and it would be hard to sleep with a rumbling stomach.

I changed into shorts and a sports bra and JS joined me on a slow 4-mile beach run as the sand would be easy on my broken foot. The sun was setting and it was a beautiful sight and I was enjoying our conversation and all of a sudden, he pulled me in and kissed me on the lips. It was unexpected and my heart felt conflicted. I was still mourning the loss of my marriage and I knew deep inside that JS was not the "one". I was grateful for his help in talking to the promoter to get me this fight. The timing of this kiss was way off, but I hugged him and told him that I needed to focus on my fight and he understood for the time being.

When we got back to his home, I was relieved to get back on the scale to see 118 pounds. I hardly slept and was eager to get on the road to Kissimmee, Florida which was about a 3-hour drive. Sports Connection would be interviewing me before the weigh-ins, so we headed out at 7 a.m. and arrived by 10 a.m. Jeff Radcliffe, the reporter who would be interviewing me came over to introduce himself and we sat on comfortable sofa chairs while the camera guy recorded. I had déjà vu thoughts from all the interviews I had during my amateur boxing career.

Jeff was impressed with my Amateur Boxing accomplishments, my Marathon Running experience and my goals and my life thus far in NYC. I was surprised at how natural and calm my responses were and then I was called to get ready to weigh in. Laura weighed in at 119.5 lbs. I got on the scale and I weighed in at exactly 118 lbs. She was a couple of inches shorter than me and had her coach with her. We shook hands after the face-off picture and went our separate ways.

There was no deep animosity between us, but she gave off a strange vibe. She smiled, but behind her smile and her eyes, I felt an intense anger and that frightened me momentarily.

It was nearly 4 p.m. when we were finished and we were due back in 3 hours, so we hurried to Denny's for my go-to meal of scrambled eggs. I felt good, but the unsettling energy from JS was nerve wrecking. "How you doing Champ? How do you feel? What round are you going to KO her?" I felt my stomach turn. I know he meant well, but I just wished he zipped up his mouth. Thankfully, Coach called and said he just landed and would meet me with Peter in a couple of hours after he got something to eat. "Hey JS, I am in desperate need of a nap. I am going to push my seat back and close my eyes for an hour and then we can head back and meet Coach and Peter. Is that cool with you?" I asked. He agreed and we both took a solid hour nap before the cell phone alarm went off.

As we were pulling into the fight venue, we saw Coach and Peter. "Hey yo, Alcivar! Looking good kid. Gotta do good tonight. Ready?" said Coach as he and Peter high fived me. Coach looked at JS from head to toe and I knew right away he did not like him, but the feeling would be mutual. I checked in with the doctor and then I was sent into Hector "Macho" Camacho's dressing room. Camacho was once a promising rising boxer, but like many professional boxers who do not have a clear vision and are misguided, he had steadily declined over the years and had gotten involved with the wrong crowd and the world of drugs and alcohol.

He looked at me like a chocolate cake and extended his hand. I shook it out of courtesy and hurried away to my own little corner on the other side of the locker room. Coach did not know how to wrap hands professionally, so we had to ask and pay a coach of another fighter which I didn't mind at the time. Coach also had a nervous energy that made me feel uncomfortable, so I welcomed neutral calming vibes. As soon as my hands were wrapped and I was dressed with my traditional short sparkling shorts and matching sports bra and my USA National boxing shoes, I started warming up. JS would go out and talk to the promoter and other people in the media and check back in to let us know how much time we had left.

This locker room was way too noisy and busy, but it was boxing and Florida after all, but I took a minute to go to the bathroom and closed my eyes for my final prayer before I went out, "God, you know how much I have sacrificed having to sell my car and all the weeks of training. Please help me have the courage tonight and help me shine if it is your will. Amen." And then I heard my ring song, "En Barranquilla Me Quedo". Hearing that song reminded me of my mom because it is where she was born and although no one ever honored me, I honored her.

I put on my "Patty Boom Boom" royal blue robe and transformed into her. She represented strength, courage, perseverance and everything needed to protect little Patricia and her dreams. I pulled the hood over my head and trotted down in between the row of filled seats and entered the ring.

The Sports Connection crew followed my every move as Coach took my robe off and the announcer introduced us to the crowd in attendance. Here we go, my 2nd Professional Boxing Fight.

The bell rang and I met Laura in the center of the ring and threw 2 hard jabs that landed and got her attention immediately. She answered back with a flurry of nervous punches all which did not land and I countered with a mean double left hook combination which did land on her left side of her face and then the bell rang. "Looking good Alcivar! Keep throwing that left hook combo but add the uppercut. She is coming with her face exposed. Calm your breathing and get back out there and don't let her breath!" said Coach in the brief one-minute break.

We were scheduled to fight for four rounds, but I was indeed breathing heavy as we had started at an intense pace with no signs of slowing down. Round 2 started and Laura came right at me, but I worked on my defense making her miss and countering off the ropes. I kept tagging her with the double hook combination and started to see the whole left side of her face swell while I started to feel shooting pains on my broken foot. Round 2 ended and the audience was cheering for both of us in appreciation of the non-stop action. As I sat in the stool, Peter poured cold water down my back which threw my breathing off! "Don't do that please!" I yelled at him. I disliked the cold water anywhere in my body as it reminded me of the awful drowning incident when I was a kid.

Round 3, Laura was still determined to somehow take this fight away from me and even tried to purposely head butt me, but I countered with the uppercuts that Coach kept yelling at me to throw and those uppercuts not only landed, but drew blood before the bell rang to end the round. "Final Round Alcivar! You are ahead, but you need to throw everything you got! DO NOT HOLD BACK! Finish her!" The final bell rang and the crowd was louder than ever. I was not going to let Laura take this fight away from me and despite the shooting pain in my foot and my heavy breathing, I threw nonstop hard punches that were dangerously snapping Laura's head back and with a minute left to end the 4th round, Laura's corner threw in the towel and the referee stepped in to stop the fight. My 2nd Professional fight ended in a TKO! I raised my hands, not because I beat Laura, but because I did not give up.

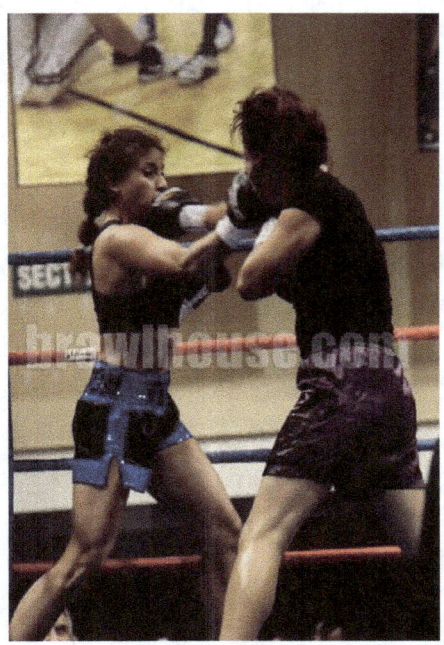

I limped back to the locker room and desperately started to untie my boxing boots. I had taped my foot too tight and asked Coach to cut the tape off my foot before he cut my wraps off. "Why the EFF is your foot taped like that Alcivar?" he asked. "I have a small hairline fracture on my 4th metatarsal and the podiatrist showed me how to tape my foot so I could go through with this fight," I replied. I think they were all in shock because no one said much after that. It was past midnight and we were all starving and the only thing open was Denny's, so we went there to grab a quick bite before we all said our goodbyes.

JS drove me to the airport the next day and promised to work on getting me my next fight as he met a promoter during my fight in Kissimmee that was putting on a card in Tampa, Florida in just 3 months from now in August. The promoter mentioned that he knew of a female MMA fighter also wanting to be on the card and that he could put us in touch with her. I made it clear to JS that he absolutely needed to jump at this opportunity and I wanted something finalized ASAP even if I had to speak on my own behalf. He had started to call me, "Baby girl" which I hated, but I felt trapped and would need to give this relationship a temporary chance as I knew that this would go nowhere. His nervous energy and the way he carried himself when he thought no one was watching made me uneasy. There were so many red flags with this guy that I did not ignore, but did not have too many options.

I was relieved to get back home to NYC where I would be working the Chase Corporate Challenge event as well as teach my bootcamp classes and work my interpreting assignments and be back with my dog, Jack. Despite the hectic schedule, familiarity is always comforting. I had also started to go back to the IDMJI Church in Woodside and knew I needed to go as soon as possible. All my insides had been in disarray after the divorce and now, I somehow felt worse even after winning my 2nd professional fight. I did not want to give up on my dreams of becoming a World Champion in Professional Boxing. As a female boxer, I knew that knock outs were unusual, so I knew I had the physical fitness, skill and mindset. Unfortunately, in women's boxing, that is simply not enough.

JS called me the following week to confirm that he had reached out to Sheri Denise Jacobs, an MMA Fighter from Tampa who agreed to fight me for again $2,500 and because of her religion, we MUST be in the ring fighting before sunset. My 3rd Professional Boxing fight was now scheduled for August 13, 2010. Between the fighter's fee, the flights for myself and Coach, it would cost me another $4,000. My funds were running low and I was praying that this situation would turn around after this fight, but it would only get more interesting and challenging.

JS had money issues. He explained that as a recruiter, he worked on commission and it had been a while since he was able to make a decent commission and was starting to fall behind on his car, apartment and other payments. I was already stressed financing and investing in my Professional Boxing career, but I did not expect to have to bail out JS as he would be on the verge of tears when we spoke. I ended up having to send him money throughout the year that we were together so he wouldn't get kicked out of his place and get gas to get to work and eat. I would say it was repayment for the emails and calls he made to the promoters, but this was another situation I prayed to get out of as soon as possible.

For the next 8 weeks, I trained, worked and prayed. I did not spar as often as I did not want to go to Gleason's Gym. There were a couple of women that did come to Coach's gym to spar with me, but it was always a big struggle. The ones that did come gave off an awful vibe, but none of that mattered to Coach or Steve. It seemed like the women that came to spar had some weird ulterior motive. Sparring was sparring and we had to take whomever was willing to come. I continued to do the strength/performance/endurance training on my own and I knew that always made a big difference.

Right before I left to fight in Florida, I received notice that I was officially accepted into the LaGuardia Community College EMT Scholarship Program that started a week after my fight. As I packed to go to Florida, I noticed the worn-out bottoms of my USA National Boxing shoes and made a mental note to replace the soles when I returned.

"Hey, Baby Girl! Welcome Home!" said JS as he greeted me at the airport. "Hey JS, good to see you! Please don't take this the wrong way, but I am worried about my weight and I am just focused on this fight," I replied. Awful memories of being stuck in that basement apartment having to pretend with Adrian crept up in my head. I hated to have to pretend how I really felt for the sake of boxing. It took me a while to realize that I had the power to end whatever was causing me distress, but in the end, we are a compilation of all our experiences.

The scale in his bathroom read 114.5 lbs. and I had signed a contract to fight at 112, plus or minus 2 pounds. This would be the first time fighting at this weight class for me. It was one of the many things I had to agree to for Jacobs to take this fight. 112 was her normal fighting weight, so I was at a disadvantage, but needed to make the best out of it once again.

I changed into my running clothes and we headed out the door to run around the Delray neighborhood which at the time was mostly an area where retired senior citizens lived, so the only thing to worry about during the run was not getting hit by a car.

We chatted while we ran and I tried to stick to talking just about boxing. But somehow in the conversation, JS alluded to me moving to Florida. The only other place I had lived in my life was in Asheville and that was because I made the ultimate sacrifice for someone I was deeply in love with. I promised myself never to make that mistake again. Besides, I was not a fan of the extreme humid tropical weather there and the constant beach and party night life. "Hey JS, my mind is completely focused on making weight and winning this fight, so I am sorry, I just cannot think about anything else," I said.

After the hour run, the scale read exactly 113 and then we packed and started our drive to Tampa for the evening weigh-ins which would be at the Wing House Bar & Lounge. Upon arrival, I checked in and almost immediately had to get on the scale. Jacobs had an intense face and looked ready with her hair already done in cornrows. She weighed in at a ready 112 ¾ lbs. and then it was my turn and the scale read 113 ½. We posed for the face-off pictures and that is the opportunity where I get a good idea of what is to come. She meant business and so did I.

If it wasn't for Jacob's demand of fighting by or before sunset, we would have been the co-main event and it would have been televised on Telemundo Channel 47, one of the most popular and watched Spanish language television networks. I needed this 3rd fight, so I had to agree to anything and everything. My focus now was rehydrating, eating and getting a good night's rest. After seeing Jacob face to face, I had to be nothing short of 100%.

I forced myself to stay in bed longer than usual, but by 6 a.m., I was fully awake and asked JS to drive us to the nearby beach to take a walk and then have a good hearty breakfast. As I walked on the beach, I paused to look at the ocean and sky and said a silent prayer. It was just what I needed and I felt good. Since my bout was the 1st bout on the card, I had to be at the "A La Carte Pavilion" event venue early by 4 p.m.

After an afternoon nap, we packed and headed to the venue where we saw Coach standing right in front waiting. "Hey Alcivar! Ready for KO #3?" he said as he high fived me. I could see that he dreaded to shake hands with JS.

I wasn't sure of the exact reasons he disliked JS, but I would need to put that aside for now. JS had one of his close friends coming to wrap my hands and work my corner with Coach, but he was nowhere in sight.

As I walked down the A La Carte Pavilion's hallway into my dressing room at 5 p.m., I saw Jacobs fully dressed in her boxing outfit and about to get her hands wrapped. We continued on to my dressing room while JS stopped in to Jacob's dressing room and said, "Hi there, no one told us you guys were ready to wrap. We would like to watch the wrapping of hands." This is a standard practice where each fight corner is allowed to send someone to watch the opposing corner's wrap their hands. There have been numerous occasions throughout the years where a fighter will purposely stick coins and other objects or substances to make their wraps lethal under the gloves. The fight Inspectors are supposed to give each corner a heads up, but this was boxing and rules were meant to be ignored. JS stayed to watch them wrap her hands while we waited for his friend Bill to show up.

With less than an hour before my fight, Bill showed up at 5:45 p.m. with his breath reeking in beer. I was furious but had to contain my anger while he wrapped my hands as quickly as possible. At 6:15 p.m., I started shadow boxing and almost slipped. The floor seemed extra slick and I would be fighting in a ring on a canvas floor, so I brushed that off and kept shadow boxing right before they yelled out my name. The lights and the venue made it feel incredibly hot, so I did not even put on my boxing robe and just trotted into the ring with the cameras in my face.

Jacobs and I met in the center of the ring for final instructions from the referee. I realized that we were the exact same height as our eyes met. The bell rang for round one and as I came rushing in to throw my hard jab, Jacobs threw her jab faster before I planted my foot and I slipped.

"ONE, TWO, THREE," yelled out the referee. I shot back up immediately shaking my head and told him that it was my boxing shoes and I had slipped. He shook his head and we continued on before the bell rang again to end the 1st round.

"That was an EFFING SLIP! Now you MUST FINISH HER! KNOCK HER OUT ALCIVAR OR YOU WILL LOSE THIS FIGHT!" yelled Coach in my ear. This was her hometown and I knew he was right. I stayed calm in front of Coach, but I knew what I had to do. I was not going to let her take this from me. The bell rang for Round 2 and even with my slippery boxing shoes, I ran to Jacobs and pinned her to the ropes like a woman possessed.

I was in fact possessed with the urge of not wanting to lose. I was fighting for that little girl protecting her like no one did. I threw the hardest punches I ever have. Jacobs not only felt the punches, but she saw and felt what I was fighting for. I heard her yell out to her corner, "STOP THE FIGHT!" but I kept on throwing punches nonstop snapping Jacob's head back multiple times until the referee stepped in between us and stopped the fight right before the end of the 2nd round. I won my 3rd Professional Boxing fight with another KO!

CHAPTER 12

Chapter Twelve - Round 12

Madre
"It isn't enough to talk about peace. One must believe in it. And it isn't enough to believe in it. One must work at it." Eleanor Roosevelt

When I returned home from Florida after my 3rd Professional Fight, I told my mom all about the fight, but the expression on her face and her words hurt more than any punch I had taken in boxing. No matter what I did, it just wasn't good enough. I could feel and see the heart of that little girl inside of me break. It would take me irreversible precious time to realize that my mom was fighting her own demons. None of what she, my father, my sisters, my family or anyone did was my fault. At the moment though, all I could feel was the immense pain of her lack of support of anything I did for my entire life. I dreaded to come to my own home.

I did not know how to talk to my mom. I blamed myself and thought there was something really wrong with me for a big portion of my life. My mom refused counseling and always would say that she is not crazy even though my younger sister and I explained to her that we all could benefit from speaking with a trained professional to help us understand certain things, but she would not budge. My mom was extremely prideful and would never apologize even when she made mistakes. She did what was done to her all of her life. Although I loved my grandmother, she was a tough lady who displayed clear preferences among her 5 chil-

319

dren and in turn, my mother did the same to my sisters and I. Except, I won the award of being the least favorite for my entire life.

She and I would not see eye to eye often. I did not know how to tell her that despite of everything, I still loved her. I was angry at her for never saying it to me either and I internalized all of my feelings. Children who are neglected, unloved and unsupported grow up feeling insecure as if something was wrong with them.

One of the biggest struggles of my life was letting go of the massive grudge I held in my heart for her. I went through many years of counseling and prayers seeking a miracle. I did not want to feel this toxicity. My mom would later on in 2020 at the start of the COVID-19 Pandemic, be diagnosed with the early stages of dementia and forgot about absolutely everything that happened in my childhood and in hers. I helped take care of my mom for the next 4 years. I took a genuine interest in her health and well-being. I took her to the neurologist every 3 months, made sure she made it to the gym throughout the week and when she couldn't, I would lead an hour workout using the stairs in the building I lived in and home weights. I also was in charge of giving her the daily prescribed medications that would help delay the onset of full-blown dementia.

In 2021, I suffered severe anxiety/panic attacks for the first time in my life for about 3 consecutive months. Counseling was not helping at all as the counselor had suggested on many occasions that my mom be put in a nursing home which only made my anxiety worse because that was not an option ever. I sincerely wanted to help take care of my mom. She was more at peace living in my neighborhood and in her own space in my apartment. She loved my dog and her daily routine.

A nursing home was never an option and I told the counselor never to mention it again as I could not possibly live with myself for even contemplating the idea. It was ironic though as my mom would constantly ask me to leave home when I was a teenager and when I did leave, she never made an effort to find me. And here I was in a situation where I could decide if my mom could stay or leave, I did not hesitate to say that as long as I lived, my mom would always have a place in my home. Life will indeed test us and give us an opportunity to do and be better.

One day as I was walking Jack during my lunch hour in the trails of Forest Park, I felt an anxiety attack creeping up in my chest. I fell down to my knees and cried and raised my hands to the sky, "God, I cannot take this pain anymore. I cannot do this by myself. I don't want to feel this resentment for my mom and you are the only one who can free me. Help me please!"

Later that day, I went to church and spoke to Brother Ronald, a long-time pastor at the Woodside IDMJI Church. I explained the situation with my mom of how she had looked the other way during years of abuse with my father, how unsupportive she was of me throughout my entire life and how I never received any love from her. "Have you ever babied your mom and made her feel special?" asked Brother Ronald. I was shocked at his question after I just finished telling him all the terrible things my mom had done to me. But Brother Ronald also knew of my athletic accomplishments and goals. "God has made you strong and special. None of this is happening by accident. Baby your mom and treat her special and you will be blessed sooner than you think," he said with a look of humility and sincerity as he laid his hands on my head and prayed over me.

I stayed for the worship services and even though Brother Ronald said something so unexpected and contrary, I felt better and continued to pray and find something to be thankful for each day. I was thankful that throughout the pandemic, I had not lost my motivation to pursue my goals, I still had my jobs and kept getting offers to do more work in my field, I had my health, my dog and most importantly, my faith.

A few months later in early 2022, my mom got infected with the Omicron Corona Virus. She became very ill with non-stop vomiting, fever and a weak heart rate which required her to be transported to the Forest Hills Hospital Emergency Room via ambulance. I remember holding and looking at the shape of her hand which was very bony and petite and resembled mine. I told her everything was going to be okay.

I also remembered when I was a kid in the hospital after wanting to die and she told me that she wished I would have done it right. I understood in that moment that I was in fact making everything right.

She was admitted into the hospital and would be required to stay for the next few days. During one of my afternoon visits, I saw my mom sound asleep in the hospital bed. She did not move as I called out her name softly. I held her hand and said, "I love you Mami and I forgive you for everything. I will let go," as tears streamed down my face. From that moment on, something and everything in my heart changed for my mom.

I did start to baby her and tried to make her feel special in any way I could, but she would not remember due to her dementia worsening. I took her to the movies with my dog, Jack on a weekly basis, I learned how to cook her favorite meals and had more significant moments with her that she would quickly forget, but would be engraved in my heart forever. I also reached out to my youngest sister who was estranged from my mom for many years and told her about my mom's deteriorating mental condition.

She came with my aunt to visit my mom in my home on Sunday, December 3, 2023. My mom was very happy to see her and hugged her tightly. We sat around the table talking for hours and eating my mom's favorite Colombian bread called pan de bono with coffee.

On December 15th, 2023, I purchased tickets to take my sister, niece and mom to a show at the Thalia Theatre in Sunnyside, Queens called, "Navidad en Colombia," meaning Christmas in Colombia which featured Colombian Holiday traditions along with folklore music and dance. It was the first time in my life I saw my mom unaffectedly happy. From the start to the end of the show, she remembered the Colombian National Anthem and sang all the traditional songs, she danced, clapped, laughed and was filled with joy for the entirety of the show. I remember looking over at her and smiling with joy as well. I had finally gotten my wish to see her truly happy for once in my life. In the past, I had tried to do similar things to make her smile and she always found something to complain about, but today, she was happy.

A couple of weeks prior, the eldest sister contacted my younger sister saying that she was going to be in NYC visiting from Florida on Saturday, December 16th and wanted to take my mom out for the day. Whenever her name came up, we always got nervous as she was mentally unstable and always had ulterior motives behind everything she did that had to in some way benefit her. She had moved to Florida in 2018 and had rarely had any communications with my mom. She had fled NYC after a domestic dispute with a former boyfriend and other legal issues.

I could not understand why I woke up with a queasy feeling in my stomach the day after having such a beautiful evening, but I kissed my mom goodbye on her forehead before she was picked up on Saturday, December 16, 2023.

It was the last time I saw my mom as the eldest sister abducted my mom and took her to Florida. I was overwhelmed with sadness, anxiety and hurt that our own sister would do such a monstrous thing, but then again, this is the type of poison that continues to get passed on unless you do everything in your power to break the cycle.

After obtaining legal assistance, we learned that the eldest had declared herself POA (Power of Attorney) over all of my mom's financial assets and made herself sole beneficiary when my mom had always had her 4 daughters. Additionally, she made herself the medical proxy and strangely opted for "no autopsy" in case of my mom's death. Throughout the following months, I prayed and tirelessly made incredible efforts with our legal team to get my mom back. As of the published time of this book, it has been just about 1 year since I saw my mom, but I was somehow at peace that before she was abducted, I had let go of all the past hurt. The resentment no longer held space in my soul. If I could go back, I only wished that it would have occurred sooner so that I would have more special moments with my mom.

I dedicated this brief chapter to my mom, Nancy Sofia Peralta because I will never know exactly what demons she was battling, but I do know that she nor anyone deserves to live in pain and I just wished I could have helped her more. I loved her more than words can ever express. I hope to see you in heaven when our time comes.

Pictured is my dog, Jack, myself and my mom, Nancy Sofia Peralta on Mother's Day, May 12, 2023 in Forest Hills, Queens, NY

CHAPTER 13

Chapter Thirteen - Round 13

Actions Speak Louder than Words
"You gain strength, courage and confidence by every experience in which you really stop to look fear in the face. You are able to say to yourself, 'I lived through this horror. I can take the next thing that comes along.' You must do the thing you think you cannot do," Eleanor Roosevelt

My classes at LaGuardia Community College for the EMT Scholarship program started immediately after arriving from Florida. I would get my workouts in at 5 a.m. and be in school from 8 a.m.- 3 p.m. Monday thru Friday and work any interpreting assignments from 4 p.m.-8 p.m. and study til midnight at times. I hardly got to see my mom, Jack or anyone for that matter for the next 6 months before I graduated with honors in February of 2011. I loved being a student again and was grateful for the scholarship and opportunity even though my boxing suffered greatly.

I was mentally drained from school and my heavy packed schedule. The sacrifice did pay off and not only did I pass the New York State Exam with above average scores, I received awards for Perfect Attendance, Excellence in Skills and Excellence in Academics. The little girl inside me was proud. It took almost my entire life to realize that making yourself and your higher power proud was good enough.

I was anxious to get back in the ring and although I had been focused on my studies, I had also been working out in the boxing gym and maintaining my fitness. JS helped schedule a rematch with Laura Gomez on March 4, 2011- less than 4 weeks after I graduated as an EMT. This time, the fight would be in in Queens, New York City with a new promoter, Felipe Gomez who was a former NYPD officer. It would be my 4th Professional Boxing fight and I would be fighting in my home town as a pro boxer for the first time. It was a pretty big deal for me even though this fight was supposed to be a tune-up.

JS had also secured another fight in Florida 4 weeks later on April 4, 2011 against Savannah Hill. I was the co-main event feature in both upcoming boxing shows which would give me the exposure I was seeking. I made it crystal clear to JS that after the Florida fight in April, I would be completely out of money to pay for any more opponents. Either the promoters paid me to fight on their card or I was truly done. Laura accepted the rematch, but was asking for $3,000 plus her flights to NYC for her and her coach. She was a tough, but willing opponent.

I took this bout seriously and got to work right away. There were many times I showed up at the boxing gym and just trained myself. I knew what to do, so I did it. Coach had opened another gym in Los Angeles, California and spent the majority of his time there now, but still managed to be at the NYC gym a couple of times a month or whenever needed.

Steve was unreliable and I had to constantly text him to be at the gym. He usually showed up if we had scheduled a sparring session with one of the female boxers he knew. I found it really strange that the women I was sparring with wanted to consistently have someone tape our sparring sessions. These women were not the ones with an upcoming event and had connections or were somehow affiliated with people from Gleason's Gym who were not exactly my supporters. I remember voicing my concerns to Coach and as usual, he paid no mind to it. "Listen, you need the sparring, so we can't be picky," he would say. However, I was the professional and I could indeed be picky and demand for no videotaping, but I would let that go which would be a big mistake in the end.

JS made it to New York City the day before the fight for the weigh-ins. We had signed a contract to fight at 115 plus or minus 1 pound. I wanted to stay in the flyweight division as I felt strong there. I weighed in at 113.5 while Laura weighed in at 118.5. I was not in a position to demand that she lose the weight as I needed to fight and I could not miss the opportunity to fight in my hometown. My mom would be in attendance for the first time in my life along with my sister, niece, friends and the entire boxing gym, so I would let that go as well.

On the day of the fight, I was able to take a short 10-minute cab ride to the venue with JS. Even though this fight was in my backyard, I felt so uneasy. And then I arrived at Cordon Bleu and saw Coach and JS interact with each other and it made my whole discomfort worse. They both disliked each other and I disliked both of them, so no wonder I felt uneasy, but I had to make the best of this challenging situation while I figured out a solution.

I changed into my new white sparkling boxing trunks and started warming up as soon as the 3rd bout was in the ring. Laura's Coach came in to watch as I got my hands wrapped and soon after that my new ring song was playing loudly- a remix that started with "En Barranquilla Me Quedo," by Joe Arroyo and then it cut into "Here comes the Boom," by P.O.D. I knew my mom would like the beginning of my ring walk song and the rest of the crowd would like the rest.

I put on my robe and starting trotting down the hallway into the ballroom and into the ring while I heard the crowd cheer and saw the images of people's faces and reactions quickly flash by. The referee called us to the center of the ring for final instructions and then the bell rang. We started exchanging punches right from the start of the bell and within the first round Laura tried to intentionally head butt me 3 different times. I looked at her like "What the hell are you doing?" and her reply look was "I don't care!" When the bell rang, Coach said, "I see what this effing girl is trying to do! Don't let her do it Alcivar!"

I felt rusty but I was not going to let this girl win in my hometown. I got the better of each round and almost scored another TKO in the final round as I caught her with a huge left hook. In the end, the mission was accomplished. I won my 4th Professional Boxing fight in my hometown in front of my mom, sister, niece, friends and gym. It would be the first and last time my mom attended one of my fights. She had agreed to go after my sister talked her into it. Nonetheless, I was glad she went. I wanted her to see what I endured. I wanted her to see my courage first hand. She had seen it throughout my childhood and now, she got to really see it again. It was a great night that I would always remember.

After the fight, I introduced JS to my family and I could immediately sense that they did not like him either. There was something about this guy that rubbed everyone the wrong way. My sister told me afterwards, that before I introduced them, she saw him flirting with women all over the venue. She warned me about him and I took that to heart. I confronted JS about how he was seen flirting with people in the crowd and that's when I saw his true personality shine. He denied everything and said that he was being extra friendly to everyone for my sake.

Before he left the next day, he logged on my computer at my home to check his urgent work emails and he forgot to log off. I realized he had not logged off his social media accounts when I kept hearing the notification alerts on my computer. I saw all the accounts he had been interacting with and email exchanges with his friends. One of the emails from JS read, "I hope we can get together soon so we can scope out some tail at the beach." My sister, Coach and my gut feelings were indeed correct. The saying, "Actions speak louder than words," was a constant reminder to believe what people do not what they say.

I did not do any celebrating and decided to go running in the trails in Central Park in the afternoon. The boxing doctor who had done my physical just the night before saw me in Central Park running while he was walking with his family. "Patty Boom Boom?" asked the doctor. I smiled through my sunglasses and stopped momentarily to reply, "Hi Doctor! Yes! It's me... I have a fight in Florida in less than 3 weeks, so no time to celebrate...enjoy the rest of your Sunday!"

My next opponent, Savannah Hill had much more experience than me as a pro boxer. This would be my 1st six round fight, so I really had no time to take it easy. I would train for the next 2 weeks to sharpen up my skills and maintain my stamina and strength. But more importantly, this was the last opponent that I would pay. I literally had spent all my savings on these 5 boxing fights. I invested in myself and prayed that somehow it would pay off. This fight was sponsored by the Susan G. Komen Cancer Foundation with the theme, "Fight(s) for the Pink" and would also be one of the featured fights being livestreamed.

I arrived at the Miami International Airport on April 1st and JS drove straight to Jupiter, Florida. The fights would be outdoors at the

Roger Dean Stadium and since my fight was the co-main event feature, it would be during the hottest part of the day. Upon arrival, I was interviewed and then we were weighed in. I saw Savannah with her husband who was also her manager. Many and most female boxers were intimately involved with someone from their boxing team and I disliked the fact that I had just joined this growing trend. However, JS did not put in one penny for me. I fully financed my first five bouts and if anything, I had to bail him out a few times due to his financial hardships. I was grateful that he spoke with the promoters which in turn helped me get on 3 boxing shows during the time we were together.

There was drama unfolding the next day when I checked in. The announcer, referee and officials were wanting to disqualify Savannah for not having appropriate footwear. She said that she always fought in sneakers and no one ever said anything which was odd. Did she not want to fight and was using that as an excuse? Thankfully, the promoter stepped in and she would be allowed to fight in her sneakers. I was angry at her and her husband for putting everyone through unnecessary stress.

I let it all go in the ring and during our 6-round fight, I was able to put on one of my best performances displaying skill and power. I am not sure how she finished on her feet, but I won my 5th Professional Bout in stellar style and was now 5-0!

It would be almost a solid year before my next fight as I stood my ground and refused to pay for any other fights. I did not have the money and I was supposed to be a professional boxer getting paid to fight **not** paying to fight. Out of desperation, Coach talked to Lou DiBella again to see if I could fight on his next boxing show. Surprisingly, he agreed to have me on his boxing show on March 7, 2012. Initially, I found it weird that he said yes right away, but then I found out that I would be fighting the woman he promoted, Keisher Mcleod and I understood. In boxing, there is always an ulterior motive behind everything. No one does anything for the sake of being nice.

This would be a big risk for me as the unwritten rule in boxing is that if you fight the fighter whose promoter is the promoter of the boxing card you are fighting in, your chances of winning are slim to none. I really did not have a choice as this would be the first time I would get paid to fight. My purse would be a measly $1,500! That's right, one thousand, five hundred dollars to fight six rounds, be the co-main event feature AND I was responsible for selling enough tickets to cover my own fighting purse. I didn't understand how one of boxing's biggest promoters was asking the fighter to sell enough tickets to cover their own purse. Was this the same requirement for Keisher?

I was sure that she was getting paid at least double since DiBella was her promoter. We would be fighting at B.B. Kings, a nightclub in Times Square.

Despite of all this, I accepted. I had enough confidence in my skill and work ethic and I would not be paying for an opponent and I did not have to rely on JS to talk to anyone and then throw it in my face. I thought this would be an opening to making good connections and perhaps self-managing my own boxing career. I had been told in the past that I absolutely needed management in boxing if I was going to make it, but no one told me to read in between the lines where management meant being asked to meet in hotel rooms or spend the weekend in the manager's getaway home to discuss a possible contract.

I knew my time in professional boxing was limited and when I was ready to walk away, I wanted to walk away with my dignity and head held up high knowing I didn't have to sleep around or was being favored by any of the judges unfairly. Up until now, I had won all of my 40+ amateur boxing fights, titles and my professional fights with hard work and skill and most importantly- I won fair and square and I intended to keep doing that.

The week of the fight, the YES (Yankee Entertainment and Sports Network) Network contacted me directly for an exclusive pre- and post-fight interview as well as film the fight against Keisher. Coach and everyone were surprised as the YES Network was dedicated to reporting on the Yankees, Brooklyn Nets and pre- and post-game shows and it would be the first time they highlighted a female boxer. I did not feel any added pressure as my background, several years as an amateur boxer and life had prepared me well, so I accepted.

The day of the weigh-ins, I took the subway to Times Square and I had goosebumps as I walked down 42nd Street and saw my name on the scrolling ad on the B.B. King's big screen "Featured Women's fight: Keisher "Fire" Mcleod vs Patty Boom Boom". Although we both signed a contract to fight at 112, we each weighed in under. I weighed in at 110.5 lbs. and Keisher at 109 lbs. She was taller at 5'8" but I had seen videos of her past fights and I was not impressed. Her team however were impressed that the non-promoted fighter was being interviewed by the YES Network. I was undefeated and Keisher had 2 losses on her record at the time. There was nothing impressive about her, but somehow, she trained at Gleason's Gym and had the connections.

JS arrived in NYC later that night and I was relieved that he checked into a nearby hotel as I did not want any distractions the night before this fight. I was already overwhelmed with having to help promote this fight and sell tickets which thankfully I sold much more than the $1,500 worth to cover my purse.

The company I was currently consulting for, Odyssey House purchased an entire VIP ringside table, my boss from the JPMorgan Chase Corporate Challenge event- Dan Brannen and another Executive from the event also purchased tickets as well as many other acquaintances, my sister and niece and a big presence from Coach's Boxing Gym would also be in attendance. I knew deep inside that many of these acquaintances were not supporters, but were people that would gladly pay to see me lose. No pressure though.

The day of the fight, I kneeled down beside my bed and said my prayers and then I took the subway into Times Square again and met JS and Coach at B.B. King's. Coach was extremely agitated and his vibe and energy made me uneasy. He didn't work with me at all for this fight, but he shows up for the big day because he had always wanted to be the show. But of course, there would be much more to the story.

As the night went on, I realized that every fighter in the "blue" corner which were the "opponents/non-promoted fighters" were losing. This was the corner I was in. My ring song started playing and we walked out with the YES Network following. Keisher and I walked to the center of the ring and then the bell rang. She had a super long reach and she was initially catching me with her long jabs, but I found my rhythm towards the end of the round and start ducking and weaving her punches and I was tagging her with hard body punches while her supporters yelled, "GET HER! She can't hurt you!"

In the 3rd round, I rushed in and before my foot hit the ground, Keisher caught me one of her long jabs and I slipped and then the referee started counting, "ONE, TWO, THREE!" I bounced back up as quickly as humanly possible and shook my head. It was clearly a slip and the crowd knew it, but I was fighting a losing battle on this card.

Nonetheless, I kept my cool and focus in spite of Coach's ridiculous yelling during the fight. He was warned a plethora of times for yelling stupidity during the fight. The fight judges kept looking over at him during the fight instead of the actual fight. The fight was action packed and I was the clear aggressor and landed the harder clearer punches and in the final 6th round, I knocked Keisher down with my left hook as she was lunging in! This was a clear knock down and the referee started counting, "ONE, TWO, THREE!"

The bell rang to end the final round and I lifted both my arms up. I knew deep inside that I had done more than enough to win and that final knock down had sealed it and then the referee called us to the center of the ring and started reading off the score cards: "55-57, 55-57, 57-55 and the winner by Split Decision.... Keisher Mcleod!" said the referee. The loud sounds of "Boo" drowned out the scarce applauses. It wasn't the first time I was robbed and wouldn't be the last, but it hurt. This was a blatant, clear robbery which was filmed and everyone present witnessed it. However, one of the judges came up to me after the fight and said, "You lost this fight because your Coach would not shut the eff up! Instead of paying attention to your fight, we were distracted by his yelling!"

Furthermore, I had learned that the promoter, Lou DiBella and Coach had some history that was not exactly good and I paid for whatever they had going on between them in the past. To make things worse, JS and Coach got into an argument. I broke down crying during the post-fight interview with the YES Network. They saw everything that had happened, but I managed to compose myself towards the end and said I would keep moving forward before I sneaked out the back door and took a cab home.

As I rode in the cab home, my sister called me, "Are you okay Patricia? I know you are sad, but I can only tell you that we are very proud of you. Just know that you won that fight. We all saw what happened. Please rest and let us know if you need anything." All she could hear was my sniffles through the uncontrollable tears, but I managed to whisper, "Thank you. I will talk to you soon."

When I got home, I prayed through tears for comfort and understanding. One of the things I struggled with throughout my life was understanding all the injustices of my life. I was in deep pain not because I lost, but of how unfair it was to have worked so hard, get paid close to nothing and still lose a decision even though I really won. However, I knew that it was also part of having faith in that everything happens for a good reason- even the unfairness.

I fell asleep in my clothes and woke up with Jack licking my face and then my phone was ringing non-stop. It was JS. I turned off my phone, got dressed and went for a 7-mile trail run with Jack in Forest Park. Throughout my run, I meditated and prayed for clarity and courage. I would not turn my phone back on until the next day. The messages from JS went from pleading for a returned call to nastiness and belittling me. I didn't finish listening to the messages as I had heard and taken enough. I called him that morning and he picked up right away and I said, "Listen, I am going to make this short. I appreciate everything you helped me with throughout the past year, but this long-distance relationship is not working out. This relationship is not healthy for either one of us, so I am putting an end to it. Please do not contact me again. Good bye."

My heart was pounding so hard, but I felt such a sense of relief as well. He would continue to harass me and even called Coach at the boxing gym for the next few months, but I ignored him and never spoke to him again. I promised myself to never ever get involved with anyone in boxing again. I dated other men throughout the years that never came remotely close to being an ideal partner. Soon after JS, I dated a Cuban guy.

He was extremely charming at first, but he had a horrible temper and he was a former alcoholic and cocaine addict but had been clean for over 10 years when I met him. I mistakenly looked past all of that not truly understanding that addictive behavior can be healed only when you replace it with healthy behavior, being honest with yourself and knowing when to seek help. He was another case where his mouth said one thing, but his actions said something completely different. I lost respect for him when I found out he pretended to have been active in the military forces. He had told many of his very close friends and other people this lie. The icing on the cake was finding emails from him to escort services.

Although that relationship was a horrible experience, it taught me so much about people with addictions, about how I had to be extremely careful not to fall into the same patterns and path that my mom once did with my own father because people with my background can easily and unconsciously fall into the same abusive cycles and patterns as their families. I promised myself to not settle. It would be a continuous process to strengthen my faith, heal past trauma, learn how to love myself and not allow anyone to treat me anything less than amazing.

After the loss to Keisher, I did not know that I was now considered an "opponent" and not a rising boxer. I was looked at this way not because I "lost", but because I was not promoted nor managed by anyone but myself. Many of the top female boxers had multiple losses on their records but were well represented.

It was all about who was your promoter or your manager. A month later, the Promoter/Matchmaker, Felipe Gomez contacted me directly offering me a spot on his boxing show on June 8, 2012. It was against Vanessa Greco who was part of that Supreme Team and Gleason's Boxing gym group who hated me. The deal was the same $1,500 purse and I had to sell enough tickets to cover my fighting purse. I accepted the fight and terms and started preparing immediately even though I was now terrified of losing. This was not a Lou DiBella fight card, but in boxing, they all know each other and no one was really your friend nor trustworthy.

Vanessa did not have a great amateur boxing career; she was shorter than me and was predictable from the videos I saw of her. I trained myself almost completely. Throughout the next few weeks, I came into the boxing gym and performed boxing drills on the heavy bags, sprinted on the track, lifted weights and set up my own sparring at the gym with some of the members.

The weigh-ins took place at the New York State Athletic Commission on 123 William Street, New York, New York which was only a 5-minute walk from Coach's boxing gym. It was the first time I was at a boxing weigh-in completely by myself. Every single boxer had people with them, but I was by myself. Vanessa showed up with a big crew and to make things more interesting, Keisher Mcleod was in her crew. They had been friends from their boxing amateur days where they were in that Supreme Team. I knew this was part of their strategy to get in my head. I closed my eyes and prayed silently, "God, you and I are a majority. If I have you, that is enough. Please help me be strong and courageous. Amen."

We were called up to get weigh in. We had signed a contract to fight at 112 plus or minus 1 pound. I weighed in at 113 and Vanessa 115- two pounds overweight. I should have demanded for her to lose the weight, but I didn't.

Her coming in over the weight limit spoke volumes and I would make her pay in the ring. We took our face off pictures for the promoter and I got to get a good glimpse of her face to face. She could not hide what she was feeling deep inside. I saw it and I would capitalize on it tomorrow night.

The boxing show took place at Cordon Bleu in Queens where I had fought Laura Gomez last year, so at least I was close to my home. I had a good routine before each fight and this would be by 7th Professional Boxing fight, so I knew what I had to do without any guidance from anyone I thought. Unfortunately, though, you cannot do everything on your own in boxing, but I sure did try.

I arrived at the venue by myself again and went straight to my dressing room where Coach arrived soon after and the New York State Inspector also checked in on me. I was focused and determined even though I found out that I was in the "opponents" corner once I realized all the guys coming back from my side of the dressing room were losing.

Felipe, the promoter and matchmaker for this boxing card fit in with the rest of the shady untrustworthy people in boxing. I was dressed, wrapped and warmed up when they started playing my ring song. I put my boxing robe and hood on and put my head down as I jogged into the ring and did not look at anyone. I could hear Vanessa's people yell, "This is your night! She is nothing!" I was always amazed and baffled of the hatred people had for me. I didn't know them and had ever done anything to them. Their hatred didn't anger me and instead made me sad.

Once the referee called us to the center of the ring for final instructions, I saw the anger and fear in Vanessa's eyes. I remembered what Coach's brother once told me before my 1st ever amateur boxing fight, "Once that bell rings, let all your fear, love and emotions unleash on whoever is in front of you!" Then the bell rang and Vanessa charged at me which I knew she would do. She did not have the power or stamina to keep up with me.

My defense was far superior than hers and I countered her every punch with hard two and three punch combinations. She tried to intentionally head butt me a few times and ended up getting the worst of it. By the final round, her people were silent as I had clearly won each and every round, but I was still very nervous as the referee read the scores from all three judges: "40-36, 40-36, 40-36 and the winner by UNANIMOUS DECISION IS.... "PATTY BOOM BOOM!" I closed my eyes and thanked God silently.

CHAPTER 14

Chapter Fourteen - Round 14

Face your fears, Live your dreams
"No one can make you feel inferior without your consent," Eleanor Roosevelt

After my 7th Professional Boxing fight against Vanessa, I struggled to get on any other boxing shows for the remainder of that year because of my lack of representation, connections and management. Coach insisted that I let his gym client, Elizabeth help manage my boxing career. I didn't think much of Liz as everyone called her. She was a crazy boxing fan whom I was forced to spar at times as a favor to Coach. She was delusional and thought of herself as a real fighter even though she never fought as an amateur or professional. She was at least 20 years my senior at the time making her be somewhere in her 50's and she had zero talent as an athlete. She was however the wife of the late Alan Vega whom was a known musician and she was a music producer, musician and attorney in the fashion industry. She had no experience in the Sports Management industry either.

According to Coach, Liz had connections and could help represent me. I hated the idea, but went along with it after Coach's non-stop insisting that turned into harassment at one point. Liz and Coach reached out to another gym member, Ronson Frank who was their close friend and who was also a fighter and a promoter of his own promotion company called Uprising Promotions. Ronson knew me very well from all

347

my amateur boxing success and he was also a member of Gleason's Gym. He was present at all the pro fights I had in NYC. He offered me $2,500 to be the Main Event on his boxing card on March 27, 2013. I would be fighting for the vacant New York State Championship belt against Eileen "The Mongoose" Olszewski. Despite having "management" now, I could not believe I was being offered only $2,500. Men or anyone else would be offered at least $10,000 for a title main event bout, but I did not know any better and I accepted.

I knew of Eileen because in my early amateur boxing days, I had sparred with Eileen who was 8 years my senior. Coach and I had been invited to the high-end gym that Eileen and her husband, Matthew Sykes Olszewski owned in midtown Manhattan that catered to the celebrity type crowd. She was coached by her husband since her amateur boxing days and had a separate manager. She was also a decorated amateur boxer with National Title wins in the 112-pound division. We had a solid sparring session back then, but she did not impress Coach enough to want to seek continuous sparring sessions. She had good ring movement, but no pop in her punches and we thought she was slow and telegraphed her punches.

She turned pro much earlier than I did and had more than twice the fights I had both as an amateur and professional boxer and practically lived in the gym. I did not have all the luxuries she did and I knew everyone considered me the underdog, so I gave her and this fight the respect and attention I gave every single bout and opponent. I had less than 6 weeks to prepare for this fight. I was already in good physical shape because of all the running and competing I did in other sports, but now the focus was on sparring and enhancing my boxing skills, speed and power. We lined up a group of women to spar with each week- Susan, Kimberly, Katya, Tiffany and Francesca. All these women also trained at Gleason's Gym and pretended to be my friends, but I knew better. Nonetheless, I had a job to do and I needed the sparring. Ronson's nephew, Steve worked with me on this fight.

Steve had never worked with a pro fighter and his input was minimal. I remember him calling Ronson the final week of training asking him advice on how to taper my training. I overheard everything, but I had never fully relied on him anyways. I did everything I could and always ran the extra mile and sparred the extra round when everyone was dead tired. I was the first one to be at the gym and the last one to leave on many occasions. I had no regrets on the work I had put in.

The night before the weigh-ins, I stopped by church to get the pastor's blessing. I remembered his words before he laid his hands over me to pray, "I will pray for you sister Patricia but God is perfect and everything that happens to us is for a good reason. He has made you a strong warrior. May God bless and protect you always."

This NYS Title fight was being held at the Five Star Banquet Hall in Queens, New York. The weigh-ins took place at the New York State Athletic Commission again in the Wall Street area in Downtown, Manhattan and once again, I was there by myself. My "manager" was away on a business trip and she was not even going to be present for the actual fight either which I found extremely odd. Everyone else was busy, so I went by myself. After the way my own team was treating me, I got a sense that no one was expecting much from me. It was clear again that I was the underdog for this fight. Both Eileen and I weighed in at exactly the same weight- 111 pounds even though we signed a contract to fight at 112 lbs. I had no one on my side taking pictures of the weigh-in or face-off, so I left immediately after.

After the weigh-in, I took the subway to Tierras Colombianas, a Colombian Restaurant in Jackson Heights and picked up a Bandeja Paisa dish to go. It is one of my favorite hearty dishes which was much needed for my bout tomorrow. This dish reminded me of my grandmother and my mom's home cooking. This dish features a thin grilled skirt steak topped with a fried egg, white rice, avocado, a small arepa, fried plantain and beans. When I got home, I turned my phone off and shared my dinner with Jack. It was important to me to have a quiet stress-free evening and this was perfect.

The next morning on March 27, 2013, I went for a light jog, stretched and enjoyed my coffee at the Starbucks near my home. I took a midday nap and at 5 p.m. I took a cab to the fight venue. When I arrived, I realized that I had forgotten my boxing robe, but with all the lights and lack of air conditioning in the venue, it really didn't matter. In the end, the robe was for show as it was only on for a few minutes when you walk to the ring walk before it was taken off in the ring.

The NYS fight Inspector that was working my corner checked in with me and would now be with me the entirety of the night. I gave the mandatory urine sample and when I was ready to get my hands wrapped, the Inspector notified Eileen's corner so that they could send someone on their team to watch which they did. Steve and Coach would be working my corner with Steve being the lead voice and I would be entering the ring first because I was the "opponent". Every fighter in my colored corner were the opponents and were losing. It was the 3rd consecutive fight where this was happening. I hated to see that, but I stayed strong and focused while I warmed up and got ready to enter the ring soon.

My ring song started playing loudly. I had no robe to put on, so I just jogged down the hallway and then down the aisles of the banquet hall and into the ring. There was a nervous applause, but no loud cheers until Eileen started to make her way in. She took her time walking down to the ring with a long red suede robe that had a huge hood that resembled the grim reaper. I looked straight at her from across the ring and she looked old. I was not afraid. I was ready. The referee called us to the center of the ring for final instructions. Her husband was looking at me with a smirk.

The bell rang and I charged at Eileen throwing solid combinations and then she purposely head butted me opening a deep cut on the top of my head and blood streamed down my face. The referee quickly stepped in and sent me to my corner where the doctor took a look at me and instructed my cut man to work on the wound. Thankfully, I had a great cut man named Richard Schwartz who quickly cleaned up the open wound and helped stop the bleeding and I was good to go for round 2.

I kept backing Eileen up into the ropes. She countered my punches with little to no effect. I did not feel any of her punches that had managed to connect. Just like in our amateur boxing days, she was slow and telegraphed her punches. I could see them coming a mile away. I continued to connect well with my combinations and up to the very end of the 8th and final round, my energy was high and I finished the round strong even staggering her a few times. There was zero doubt that I had won. When I walked back to my corner at the end of the 8th round, Coach said, "You are the new New York State Champion...no doubt!"

The referee called us to the center of the ring and read the scores. "**Judges**: John McKale 78-74, John Signorile 79-73, Robin Taylor 77-75. And your winner by Unanimous Decision and the NEW NEW YORK STATE CHAMPION IS.....PATTY BOOM BOOM ALCIVAR!" I dropped to my knees and covered my face in disbelief crying before the NYS Athletic Commissioner, Melvina Latham picked me up and put the beautiful leather gold and gemstone trimmed belt around my waist.

It was a surreal moment that I will never ever forget. Even though all the women I had sparred with were present for the fight, they all disappeared once I was announced the winner. In fact, no one from Coach's boxing gym stayed for any pictures and left as soon as the scores were announced with the exception of my corner. It was clear that no one expected nor wanted me to win, but I did and no one could ever take that win nor that belt away from me. I will forever be the New York State Women's Boxing Champion!

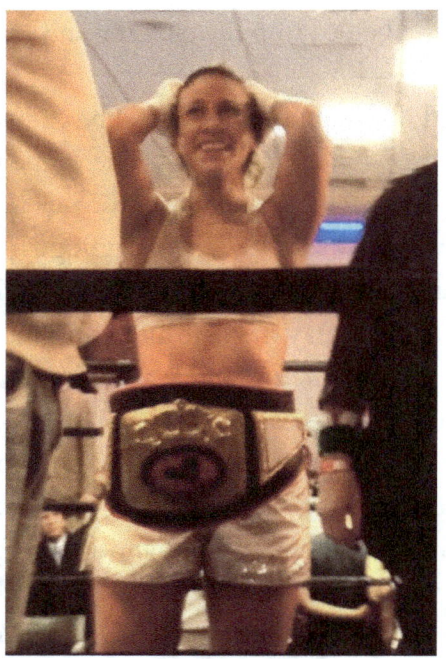

Shortly after winning the NYS Boxing Title, the United States Embassy contacted me about a speaking opportunity in Dushanbe, Tajikistan. They were looking for an inspiring and accomplished female athlete to speak and present for 10 days to the young women and athletes in Tajikistan after Tajik female boxer, Mavzuna Chorieva won their country a Bronze Medal in the 2012 Summer Olympics. I was honored and was surprised since there are so many talented successful American female athletes.

The U.S. Embassy paid for my flight, food, daily stipend, athlete's speaking fee and transport me in a safety vehicle everywhere while in the Middle East. It was my biggest pay day as a Professional Boxer and I was humbled to tears. I remembered the public speaking class I really did not want to take in North Carolina, but felt this poking sensation as if I had to, so I did and I excelled in that class and now, I was going to put everything I learned to good use. I worked on my PowerPoint presentations together and had electricity run through my body as I included pictures of my recent championship win. I was finally going to live part of my purpose- to use my story as inspiration to others. This was my first international trip outside the United States and I was flown first class via Turkish Airlines on April 15, 2013.

Upon arrival, I was greeted by the United States Embassy Representatives and was taken right away for a radio appearance on Radio Vatan who had a significant sized audience. I was welcomed with the warmest greetings from the people, children and locals. They handed me multiple bouquets of flowers and a "toque" hat, a beaded necklace, scarf and a purse as part of their welcome. I was deeply moved with emotions of gratitude being welcomed this way by people that knew my story, but I had never met. Even after winning the 1st ever USA Women's National Boxing Championships or winning the NYS Title recently, I was never given flowers or welcomed this way ever. I was nervous speaking via a Tajik Interpreter, but throughout the days I realized that what the people truly saw and heard was my heart and intentions and that spoke volumes. No interpreter or translator was needed for that.

Every one of the 12 presentations I gave was packed to capacity and went way over the allotted time. I spoke at the Khatlon Sports Center and also performed workouts and demonstrations for the Tajik Girls Boxing and Martial Arts Program. I was transported to Kulob for a speech to all the students participating in the USG Alumni Engagement Innovation Fund and I also spoke to the university students at the

American Corner Kulob. But, one of my most treasured moments was being invited by Mavzuna Chorieva to her home for "tea".

When I arrived at her home, she had a banquet of food all laid out on the table. She had recently become a new mom and we spoke as if we knew each other for years. She gifted me with the pink gloves she won the Bronze Medal with. I did not want to accept them as it was something she earned and deserved, but not accepting it would be an insult in her culture or in any culture for that matter. To this present day, I have no words to explain what I felt for that incredible gesture and my only hope was that she knew how her kindness affected me for the rest of my life.

I returned to New York City a few weeks later in the early summer and received a call from Coach, "Hey Alcivar, we got an offer to fight for a World Title!" he said. I almost jumped through the phone and replied, "Whoa! What? Absolutely! When and against who?" after a brief pause, he said, "It would be a rematch with Eileen but it would be for a World Title this time. You HAVE to take this fight Alcivar!" And just like that, my excitement disappeared. In sports and in everything I did, I found motivation in rising up against obstacles, defying the odds and challenging myself. I clearly won an 8-round Title fight against Eileen and there was zero doubt in anyone's mind including the judges that I had won. There was absolutely nothing to prove. "Coach, I don't want this fight even for a World Title. I would rather wait for a different opponent. Tell Liz to find me another fight," I said before I hung up.

I sparred Eileen **twice** in our amateur boxing days and fought her for 8 rounds as a professional and hands down won every single round. Additionally, I did not like her husband or her people and I did not want any part of her. I was truly done dealing with anything that pertained to Eileen. There was no controversy or debate on who won our last fight, so I did not understand why Coach even considered this offer. I found it really strange, but I was relieved that I had the courage to stand firmly on what I wanted and said my piece. I was still dating the Cuban guy at the time who saw how upset I was after speaking with Coach. He was present for the NYS Title fight with Eileen and also thought there was no benefit in fighting her again, so I let it go and decided to look for a running race where I can go all out and release this anxiety as I had a bad feeling this was not over. I signed up for a Spartan Beast event that weekend that helped me clear my head.

Then exactly two weeks later, Coach called again, "Alcivar, you **MUST** take this rematch or else Liz and I are done working with you. The goal has always been to get a World Title fight, so just fight this chick one last time. You beat her easily once, so just do it again," he said. I was in disbelief of what I was hearing. Coach and Liz were bullying me into taking this fight and I found myself in a very difficult situation yet again. Coach was now giving me an ultimatum as he knew I didn't have any other place to train and my financing was nonexistent. "This is not fair Coach! I don't know why you and Liz are forcing me to take this fight. I am not happy about this at all, but whatever," I replied.

Everything in my body and soul told me not to take this fight, but in late July, I felt forced to sign a contract with their good friend Ronson Frank from Uprising Promotions to fight Eileen yet again on September 25, 2013. I was sure Ronson had a side deal with Eileen's Team as everything he did was to her benefit.

Throughout the 6 weeks that I had to train for this rematch, I received the most hateful and threatening direct messages via Facebook messenger. One of them read, "You are going to get the worst beating of your life on September 25th." Another read, "Mark my words, you are going to die on the 25th!" Other strange things also occurred like I was never able to watch the video of the first fight I had against Eileen. For some reason, Ronson made every excuse in the book to not show us the video and Coach and Liz didn't insist as much either.

For this fight, I worked with Angel, my former sparring partner from my amateur boxing days who had now become a trainer as Steve, Ronson's nephew disappeared completely. I trained just as hard as I possibly could while maintaining my full-time jobs. I had sparred up to 12 rounds multiple times in preparation for this fight and I was looking really sharp. I was already weighing 112 pounds a few days before the official weigh-in, so I was indeed ready. However, I kept having these uncomfortable feelings that did not go away ever since I signed the contract for this rematch. I kept hearing Father Joe's words echo in my head, "Patricia, you have God-given instincts. Listen to them."

The day of the official weigh-ins at the NYS Athletic Department, Angel was the only one that accompanied me. Coach and Liz were conveniently busy. Eileen had her husband, manager and friends, but what made an impactful statement of what type of backing she had was when Liev Schreiber, a popular American actor, director, screenwriter and producer made it known he was in Eileen's team. He took pictures with a professional camera and he was bossing people around. The word was that she split her time training in Los Angeles and NYC in an elite camp. It was also notable during the weigh-ins that she had muscles coming out of her ears which was impressive for a woman in her late 40's to build this type of physique in just a few months.

We both weighed in at exactly 111 pounds again. Liev Schreiber kept giving me dirty looks trying to intimidate me which was amusing to me. Eileen and her husband, Matthew had celebrity clients from the high-end gym they owned, but this "client" seemed heavily invested in this fight. We posed for the media pictures and then I told Angel I wanted to get the hell out of there. Everything felt off for this fight.

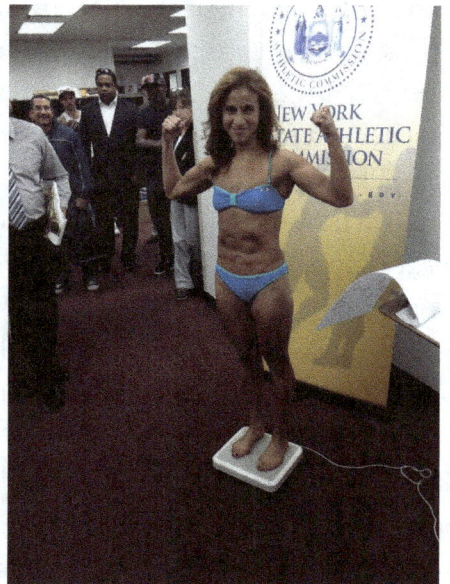

Angel went back to the boxing gym and before I went home, I made a quick stop at church. As I sat there and prayed, I had an overwhelming sense of peace. Throughout my entire life, I have always taken pride in all the hard work I put in everything from relationships to work, school, running, boxing and competitions. I let the anxieties go and left it to God. I turned myself off from the world and went home to rest with my dog.

The next day, I took a cab to 5 Star Banquet Hall at 5 p.m. and met Angel there. Coach would be working my corner with Angel being the lead in the corner. The fight Inspector checked in and I gave the required urine sample. When it was time to get my hands wrapped, Eileen's corner opted to **not** send anyone to watch me wrap which I found strange as they did in the 1st fight and this was a World Title bout, but it was one of many strange things that kept happening for this fight. Even though I was the current Champion and Title holder, Uprising Promotions had me as the "opponent" and I would be coming into the ring first. It was apparent of the influence that Eileen and her people had with Ronson Frank and the NYS Athletic Commission. I tried to brush that off with the mentality that all my hard work always paid off in the end.

Angel put Vaseline on my face and I was ready to go as soon as my ring song started playing. I trotted down the aisles and into the ring without a fancy robe or anything. Eileen made her grand entrance and then the bell rang to start the first round. Eileen threw a one-two combination (jab and right hand) and I saw black spots immediately and I felt my right eye swell up right away. Something was really wrong! I was not fighting a woman here. I had sparred men in the past and women up to 30 pounds heavier than me and this power was unreal. I had fought Eileen just 5 months earlier and walked past her hardest punches. As the bell rang to end the 1st round, I understood why everything in my soul told me not to take this fight.

I went back to my corner and I realized that I may indeed die tonight in the ring, but I was not going to quit. I did not hear anything Angel was telling me. I just closed my eyes and prayed silently, "God, just give me the strength not to quit. I am fighting an unfair fight here and all I have is you." I kept charging at Eileen despite the freakish strength of every punch she was throwing at me. Any and every punch she threw felt as she was crushing my skull. In over 40 amateur boxing fights, all my professional fights and sparring sessions throughout the last 10 years, I had never felt this type of power.

I did not know what round I was in when I went back to my corner and I did not hear anything anyone was saying to me. However, I do remember a round near the end where I closed my eyes and tears were coming down and I mentally prayed, "God, if this is the end for me, I hope I have done you proud."

I went out for the final round charging as I had for every round and taking every brutal punch Eileen threw. I never backed away and never gave up. My nose was bleeding profusely and my right eye was now completely shut and then the referee stepped in and stopped the fight. When I went back to the corner, the first words out of Coach's mouth were, "That Effing girl cheated." The doctor came in and started looking at my eye and I was immediately taken to the dressing room to get my vitals checked.

I went to the Emergency Room on my own and by the grace of God, I was relieved that my orbital bone nor my nose were **not** broken even though it felt and looked like it was. The doctor said that I took some heavy blows and he was also relieved that nothing except a couple of ribs were broken. Despite this horrible outcome, my faith was not affected. I did not nor would I ever give up on God. I was not angry and instead, I was sad and hurt of how low people would stoop to win and what people would do for money. I was not sure up to what extent, but my team had also betrayed me and sold me out.

I remember asking both Liz and Coach to ask Ronson for the video of this fight. Asking became insisting and then harassing, but nonetheless, Ronson would never let me see the videos or pictures of either the first or the second fight even with Coach and Liz supposedly asking for it. What was most impactful was that one of the former interim NYS Athletic Commissioners and Boxing Judge, John Signorile called the gym to see how I was. He knew me from my amateur boxing days and he saw every single of my professional boxing fights in NYC including the first and second fight with Eileen and he said, "Something was not right with this girl for the second fight. Patty is one of the most talented female boxers I have ever seen and I never saw her lose a round like that and I knew something was wrong when her eye swelled up from a jab within the first round."

However, for both of my title fights against Eileen, the NYS Athletic Commissioner was Melvina Lathan. John Signorile was present for both fights as well. I had also found out that Eileen was sparring men in Freddie Roach's popular boxing gym in Los Angeles named Wild Card for the second fight and not even the men wanted to spar with her. The strength she strangely developed was freakish.

It is not the first or the last time these types of things happen in boxing. Boxing has always been surrounded with shady people doing shady things. In 1983, Carlos "Panama" Lewis who was an American boxing trainer, was convicted of tampering with the gloves of Luis Resto for his fight against Billy Collins Jr. Billy's face was deformed after their fight which led to the investigation as Resto was not known for his punching power. Unfortunately, justice was not done in time as Billy suffered from depression and died shortly after their fight from an alleged suicide.

There have been countless reported and unreported incidents where boxing commissioners, judges, promoters, managers and trainers get paid off to sell out a fighter. Where fighters take Performing Enhancing Drugs (PEDs) that mysteriously go undetected among other unfair advantages. I did not have Coach, Liz or anyone fighting for me. I was now in a sport I no longer loved. I had never given up on anything in my life, but how could I remain in a sport where I literally had people wanting to kill me and almost did. I knew the end was near but it would take one final shot....

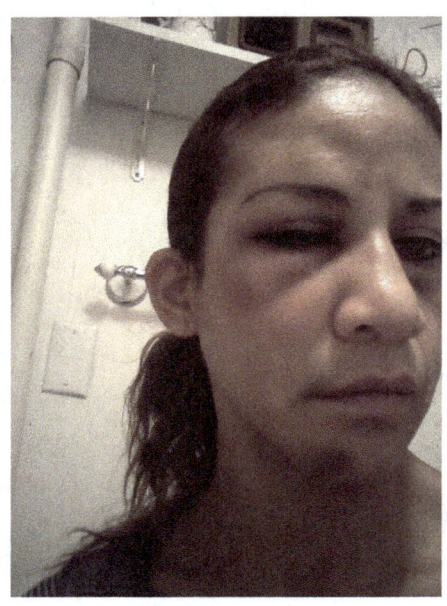

Chapter Fifteen - Round 15

Let go, Let God
"A stumbling-block to the pessimist is a stepping-stone to the optimist." Eleanor Roosevelt

On a recent mountain climbing trip, the Climbing Guide asked the group what "super powers" each person had, if any. The replies ranged from being able to eat anything at any time to sleeping anywhere at any time. When I thought about it, I realized that one of my "super powers" is having an incredibly high tolerance for pain. I mean, I feel the pain, but by the grace of God, I am able to keep pushing forward despite the pain.

After the second fight with Eileen Olszewski in 2013, I took a break, but fought again in 2014 and three more times in 2015. I never got a real boxing manager or promoter and never left Coach's gym, so I was continuously looked at as an "opponent" and not a rising boxer. Whatever Eileen did during that 2nd fight seemed to be the trend because I fought Keisher Mcleod for a second time in 2015 and almost the exact thing happened as with the 2nd Eileen Olszewski fight. Keisher's corner did not even care about sending someone to watch my corner wrap my hands and her strength for the 2nd fight was completely different. I couldn't and didn't say anything and instead for the first time in my boxing career, stayed away from her punches and didn't charge in at all.

A simple jab that had the power she never had in our first fight at B.B. Kings, left permanent eye floaters in my right eye.

In the late summer of 2015, I signed a contract to fight Cristina Fuentes in her hometown of Laredo, Texas for a World Title. My thinking was that Cristina and her people lived far away from all the nonsense in New York City, so perhaps I had a better chance of getting a fair shot even though I would be fighting in her backyard. Furthermore, in boxing, you could not hide anything as everyone knew each other, so I was doomed from the start, but I didn't know it at the time. I always stayed positive until the very end. Our fight would be the main event on August 14, 2015 in the Laredo Arena. Cristina was a seasoned fighter, so I trained tirelessly for 6 weeks with Angel at Coach's boxing gym.

If there is something that I will be forever known for, it is my discipline and commitment to whatever my goal is. I always arrived ready and in shape. I weighed in at a very ready 110.5 lbs. even after taking a flight the night before. As we took the face-off pictures, I had to look down at Cristina as she was significantly shorter than me. She had a sizeable group with her and once again I realized that I was clearly the opponent trying to pull an upset win over the favorite fighter. I had the skill, stamina and strength, so I never lost hope even though I would not only be fighting just Cristina. It was her manager, her promoter, her friends and family and whatever other influencers she had behind her.

We quickly left to find something to eat before heading to our hotel and I did not realize how close we were to Mexico until we clearly saw the Mexican Border in big letters. One of the things I knew from boxing was how loyal boxing fans were to their fighters especially in Latin America, so I was definitely going to have my hands full for this fight. I ordered a big plate of rice and a steak with avocado and was good to go back to my room and rest. I prayed, "God, please help me fight to the best of my ability and protect me and everyone with me tomorrow night. Amen."

Arriving at the Laredo Arena the next day took my breath away momentarily as it was their version of New York City's Madison Square Garden. I had worked hard all my life in everything that I did especially boxing. I had earned my right to fight here even though the money I was getting paid did not reflect that at all. I found it odd that my hands were starting to shake when it was time to get them wrapped as that had never happened before despite the normal nerves before any fight.

Throughout the years, I took notice of the clues and signals my body was sending to alert me when something is not right. I started to jump rope in a corner to take my mind off whatever it was that I was feeling. I broke a sweat and started to hit the pads and shadow box and then they came to escort me to the ring. I didn't care that Cristina had a huge following and that everyone was cheering for her. I was focused on performing my best and as soon as that first bell rang, I fearlessly came straight at her throwing combination of punches. She was strong, but I didn't care and kept throwing over her punches. The crowd appreciated that and were cheering both of us now. I maintained the same energy throughout the next 3 rounds and I was now ahead on the scorecards.

However, in round 4, the significantly shorter Cristina blatantly jumped up and purposely and intentionally head butted me. The head butt opened a 6-inch gash above my left eye where my bone was now visible. The referee stepped in and stopped the fight. Coincidentally, if there is an "accidental" head butt before the end of the 4th round of a boxing fight, then the fight is ruled a "no contest" and no winner or loser is declared and that is exactly what happened.

I was in disbelief and as I was walking back to my dressing rooms, boxing fans knew what had really happened here and were cheering me on wanting to take pictures with me and get my autograph. The fight doctor presented me with 2 options: Go to the Emergency Room to get stitches or get stitched up right there in the dressing room. Coach did not want to go to the Emergency Room, so I opted to get stitches in the dressing room.

It was not until the doctor put the first stitch that I realized there would be no anesthesia! I have taken significant pain in my life, but six stitches above my left eye without anesthesia stands out as one of the biggest. The doctor also said I would need to take 8-12 months off from getting hit as this injury was in a very delicate part of my face where any blow to the same area would make that spot easily open back up.

I did not cry this time and instead felt a sense of relief. This terrible incident was typical behavior in boxing and I felt as if the powers above allowed this to happen before something worse did. Laura Gomez attempted many times to injure me with head butts and so did Vanessa Greco and Eileen Olszewski. This horrible incident was a blessing in disguise and I was thankful. In every unfair fight, the crowd saw exactly what had happened and I knew deep inside what type of athlete I was and I took pride in that. I had accomplished what many thought I couldn't in boxing by winning the following titles: New York City Golden Gloves, the first ever USA Women's National Boxing Championship title, the first ever International Women's Boxing title (USA vs Canada), Metro Boxing Championship title, Western Boxing Championship title in Kentucky and the New York State Boxing Championship title as a professional boxer. I was also the first ever female to be named "Athlete of the Year in boxing" as voted by the United States Olympic Boxing Committee.

As Bob Swoap would once tell me, "No one will ever take away the fact that I won all those titles. I will Forever be a Champion. Period."

Even after the infamous headbutt in 2015, I continued to stay busy working, running and seeking my next goal. I had started to hike again and found comfort in the great outdoors. One of my personal training clients, Jess, who was also very wealthy asked me to be her temporary part-time personal assistant while she found someone who could do it full time and permanently. I agreed not knowing that this position would require me to travel with her on many occasions.

A few days before my birthday in December, Jess asked me to travel with her to Utah. I did not want to go on my birthday weekend, but she promised it would be worth my while once I helped her move from one condo to another in Salt Lake City. We took the first flight out in the early morning and I felt my insides get filled with this unfamiliar feeling of fullness and emotion to see the snow and the beauty of the mountainous landscapes as we got picked up from the SLC Airport and got driven to Alta, Utah which was near all the major ski resorts. I could not understand why my head was pounding until Jess explained that we were at 6,000 feet above sea level. It was my first time experiencing any sort of altitude, so that definitely explained it.

We got to work right away. She wanted to prove to her father-in-law that she was capable of moving and having everything ready without "professional help". The new condo was only across the street, so I kept running back and forth with heavy boxes on my shoulders which motivated her to do the same. I was on a mission to help Jess and I also wanted to get done as soon as possible so I can rest and go on whatever birthday adventure Jess had planned for us the next day. We worked hard for about 8 hours straight and I was ecstatic when she said that we were done just as the sun was setting.

Jess walked into the room I was staying in with a very concerned look and said, "Patty, you have to come with me to the Urgent Care right now!" I jumped up off my chair and followed her to the car. As we drove to the nearby Urgent Care, she explained that when we were moving all the heavy boxes, one of them fell on her and may have punctured one of her breast implants as she could hear a weird swooshing sound.

The doctor examined her and said she was not in any immediate danger and that breast implants have to be replaced every 10 years and she was due. However, she would not be able to go on the adventure she had planned with me. "Patty, you will be fine to go by yourself. The guide is a good friend of mine and will take care of you. His name is Quino and he will pick you up tomorrow at 5 a.m.," said Jess. I woke up at 4 a.m. and saw that she had left her winter jacket, ski pants, gloves, wool socks and back pack for me to borrow and wear.

At 5 a.m. sharp there was a loud knock and I quickly ran down to answer it. "Hello Patty, my name is Quino and I am here to take you on a little adventure today," said the tall slim Latin Guide. I had absolutely no clue what I was in for, but I replied, "Hi Quino! I have no idea what we are doing today, but I am sure I have never done it. Jess cannot come with me today, so I am nervous!" I said laughing as I got in his truck. We drove about half an hour to the start of the trail to climb Toledo Peak, 10,360 feet via the West Ridge. As we pulled into the parking lot, he took out snowshoes, crampons, an ice axe, poles, a helmet and a harness for me. My eyes were wide open and I asked, "What is all this?" Quino laughed and said, "This is really your first time alpine climbing, huh? For now, I will help you put those snowshoes on.

Pack the ice axe, crampons, harness and helmet in your backpack." I felt like a big baby as he also helped me get my rented boots on and just about everything, but I kept smiling the entire time. I had no idea what awaited, but deep inside, I knew it was going to be amazing and just what I was looking for all this time. We started snowshoeing right from the parking lot. The snow and surrounding landscapes were heavenly! I tried to match Quino's pace, but felt so out of breath. "Patty, take it easy. It's okay if you are behind me. This is your first time climbing a mountain in high altitude. Pace yourself," said Quino.

I took a deep breath and had no choice but to slow down. As we reached the mid-way point, Quino said, "Patty, you have done very well. For first time climbers, this is the point we usually turn around, but I understand you are an athlete and you are in very good shape. I will leave the decision up to you if you would like to turn around here or continue. If we continue, it is about 2-3 hours to the summit. I was out of breath and my legs were burning, but I felt this poking sensation letting me know that I needed to continue. I needed to know what it felt like to see and reach the summit.

"I am not going to lie Quino. This is hard, but I can continue. I want to reach the summit," I said. So, we took a small break to hydrate, eat a snack and put on my harness, crampons, helmet and ice axe. I could not believe how incredibly sharp these crampons were until I tripped on them and immediately cut the sides of the ski pants open. I laughed at myself non-stop. It felt good to learn and to be in such a peaceful beautiful place.

After another hour of ascending some steep sections, we reached a challenging rock-climbing section. "Patty, you have to use the front points of the crampons to climb. Watch me first and do exactly as I do. Make sure 3 points are always on a rock. Either two hands and a foot, or two feet and one hand so you are secure. The rocks had sharp edges and some had icy spots which made my legs tremble with fear, but somehow, I got through the two long rock-climbing sections before we started walking on a narrow ridge. I was exhilarated and my heart wanted to burst. "Patty, why are you always smiling?" asked Quino.

"Isn't it obvious Quino? I am happy! I have lived in New York City most of my life. I have never experienced beauty like this. This is very challenging, but no one is trying to knock me out and somehow, I feel loved here in the Mountains," I replied. Soon after, Quino stood behind me and said, "I will let you walk alone from here Patty. Walk to the end where that rock is sticking out and that is the summit." I felt an immediate lump in my throat and my eyes watered up. I walked to the end and I felt the sun and mountain's embrace. I looked up at the sky as tears streamed down my face. "Thank you, God." Right then, I realized this is where I belong. This is what I was meant to do....

Epilogue

Although I never officially retired from boxing, in my mind, I could walk away with my head held up high knowing that I did not have to sleep with any of the big promoters or managers to get a fair shot. My boxing purse for a fight did not exceed $2,500. In 13 professional boxing fights, I earned a total of $15k while any other boxer would make at least that per fight. I conducted myself with class and as a true professional athlete. I was always in shape and prepared, but most important of all, I was loyal to Coach despite of his betrayals.

The purpose of this first book was to share what is possible through faith, determination and the will to never ever give up. Being abused by the people you love does not have to define your future. Healing is a life-long process in which you must be proactive on a daily basis. A big part of my personal healing came through forgiving those who hurt me the most once I realized that forgiveness did not mean I would forget what was done to me. Instead, I no longer allowed myself to dwell in anger, sadness or resentment. I could not have let go unless I completely surrendered to my higher power and asked for help. It is the most vulnerable and humbling feeling in the world.

I forgave my father for all the years of abuse. I forgave my mom for not protecting me and providing the love I have longed for my entire life. I forgave my family for turning their backs on me. I forgave Coach for betraying my trust. I forgave the women in boxing who did not fight me fairly. Each act of injustice throughout my life brought me closer to God and instead helped me excel.

To that little girl inside me, "I love you and I will protect you and help you continue to live the life you deserve."